THE ROMAN FRONTIER
IN BRITAIN

The Roman
Frontier in Britain

*Hadrian's Wall, The Antonine Wall
and Roman Policy in the North*

DAVID SHOTTER

Carnegie Publishing, 1996

First published by Carnegie Publishing Ltd,
18 Maynard Street, Preston PR2 2AL

ISBN 1-85936-015-7

Typesetting and origination by Carnegie Publishing, Preston
Printed and bound by The Alden Press, Oxford

Acknowledgements

I T IS A PLEASURE to acknowledge help which I have received from
various sources in the preparation of this book: for advice at various
points and for permission to use in advance of its publication the results
of his work on the Solway Plain I should like to thank especially
Professor Barri Jones of Manchester University. Thanks are also due
to Barri Jones and Manunair for permission to use photographs for
plates 5, 6, 11, 12, 17, 18, 23, 25, 28, 31, 35, 38, 46 and 54; to Dr
Adrian Olivier and Lancaster University Archaeological Unit for plates
8, 51, 53 and 55; to the Trustees of the British Museum for plates 1,
2, 3, 16, 36 and 39; to the Cambridge University Committee for Air
Photography for plate 9; to the Grosvenor Museum at Chester for plate
4; to Historic Scotland for plate 30; to the Trustees of the Senhouse
Roman Museum at Maryport for plate 27; and to Joe Thompson
(formerly of Lancaster University) for plate 50.

My thanks are also due to the History Department at Lancaster
University for financial help in the preparation of the plates, and to
Miss Susan Waddington of the History Department for her help in the
preparation of the manuscript.

Contents

Acknowledgements		v
List of Plates		viii
List of Figures		x
Roman Governors of Britain		xii
Roman Emperors		xiii
Events of Roman Britain		xv
	Introduction	1
1.	The Roman Idea of Empire and Frontiers	3
2.	The Invasion of Britain	15
3.	Objectives and Realities	23
4.	Flavian and Trajanic Frontiers	41
5.	Hadrian's Wall	55
6.	Fortifications on the Cumberland Coast	72
7.	A Renewed Offensive: the Antonine Wall	82
8.	Frontier Hostilities	98
9.	The Third and Fourth Centuries	107
10.	Britain within its Frontiers	125
	Epilogue	143
	Classical Sources	145
	Coin Evidence	151
	Disposition of Legions	155
	Notes and References	161
	Bibliography	168
	Index	173

List of Plates

1.	The 'Piercebridge ploughman'	3
2.	*Denarius* of Claudius	18
3.	Bronze head of Claudius	21
4.	Lead water-pipe, Chester	27
5.	Campaign camp, Rey Cross-on-Stainmore	29
6.	A Stainmore watchtower	30
7.	Timber gateway, Carlisle fort	31
8.	Rampart corduroy, Ribchester fort	32
9.	Campaign camp, Dalginross	38
10.	The Stanegate road, Vindolanda	42
11.	The forts at Nether Denton	45
12.	The forts at 'Burgh I'	46
13.	The watchtower at 'Burgh I'	47
14.	Finglandrigg: the running ditch	47
15.	The fort at Hardknott Pass	51
16.	*Britannia – as* of Hadrian	54
17.	Hadrian's Wall at Cawfields	57
18.	Cawfields milecastle	61
19.	The goddess, Brigantia	62
20.	The fort at Housesteads	65
21.	The turf wall, Appletree	67
22.	The fort at Bewcastle	68
23.	The fort at Beckfoot	73
24.	The milefortlet at Biglands House	74
25.	Tower 2B, Campfield	75
26.	Rampart turves, Biglands milefortlet	77
27.	Altar of Marcus Maenius Agrippa	79
28.	Palisade, Silloth	80
29.	Antonine Wall ditch, Watling Lodge	90
30.	Antonine Wall, Rough Castle	91
31.	The fort at Ardoch	93
32.	The fort at Birdoswald	100
33.	The stone granaries, Birdoswald	101
34.	The stores building, Corbridge	102

35.	The fort at South Shields	103
36.	*Denarius* of Septimius Severus	105
37.	Milestone, Brougham	108
38.	The fort and *vicus*, Vindolanda	109
39.	Radiate of Carausius	112
40.	Housesteads fort: 'chalet barracks'	116
41.	The 'Wery Wall', Lancaster	117
42.	The late fort at Caer Gybi (Holyhead)	117
43.	Portchester Castle: wall and bastions	118
44.	'Hall building': Birdoswald fort	123
45.	Blocked gateway: Birdoswald fort	124
46.	The fort and *vicus* at Old Carlisle	126
47.	'Strip house': Vindolanda	127
48.	Bath-house: Hardknott fort	128
49.	Iron-working hearths: Manchester	130
50.	Cocidius plaque: Bewcastle	131
51.	Marsyas statuette: Papcastle	133
52.	Temple of Mithras: Carrawburgh	134
53.	The cemetery: Low Borrow Bridge	136
54.	Romano-British landscape: Eller Beck	137
55.	Romano-British farmstead: Castle Hill, Leck	138
56.	Romano-British farmstead: Colt Park, Ribblesdale	140
57.	The fort at Whitley Castle	141
58.	*Solidi* of Theodosius I and Valentinian II	152

List of Figures

1.	The Roman Empire in A.D. 14	10
2.	Probable locations of the tribes of northern England and southern Scotland	24
3.	Agricolan 'campaign camps' in northern Scotland	33
4.	Flavian forts of the Forth–Clyde isthmus	34
5.	Flavian forts in Scotland.	36
6.	The Stanegate-*limes*	
	i) Phase 1 (*c.* A.D. 90)	43
	ii) Phase 2 (*c.* A.D. 100)	49
7.	Northern England and southern Scotland	56
8.	Hadrian's Wall	58–9
9.	Hadrian's Wall – section	64
10.	The Cumberland coast	76
11.	The Antonine Wall:	
	i) Probable initial plan	88
	ii) Final arrangement	88
12.	Scotland in the Antonine period	95
13.	Severan sites in Scotland	104
14.	Coastal defences of the third and fourth centuries	114
15.	Castle Hill, Leck: Romano-British farmstead	139

Abbreviations

Arch. Ael.	*Archaeologia Aeliana*
Arch. J.	*Archaeological Journal*
BAR	*British Archaeological Reports*
CW	*Transactions of the Cumberland and Westmorland Antiquarian and Archaeological Society*
JRS	*Journal of Roman Studies*
MAB	*Manchester Archaeological Bulletin*
PSAS	*Proceedings of the Society of Antiquaries of Scotland*
RIB	*The Roman Inscriptions of Britain*
RIC	*The Roman Imperial Coinage*
Scot. Arch. Forum	*Scottish Archaeological Forum*

Roman Governors of Britain
(selective list)

A.D.	43–47	Aulus Plautius
	47–52	Ostorius Scapula
	52–58	Didius Gallus
	58–59	Quintus Veranius
	59–61	Suetonius Paullinus
	61–63	Petronius Turpilianus
	63–69	Trebellius Maximus
	69–71	Vettius Bolanus
	71–74	Petillius Cerialis
	74–77	Julius Frontinus
	77–83	Julius Agricola
Between 83 and 101		Sallustius Lucullus
		Metilius Nepos
		Avidius Quietus
	101–?	Neratius Marcellus
	115–118	Atilius Bradua
	118–122	Pompeius Falco
	122–125	Platorius Nepos
	131–134	Julius Severus
	134–138	Mummius Sisenna
	138–145	Lollius Urbicus
	155–158	Julius Verus
	161–163	Statius Priscus
	163–166	Calpurnius Agricola
	175–178	Antistius Adventus
	180–185	Ulpius Marcellus
	185–187	Helvius Pertinax
	191–196	Clodius Albinus
	197–202	Virius Lupus
	202–205	Valerius Pudens
	205–207	Alfenus Senecio

Roman Emperors

31 B.C.–A.D. 14		Augustus
A.D.	14–37	Tiberius
	37–41	Gaius (Caligula)
	41–54	Claudius
	54–68	Nero
	68–69 (Jan)	Galba
	69 (Jan–April)	Otho
	69 (April–Dec)	Vitellius
	69–79	Vespasian
	79–81	Titus
	81–96	Domitian
	96–98	Nerva
	98–117	Trajan
	117–138	Hadrian
	138–161	Antoninus Pius
	161–180	Marcus Aurelius (jointly with Lucius Verus, A.D.161–169)
	180–192	Commodus
	192–193	Pertinax
	193	Didius Julianus
	193–194	Pescennius Niger
	193–197	Clodius Albinus
	193–211	Septimius Severus
	198–217	Caracalla
	209–212	Geta
	218–222	Elagabalus
	222–235	Severus Alexander
	238–244	Gordian III
	244–249	Philip I
	249–251	Trajan Decius
	253–259	Valerian
	253–268	Gallienus
	259–273	'Independent Empire of the Gauls'
	259–268	Postumus

269–271	Victorinus
271–273	Tetricus I and II
269–275	Aurelian
284–305	Diocletian
286–308	Maximian
287–296	'British Rebellion'
287–293	Carausius
293–296	Allectus
293–306	Constantius I
306–337	Constantine I
337–350	Constans
337–361	Constantius II
351–353	Magnentius
360–363	Julian
364–375	Valentinian I
364–378	Valens
367–383	Gratian
375–392	Valentinian II
379–395	Theodosius I
383–388	Magnus Maximus
392–394	Eugenius
395–408	Arcadius
395–423	Honorius

The Events of Roman Britain

B.C.	55–54	Incursions of Julius Caesar.
A.D.	43	Invasion of Britain; annexation of the south-east.
	60–61	Rebellion of Boudicca.
	c.60–69	Increasing restlessness in the north; Roman intervention required.
	69	Roman civil war; breakdown of the treaty with Cartimandua.
	71–74	Annexation of the Brigantes by Cerialis and Agricola.
	77–83	Governorship of Agricola; annexation of Scotland.
	87	Withdrawal of a legion from Britain; evacuation of Scotland and development of Stanegate frontier; consolidation of occupation in north-west England.
	c.110–120	Disturbances in northern Britain (?); further withdrawals of Roman troops (?).
	118–119	Victories won under Pompeius Falco.
	121–122	Hadrian's visit to Britain; start of work on Hadrian's Wall and the coastal system.
	c.125	Inception of 'fort phase' on Hadrian's Wall (completed by c. 138).
	143	Renewed invasion of Scotland; building of the Antonine Wall.
	c.157	Break in occupation of the Antonine Wall, followed by selective re-occupation.
	c.163	Abandonment of the Antonine Wall; re-occupation of Hadrian's Wall and the coastal system. Evidence of instability in the north.
	180	Governorship of Ulpius Marcellus; disturbances in the north.
	192	Death of the emperor, Commodus; renewed political instability; eventual emergence of Septimius Severus (197).
	209–211	Severus in Britain; campaigns in northern

	Scotland, leading to an 'accommodation' with the Scottish tribes.
c.250	Beginning of fortification of the east coast.
259–273	'Independent Empire of the Gauls'; establishment of *Civitas* of the Carvetii (?).
287–296	Rebellion in Britain of Carausius and Allectus.
c.306	Refurbishment of northern sites against hostilities from Scotland.
c.330–340	West coast defences put in hand; increasing instability in the north.
351–355	Rebellion of Magnentius.
367	'Conspiracy of the barbarians'; followed by refurbishment of many northern sites and inception of watchtowers on the Yorkshire coast.
383–388	Rebellion of Magnus Maximus; instability on all frontiers.
c.395	Stilicho in Britain.
c.400	Gradual breakdown of order and administration.

Introduction

THE frontiers of the Roman empire provide some of the most dramatic surviving monuments to its power and to the vision which it represented. Through Europe, Asia Minor, north Africa, as well as in Britain, natural barriers were enhanced by man-made features to 'separate Romans from barbarians' and to provide a line behind which a wide variety of native populations were given the opportunity to share in the prosperity and way of life of a Romanising empire.

It was an exciting vision. Never from their earliest days, as the emperor Claudius once reminded the senate, did the Romans seek to impose themselves in such a way as to stifle local aspiration. Through the medium of Roman citizenship participation in the empire was widely available. It might on occasion be dignified as a civilising mission, but in reality Rome saw her empire as a way of making herself safer; ultimately, major enemies lurked and threatened beyond the frontiers – such as the German tribes beyond the Rhine and the Danube, and the kingdom of the Parthians beyond the Tigris and Euphrates. Major upsets were caused at various times by these people; in the last decade of the second century B.C., the Germanic Cimbri and Teutones penetrated northern Italy, and again in A.D. 9 German tribesmen annihilated three complete legions (XVII, XVIII and XIX) in the Teutoburg Forest. Both of these disasters were etched on the Roman memory as strongly as were the losses of armies at the hands of the Parthians in 53 and 36 B.C. Nor were the Romans wrong in their analysis, for these were the sources of the difficulties which later contributed to the eventual decline and fall of the Roman empire.

Thus Rome developed the philosophy of keeping these enemies at bay, by surrounding herself with an empire of willing subjects, whose willingness was bought quite cynically with privileges. There is certainly no need to assume affection on Rome's part towards this empire; a writing tablet from Vindolanda refers to 'nasty little Brits', whilst easterners are described by the satiric poet, Juvenal, as the sewerage of the Syrian river, Orontes.

Britain is particularly rich in frontier monuments, which serve to remind us not only of the power of Rome, but the degree of her engagement in so far-off a province. Whilst we may argue about the existence or otherwise of intermediate and temporary frontier zones in southern England, in the approaches to Wales, and through the midlands, there is no doubting such 'frontiers' as the Gask Ridge, the Stanegate, Hadrian's Wall, the coastal defences of Cumbria and the Antonine Wall. From all of these, substantial evidence can be seen on the ground, as well as through the medium of aerial reconnaissance. These allow us to ask questions about the purpose of Roman frontiers in Britain – indeed about the occupation as a whole. Most of them, too, survive in some of the most wild and unspoilt areas of British countryside, thus evoking powerful images about the conqueror from the Mediterranean. Our study is also enhanced by the survival of documentary evidence – not least the wooden writing tablets from Vindolanda which not only bring alive the quality of existence in a Roman 'frontier zone', but enable us to enjoy an almost unique insight into life in the province of Britain.

It is not intended that this book will simply recite phases of construction, as elucidated by the work of archaeologists, though inevitably this evidence has to be grasped; our main concern is to attempt to answer some of the many problems still remaining, and to show how, in Britain just as much as in provinces closer to Rome, life was about the interaction of Roman and native, as they both sought to profit from the fruits of a prosperity that was the *Pax Romana*.

The Roman Idea of
Empire and Frontiers

LIKE so many things in Rome, the concept of frontier (*limes*) had its origins in a long-distant agricultural past; a *limes* was a bank or path, usually of stone, which separated property from property and field from field. This clearly in its turn derived from a simpler bank formed by the turning of a furrow in a manner still kept ceremonially alive in the days of empire – as the 'Piercebridge ploughman' demonstrates.[1]

Originally, Rome emerged from a scatter of hill-top villages in the early years of the sixth century B.C., to form a unified city, which protected itself with an earth bank – the precursor of the so-called Servian Walls.[2] This was designed to demarcate Roman territory, as well as to offer a protection against local enemies; for many years in the sixth and fifth centuries B.C., Rome was occupied with the vital business of preserving its own territorial integrity, for the site of Rome, exercising a crucial control over traffic along the lower Tiber Valley, was viewed jealously by neighbours. The political organisation of early

1. The 'Piercebridge Ploughman'. The figurine, which was found at Piercebridge in Co. Durham, represents the formal act of turning the furrow to denote the area to be devoted to a town or property.

Rome reflected its military preoccupations, for the *comitia centuriata*, the chief assembly of the Roman people, was organised in military groupings and represented the 'nation at war'. It was an unquestioned axiom that those whose wealth enabled them to make the greatest contribution in wartime – *tributum* was notionally a loan that was contributed to the war effort – should also enjoy the greatest political privileges. Similarly, the kings (until *c*.450 B.C.) and then the consuls and praetors exercised both civilian and military control. The legion comprised those who were 'chosen' – the levy (*lectio*) was the choice made on the basis of wealth – to serve the military machine in a manner that was appropriate to their resources.

Gradually, Rome's immediate neighbours were beaten back, and Roman territory expanded; certain precepts in dealing with conquered territory were enunciated early – the granting to conquered enemies of rights of citizenship, the founding of towns (*coloniae*) in conquered territory, which both heralded the conqueror's culture and provided a military reserve, the confiscation of land for settlement purposes (*ager publicus*), and the making of treaties with those on the fringes of conquered territory and beyond. By the middle of the third century B.C., most of Italy was either subject to Rome or enjoyed treaties with her. On three sides, Roman Italy was bounded by the sea, and on the fourth by the river Po and the Alps. It made sense then, as later, to utilise natural features as boundaries.

It was Rome's new role as 'mistress of Italy' that led to further conflict and on a wider geographical scale; for conquests in Italy – particularly of the Greek city states in the south – imposed foreign obligations on the fledgling imperial power. Thus Rome 'inherited' the quarrel, based mainly on commercial rivalries, which these 'western Greeks' had with the north African power of Carthage. She also had to oppose the efforts of certain Greeks from the mainland to deliver their kith-and-kin from the barbarian's (that is, Rome's) clutches; and the resultant responsibilities in mainland Greece led to Rome's involvement in the turbulent politics of the Hellenistic kingdoms of Asia Minor. None of this imperial growth was deliberately sought, as is demonstrated by Rome's early inadequacy when it came to handling the requirements and opportunities posed by its new territories.

The Roman army consisted of property-owning farmers, deriving from a time when it was feasible to combine the needs of the land with an annual campaigning cycle. Such an army was not comfortably capable of extended campaigns or of undertaking garrison duties. The levy was received with increasing resentment, and the ever-growing need for troops led to violence in Roman politics, first by the rivalries engendered by the proposition of land-resettlement programmes, then by Marius' reform (in 107 B.C.) which opened military service to *all* citizens but failed to take adequate note of the need to provide for the resettlement of time-expired veterans. The army thus became a 'floating weapon' ready to follow whichever politician offered it the most. It was not until the time of the first emperor, Augustus (31 B.C.–A.D. 14), that measures were introduced which provided for full professionalism through the introduction of fixed terms of service, and which lowered the military profile by putting all the troops in garrison in provinces on the fringes of empire. It is no exaggeration to say that Rome's long-standing failure to deal adequately with the problems caused to the army by imperial growth led to the demise of the republic at the hands of armed adventurers, and its replacement by a new monarchic system dominated by emperors (the principate).

Rome's unpreparedness for the growth of empire led to other problems: first, there was no real system for the government of the newly acquired provinces; eventually, a system of sorts was devised whereby those who had been consuls or praetors in Rome were required to follow these posts with a year as a proconsular or pro-praetorian governor of a province. This proved disastrous, because such posts were the preserve of the aristocracy whose 'qualification' was nominally that they were so wealthy as not to need a salary. However, many Roman aristocrats were wealthy in land, but suffered from what we would nowadays term 'cash-flow problems'. To undertake the bribery of the electorate necessary to secure election in the first place, many candidates for office borrowed heavily, and saw their year in a province as a heaven-sent opportunity to satisfy creditors and put aside a 'nest-egg' for the future. Provinces had little or no chance of redress, since the juries of the extortion court in Rome were filled by men who had either been as guilty as the accused in the past or who hoped to be in the future.

Secondly, Rome had no 'civil service' in the early days of imperial growth, and so no group of 'government employees' to whom it could turn for tax collection and the operation of state enterprises. Instead, such jobs were undertaken on a profit-making basis by companies formed out of Rome's second social group, the equestrian order. The 'tax assessment' of a province was effectively the amount bid by the company that was successful in the bidding process in Rome; such a figure might bear little relationship to the ability of provincials to pay, and in such circumstances the same equestrians might change roles and become moneylenders charging exorbitant rates of interest on loans that they made to people so that they could pay their taxes.

Thirdly, the influx into Rome and Italy of the profits of empire – money and prisoners of war – severely distorted the traditional way of life. Money fuelled the growing problem of corruption in public life, particularly at election time, whilst prisoners-of-war were sold as slaves and took over many of the jobs previously done by Roman families for themselves. The removal of the much-prized principle of self-sufficiency all but destroyed the coherence of the Roman family.

Fourthly, the Roman army had long consisted of two groups; the legions provided the infantry whilst the allies made up much of the cavalry of the Roman army. The legions had to be recruited from property-owning Roman citizens, whilst the allies were made up of property-owning Italians who were either non-citizens or who enjoyed an intermediate status, called 'Latin rights'. Until c.200 B.C., these two groups shared on an even basis the dangers and rewards of warfare; but gradually Roman arrogance bred a sense of superiority over Italians, and differential attitudes were introduced over privileges and rewards. Very soon, Italians came to see that their sole salvation lay in acquiring Roman citizenship; when this was refused, they went to war with Rome (91–89 B.C.) to achieve it.

All of this had come about because the small city state of Rome and the privileged, but paternalistic, élite that governed it was totally unprepared for what imperial growth would bring; there was no 'philosophy of empire', and the vacuum was filled by mere greed and corruption. Further, since there was no view of the purpose of empire, no thought was given to what territory should be acquired or to how it should be handled. Had such a situation continued indefinitely, the result would have been disaster for conquerors and subjects alike; the Pax Romana of the pre-Augustan period was indeed a desolation.

Change had to come; and fortunately for Rome and the empire there were men who recognised the dangers of doing nothing. In 70 B.C., one of the most notorious cases of provincial maladministration was brought to court, when the people of Sicily persuaded Marcus Cicero to prosecute their case against Gaius Verres. Cicero was as much concerned with the demoralisation of the Roman governing class as with anything else; we should not be too convinced of the notion of Roman humanity towards provincials, as five years later the same Cicero offered to defend another aristocrat arraigned on similar charges – and only because temporarily he needed a political alliance with the man concerned. In the late 50s, Pompey changed the rules concerning the appointment of provincial governors to reduce corruption, though he was less concerned with the effect upon provincials than with the damaging uses to which such ill-gotten gains were put in Rome.

Perhaps the first significant figure to entertain positive and coherent views about the empire was Julius Caesar who, though not having the title, in effect became Rome's first emperor in 49 B.C. Before that, however, Caesar had enjoyed nearly a decade of control in Gaul. We do not need to dwell for the present purpose on all the circumstances of this tenure, since at least in part Caesar's conduct was fashioned by his view of political rivalries in Rome.[3] Caesar needed success and good publicity from his Gallic command, and evidently found contemporary arrangements in Roman Gaul unsatisfactory from that point of view.

When Caesar went to Gaul in 58 B.C., the province consisted of the coastal strip which linked Italy with Spain, and which had a northern land frontier which consisted essentially of tribes dominated by subsidised 'client rulers'. The chief problem in the area was the disturbance caused in northern Gaul by the German chieftain, Ariovistus, who was forced by pressure to his rear to cross the Rhine, seeking new lands in Gaul. Caesar recognised that the answer to this was to take Roman territory up to the Rhine, and treat the river as a frontier which could then be policed to prevent such incursions. His fears about the integrity of this new, enlarged, province persuaded him that Britain required attention also. Here, however, his 'solution' was to treat the sea as the frontier but to introduce some element of political management into the tribes of south-east Britain – a discernible frontier, but with political management exercised over a zone beyond it.

When Gaul was finally pacified in 51 B.C., Caesar was able to demonstrate his ideas on the proper management of a province; these included closer supervision of the conduct of governors and particularly of financial officials. Caesar was the first to see the advantage of having taxation liability properly assessed and the resultant taxes collected by officials *employed* by Rome – the first steps towards the creation of an overseas 'civil service'. The second major plank of Caesar's reforming 'broom' was the generous extension of the benefits of Roman citizenship to Gallic leaders in an effort to encourage not just their support but also their active participation in locally based administration. He thus advocated the principle of a fair and just administration sent by Rome to a province which was encouraged to take responsibility for much of its own government at a local level; for the first time, therefore, leading provincials had a stake in their own well-being, and were encouraged to believe that becoming a Roman province provided a gateway to prosperity, rather than exploitation.

Caesar was not led to this view necessarily by an altruistic humanitarianism; his policy was based upon pragmatic ideas – that provinces would be more willingly co-operative, if encouraged in this way. In its turn, this would be from Rome's point of view far more effective, and therefore economical; a province's prosperity could be realised to the obvious advantage of Romans and provincials alike, and if this was achieved willingly then there would be less need for the presence of a large and costly garrison army; Caesar's 'philosophy of empire' was that Rome would gain protection from more distant enemies, if surrounded by a 'buffer' of such co-operative provinces. This would be best achieved if the empire was not only held together by sharing in a common culture, but also physically contained within clearly observable and defendable frontier lines, such as the Rhine and the Ocean provided in the case of Gaul.

Caesar's ideas did not die with him in 44 B.C., even though many of his contemporaries will have regretted the passing of the age of exploitation. In 31 B.C., Caesar's great-nephew and adopted son, the future emperor Augustus, emerged victorious over all his political rivals. By then there was a wide acceptance of the fact that Rome needed a centralised form of government if the urge towards destructive factionalism was to be checked. In a reign that lasted until his death in A.D. 14, Augustus set about building upon many of Caesar's ideas.[4]

For the first time, both senators and members of the equestrian order were made to understand that they were parts of an administrative service, salaried by the state, and dependent upon the patronage of an emperor who could sack them (or worse) if they did not conform to his wishes; those with jobs in the provinces were there to keep the peace, encourage enthusiasm for the *Pax Romana*, collect fairly assessed taxes, and to realise a province's social and economic potential. Such standards could now be applied across the board. Augustus and the majority of his successors were hard on non-conformism: Tiberius (A.D. 14–37) pronounced that he wanted his 'sheep sheared, not flayed', and was tough on those who failed to deliver. Claudius (A.D. 41–54), whilst he encouraged provincial participation, was firmly hostile to those local leaders who tried to build up for themselves positions that were too powerful. Even Nero (A.D. 54–68), that much-maligned emperor, tried to introduce reforms to the taxation system which would have spread prosperity further down the social ladder in provinces. It certainly became easier for provinces to instigate the prosecution of maladministrators, though they probably still did not see much in the way of reparation in such cases. On the Augustan situation in the provinces, the historian, Tacitus, gave this favourable judgement:

'The new order was popular in the provinces. There, government by the senate and people (that is, the republic) was looked upon sceptically as a matter of sparring dignitaries and extortionate officials. The legal system had provided no remedy against these, since it was wholly incapacitated by violence, favouritism, and – most of all – bribery'.[5]

Undoubtedly, however, the greatest problem that the republic had faced was the ease with which its army was utilised by individuals in the service of their own advancement. This was possible because, since the reforms of Marius in 107 B.C., the legionary army had been recruited from Roman citizens irrespective of their property status; they were still, however, recruited on a campaign basis, and no institutionalised provision was made for their demobilisation. This lack of structural integration into the state required reform.

Augustus' reform was thorough; he gave the legions for the first time fixed service conditions, and he established a fund that was kept topped-up from the receipts from taxation in order to buy land and pay out retirement gratuities. Although notionally this was done in the state's name, the army was well aware that Augustus was its real benefactor. But since Augustus was regarded as the 'head of state', the old conflicts and rivalries seemed no longer relevant. The principle of non-citizen service by the 'allies' was also enshrined in the broadly based recruitment of auxiliaries; these were levied in the provinces for service in mostly small units of infantry and cavalry, and, like the legionaries, were given fixed terms and generous discharge settlements. At first, they served under Romanised, 'local', commanders.

This reorganised army was made up of 28 legions (see Appendix III) – or a little in excess of 150,000 men – along with auxiliary troops amounting to a similar number. This number of men was held by Augustus to represent a reasonable compromise between what was needed to service commitments and what was tolerable politically and economically. Increasingly, and particularly as Roman citizenship spread, this army contained fewer and fewer Italians, which marked a sharp contrast with the days when all Roman armies were levied in Italy, departed from there to fight their wars, and returned there when a campaign was over.

Politically, Augustus performed a delicate balancing act to secure the

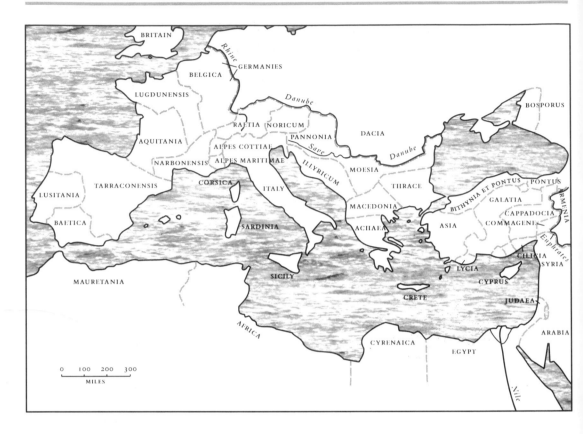

Figure 1. The Roman Empire in A.D. 14. Augustus' stabilising of Roman politics and his reform of the army allowed Rome for the first time to think of an empire with clear frontiers. Most of these took a considerable time to achieve, though Augustus himself contributed to developments along the Rhine and the Danube, and in the east.

support of the old aristocracy: it was crucial to avoid any overt appearance of monarchism, for, in constitutional fiction, Augustus was an 'officer with a special mandate'. The presence in Italy of in excess of 300,000 troops would, of course, have destroyed that fiction, and opened Augustus to charges of military dictatorship. It was thus a vital compromise to keep these troops away from Italy; the obvious alternative for those who were not actually fighting was to hold them as garrisons in the provinces; most of them, not surprisingly, were kept in permanent garrisons in the frontier provinces, where they rapidly developed feelings of superiority over those whom they garrisoned – as was certainly true of the armies in Germany and Britain.

The availability of such an army for the first time in Rome's history facilitated the development of a proper frontier policy. Effectively, in Augustus' lifetime this consisted of the choice of natural barriers, such as rivers, which served to demarcate the territory of the empire from non-Roman territory beyond. It was the aim that territory within the frontiers should either be organised into provinces or left as 'client kingdoms' in the hands of pro-Roman rulers. In the east, Asia Minor was made up of Roman provinces around the coastline with client kingdoms in the

interior; the river Euphrates effectively separated these from the kingdoms of Parthia and Armenia, the latter of which Rome attempted with
varying success to use as a client kingdom. In north Africa, the coastal
lands of the Mediterranean were organised into provinces and client
kingdoms, whilst their southern frontiers were effectively provided by
the Sahara.

Much of Augustus' attention, however, was devoted to Europe;
essentially, it was planned that the frontier should consist of the river
Danube, to mark the northern limit of the empire, together with a
north–south river. Augustus probably originally worked towards the
Elbe for this purpose, but after the great disaster near Osnabrück in
A.D. 9, when three entire legions were lost under Quinctilius Varus,
he had to content himself with the Rhine; he formed the western bank
into two 'military districts' – Upper and Lower Germany – and stationed
eight legions in them. As in Britain, the fortresses and forts for these
troops acted as social and economic magnets for local people, who, as
Dio Cassius describes them, 'became assustomed to hold markets and
to meeting in peaceful assemblages'; he goes on,[6] 'they had not,
however, forgotten their ancestral habits, their native manners, their
old life of independence, or the power derived from arms. Hence, so
long as they were unlearning these customs gradually and by the way,
as one might say, under careful watching, they were not disturbed by
the change in their manner of life, and were becoming different without
knowing it'. However, as we shall see in the case of Hadrian's Wall,
the frontier in Germany did not consist solely of the river, for the
existence of bridges across the Rhine demonstrates that the linear
frontier was itself part of a wider zone – in the case of Germany, the
river and territory on either side of it.

Augustus left his successor, Tiberius, an essentially stable empire, and
he laid upon him the firm advice that the empire should be kept within
its existing limits.[7] Although some ascribed this to Augustus' fear that
he might be outshone by imperial successes on Tiberius' part, it is
more likely that he was partly acting under the shock of the Varus
disaster; but partly too his advice was really a reiteration of his long-held
view that the acceptable size of the army did not allow for imperialist
adventures. Nor did he wish to concentrate too many troops in any
one area; events were to show that this could offer scope to an
over-ambitious commander and encourage a damaging *esprit de corps* in
individual army groups. We can see in the events of the civil war of
A.D. 68–69 how candidates sought first to benefit from such *esprit de
corps*, and then to disperse it by legionary movements.

Although some minor and temporary shifts of policy occurred in parts of the empire over the ensuing decades, the Augustan view generally held, and such fighting as there was was concerned with strengthening existing frontiers. The evidence of aerial photography has indicated that at some stage both the southern and eastern frontiers of the empire were enhanced by palisades. The most comprehensive activity, however, concerned the Rhine–Danube frontiers; here there was a potential awkwardness in the area between the headwaters of the two rivers, which was known as 'the tithe lands' (*agri decumates*); to close off this gap, the Romans over a period of more than a century established a man-made fortification – the *limes Germanicus* and *limes Raeticus* – which consisted of roads, ditches, palisades, forts and watch-towers and which eventually ran from Regensburg (on the Danube) to Mainz (on the Rhine). As Agricola was defeating the Caledonians at *Mons Graupius* in A.D. 83, the emperor, Domitian, was personally directing operations against the tribe of Chatti at the northern end of the *limes Germanicus*. Tacitus could not resist comparisons which favoured his father-in-law, Agricola, though there can be little doubt that success in Germany was more crucial – and real enough.

The control of tribes on the northern bank of the Danube was also a problem which had exercised Augustus, and which continued to give trouble. It was to deal with this that troops were withdrawn from Britain in the 80s; it was the reason for Trajan's Dacian wars and his eventual organising of the province of Dacia on the river's north bank; and it explains the attempt by Marcus Aurelius in the mid-second century A.D. to push Roman territory northwards on the western end of the Danube, reviving thoughts of an Elbe frontier.

There were changes, not surprisingly, to the organisation of the empire over the period, some of which were occasioned by the growing Romanisation of the provinces, and some by lessons learned along the way. For example, following difficult experiences with auxiliary troops and their commanders during the civil war of A.D. 68–69, a new command structure was devised by Vespasian which introduced senior officers of equestrian standing, who enjoyed mostly short-term appointments, to replace the practice of using local commanders. Also, auxiliary troops were moved around more in order to prevent the formation of dangerous loyalties. Over the years, however, the auxiliary troops, which had been intended originally to provide an element of diversity in the Roman army, tended to become more like the legions. To answer this, Hadrian brought in the so-called 'irregular' troops to reintroduce diversity to tactics, and lend the kind of variety which had originally been provided by the auxiliaries. Since many such troops were recruited from the frontier areas of the empire, it was inevitable that some should level the charge that Hadrian was accelerating the 'barbarisation' of the Roman army, thus looking ahead to a time when an increasing amount of frontier defence was to be entrusted to people for whom Rome held little significance or loyalty.

The other main areas of change were social and political; grants of Roman citizenship in the provinces accelerated, culminating in A.D. 212 with Caracalla's extension of the rights to all free-born provincials. The implications of citizenship grants were considerable; not only were citizens eligible for legionary service, but if they were sufficiently wealthy they could pursue political careers locally or in the broader imperial administration. By the later first century A.D., many provincials were members of the senatorial and equestrian orders, and could thus be appointed to posts in the civilian and military command structure. Because the level of financial qualification was lower, more provincials aspired to membership of the equestrian order, and emperors were creating an increasing number of posts in the imperial service for equestrians. This could be regarded as the logical conclusion of the tentative experiments in the extension of Roman privileges initiated by Julius Caesar in the mid-first century B.C. Senators could look to a series of posts in Rome culminating with the consulship, whilst in the provinces they could be legionary commanders or provincial governors. For equestrians there were jobs as junior officers in the legions and commands of auxiliary units; there was also a wide range of procuratorial posts at various levels of seniority in the financial and property sides of the imperial service.

Emperors tended, as they became more suspicious and fearful of the ambitions of senators, to entrust more responsibility to equestrians. An important stage in these developments was reached in the late second century A.D., with the reforms of Septimius Severus (A.D. 193–211). Severus relied heavily for his own rise to power upon the army; he repaid the loyalty of the army not only by making improvements to service conditions, but also by making promotion through the ranks of the army the chief route to entry to the administrative service; for ex-centurions automatically won equestrian status.[8]

It has been rightly observed that this was less a dictatorship exercised *through* the army than a dictatorship exercised *by* the army. The logical conclusion was that ordinary soldiers could entertain limitless aspirations, and it was partly their realisation of this that led to the anarchy of the mid-third century A.D., which, combined with severe economic problems, almost brought the empire to its knees. The Roman army became more concerned with its own political and financial aspirations than it was with defending the frontiers; the integrity of the frontiers inevitably suffered, and separatist movements, such as the *Imperium Galliarum* ('independent empire of the Gauls' – A.D. 259–273), which involved Britain, appeared. Under these conditions, it is not surprising that some frontier zones were 'repopulated' by people from beyond the frontiers – themselves reacting to population pressures being exerted upon them.

The empire in the 260s and 270s was close to collapse, and it was only the organisational flair of Diocletian, 'the greatest statesman of the Decline', that arrested it – for the time being at least.[9] But the cost was high; such was the suspicious nature of Diocletian's temperament that a major feature of his reform was the fragmentation of organisation and command in the provinces, in an effort to prevent the possibility of coherent action being mounted against him. In the long run, this fragmentation was the death-knell of an empire the success and prosperity of which had derived from its very coherence. The effects of this in Britain we shall examine in a later chapter.

Britain did not, of course, become part of the Roman empire until many of the difficulties outlined in this chapter had themselves passed into history. We have, therefore, the opportunity to relate policies which were put into effect on the frontier(s) and within the provinces of Britain with what happened elsewhere in the empire. Although further away from the empire's centre, there is every reason to believe that a high level of commitment to Britain was maintained, and that in the latter years, the status of an 'offshore island' with its own unique frontiers was increasingly appreciated.

2

The Invasion of Britain:
A Frontier for Western Europe

I T IS UNCLEAR at what point in the history of the Roman occupation of Britain a 'frontier policy' emerged; there were certainly roads or fortified lines which temporarily marked distinctions between conquered and unconquered territory. However, it appears that until late in the first century A.D., the Roman objective had been to embrace the whole of England, Scotland and Wales in the province of *Britannia*. It was with this objective that the army of the emperor, Claudius, embarked on the Gallic coast in A.D. 43.

However, in the century preceding the Claudian invasion, Roman policy towards Britain could hardly be described as either well developed or dynamic. Julius Caesar's two incursions of 55 and 54 B.C. had less to do with a long-term strategy for Britain than with the security situation in Gaul and with Caesar's own political position in Rome itself. However, as we have seen, in one respect Caesar's contribution was particularly important; he was one of the first Roman politicians to entertain what might be dignified with the description of an 'imperial philosophy'. Whilst this may not have been particularly sophisticated, it did have implications for Britain in the longer term. Caesar's aim was that Rome and Italy should be protected from its real enemies in the north and the east by a 'buffer' of provinces; to be effective as a 'buffer' these provinces had to enjoy reasonably fair and sound government. Caesar himself adumbrated this by the conquest of Gaul up to the river Rhine and the institution of measures to secure good government, with local participation, within the newly constituted Gallic provinces.

Events in Rome, however, prevented Caesar from developing any plans he may have had for Britain, and it was not until the 30s that any kind of stability began to return to the internal politics of the city. Following his victory in 31 B.C., Augustus was able to give more thought to arrangements in the empire. In the early years of his reign at least, 'sources close to the government' on a number of occasions heralded an imminent invasion of Britain. This, however, did not materialise; indeed, by the end of his life in A.D. 14, Augustus, as we have seen, offered his successor, Tiberius, very firm advice that the empire 'should be kept within its current boundaries'. This, of course, left Britain outside the empire. In the event, Augustus was able to keep Britain at bay; the effect of Romanisation in Gaul was that some groups in southern England began to enjoy the material culture of the Mediterranean, and thus to a degree to adopt Roman habits. This is vividly illustrated by the use of the vine leaf as a motif on some Iron Age coins and of Latin for the legends. Not surprisingly, some reacted to this; north of the Thames, Cunobelinus valued nationalism and independence, though not to the point of injudiciousness; he had some kind of treaty with Augustus, possibly as 'king and friend of the Roman people', and on at least one occasion – in A.D. 16 – he showed his good faith by returning to Rome some soldiers from the Rhine who had been swept across the North Sea by atrocious weather.

Over the next quarter of a century it was no doubt the hope in Rome that the good sense and pragmatism of Cunobelinus and the tension between pro- and anti-Roman groups in Britain would be sufficient to obviate the need for Roman intervention. However, during this period both the threat and attraction of Britain were demonstrated: a rebellion in Gaul in A.D. 21 was led by a Romanised Gaul by the name of Julius Sacrovir – the name means 'holy man' and prompts the suggestion that the rebellion had religious (Druidic) undertones and may therefore have had a 'British dimension'. At the same time, Strabo, (writing during the reign of the emperor, Tiberius), indicates the economic connections between Britain and Gaul and the developing strength of Britain in his reference to the fact that British items for trade included an exportable grain surplus.

By the late 30s, the period of stability between Britain and the Roman empire across the English Channel was clearly approaching its end; the pressure on Rome's chief ally, Verica of the Atrebates, was growing, and the death of Cunobelinus in c.A.D. 40 removed a key player. His sons were at once more aggressive and more grasping; it is little wonder that in A.D. 40, Caligula used the opportunity offered by the submission to him of Cunobelinus' third son, Adminius, to mount a demonstration of Roman military might on the Gallic coast. Adminius had been driven out by the aggressive imperialism of his brothers, Caratacus and Togodumnus, who also succeeded in driving Verica out of Atrebatic territory; there was a danger that if this treatment of Verica went unnoticed, then other pro-Roman rulers around the empire might start reviewing their positions.

When Caligula was assassinated in A.D. 41 and succeeded by his uncle, Claudius, the new emperor had to give Britain considerable thought. Fundamentally, he had to decide whether the time had come to consider incorporating Britain into the empire or whether the Gallic coast should be defended in such a way as to preclude any chance of interference from south-east Britain, which he had now to regard as hostile territory. There was, in fact, little in favour of this latter option; not least, it would have meant the stationing in western Europe of so many troops as to constitute a threat to the empire's (and his) political and military stability. Such a garrison army would have had to be supported from existing resources rather than, in the event of a successful invasion of Britain, utilising the resources of the newly conquered territory. Further, a military campaign of this nature would not just lend a military respectability to an unlikely candidate for the throne: it would also give him the opportunity to demonstrate that, despite having been raised to power by the praetorian guard in Rome, he was anxious to win the support of the legionaries who traditionally envied and hated the praetorians for their favourable conditions of service. Further, it would be to bring to its logical conclusion the work started by Julius Caesar; there can be little doubt that Claudius' dynamism and sense of history put him in sympathy with the 'world-view' of Julius Caesar and compelled him to embrace the whole of Britain in his intentions. The empire's frontier was thus to be advanced in the north west from the Gallic coast to include the island which had for so long proved elusive.

The invasion force of A.D. 43 consisted of four legions – II *Augusta*, IX *Hispana*, XIV *Gemina Martia Victrix*, and XX *Valeria Victrix*, with detachments at least from others, including VIII *Augusta*;[1] sailing from Boulogne, the force established its initial bridgehead at Richborough, on the Kent coast. Although the first season of campaigning was hard, it culminated in the capture of Cunobelinus' old capital at Camulodunum (Colchester); Claudius joined his army for its triumphal entry into Colchester, thus emphasising the political importance attached by the emperor to the whole project. From this enlarged bridgehead, prongs of invasion were launched deeper into Britain – northwards towards Lincoln (IX *Hispana*), north-westwards towards Wroxeter (XIV *Gemina Martia Victrix*), westwards towards Gloucester (XX *Valeria Victirx*),[2] and south-westwards towards Exeter (II *Augusta*).[3] Little detail is known of these advances, save for the last, for which the commander was the future emperor, Vespasian;[4] Suetonius[5] relates that Vespasian conquered the Isle of Wight (*Vectis Insula*), reduced two strong tribes (presumably the Durotriges and the Dobunni of the west country), and stormed more than twenty hillforts (including presumably those at Hod Hill and Maiden Castle). We may assume that Vespasian's chief opponent was Caratacus, the son of Cunobelinus, who was now essentially masterminding resistance to Rome until he was handed over in A.D. 51 by Queen Cartimandua of the northern tribe of the Brigantes.

It was at one time fashionable to think of the province being expanded from the original bridgehead reaching during the 40s a 'frontier' marked by the Fosse Way, a road running from the Humber estuary south-westwards to Exeter.[6] Superficially, the idea of a Fosse Way frontier is attractive, particularly since Tacitus[7] talks of the governor, Ostorius Scapula (A.D. 47–52), preparing to 'tame everything on this side of the rivers Trent and Severn'. However, this would appear to refer to a decision to institute the full paraphernalia of provincial administration into the area so far won, rather than suggesting a halt to military advance on the Fosse Way.

Indeed, there are features which indicate the impropriety of thinking of the Fosse Way as a frontier in the sense of Hadrian's Wall. For example, it does not appear to have been conceived or built as a unity. Nor were troops concentrated behind it; indeed, legionary and auxiliary troops were disposed on both sides of it, suggesting that it was not a statement of the limit of Roman authority, but, at most, a line of lateral communication which might serve as a convenient 'jumping off' point for further advance and in time a rearward area where the troops' supplies might be concentrated. As more military sites come to light, it is clear that the notion that large groups of men were placed in a static condition along a frontier line is erroneous; the legions were split into smaller groups, or *vexillations*, and were based in the so-called 'vexillation fortresses' (large forts of twenty to thirty acres).[8] It is an attractive idea that this development might reflect the changing nature of warfare in Britain, once the original unified resistance had been broken in the campaign of A.D. 43.

The military advance, in other words, was not stopping in these early years, though its nature and pace had to remain fluid in order to facilitate responses to changing situations; Ostorius Scapula and his successors, Didius Gallus (A.D. 52–57) and Quintus Veranius (A.D. 57–58),[9] had to remain alert to the possibility of difficulties arising in places other than in the western campaigning areas. The establishment of the administrative infrastructure in the south-east, and particularly the organisation of Colchester as a veteran-*colonia* and administrative capital of the province caused resentments amongst the tribes of the east coast

2. Denarius of Claudius. The coin, which was issued in A.D. 44 to commemorate the successful invasion of Britain in the previous year, depicts a triumphal arch which represents those erected in Rome and Colchester: the legend is DE BRITANN (['Commemorating victory over] the Britons').

(The Trinovantes and Iceni).[10] Further, the institution at an early stage of a treaty with Queen Cartimandua of the Brigantes went a long way towards securing the northern flank of Roman military operations, although such was the factional nature of Brigantian politics that the treaty did not reduce the tribe to complete quiescence.

Further, campaigning in Wales did not prove to be easy; in the first place, the terrain was not ideally suited to legionary tactics, and more use may have had to be made of auxiliaries. Secondly, the full force of Caratacus' re-emergence as a national leader was felt in his organisation first of the Silures (of south Wales) and then of the Ordovices (of north Wales). It is clear that Roman troops encountered considerable difficulties in this; for although in A.D. 51 Caratacus fled to Cartimandua expecting sanctuary but receiving betrayal when it looked as if the Roman *coup de grace* was imminent, the following year was marked by the death, whilst in office, of Ostorius Scapula. As Tacitus says,[11] he was worn out by his responsibilities.

Throughout this period of campaigning the bases of the troops were brought closer to the action; although *close* dating of some of the military sites is not possible, it appears that Wales was in effect separated from England by a line of fortresses and forts from Chester, to Whitchurch, Rhyn Park (Oswestry), Wroxeter, Leighton, Leintwardine, Clyro, Abergavenny, Usk, Gloucester and Circencester. Whether this was ever viewed as a frontier – a Roman precursor to Offa's Dyke – is uncertain, although the northern part of it must have operated in that capacity until north Wales was finally incorporated into the province in Flavian times.[12]

Despite the implication of Tacitus[13] that little was done by Didius Gallus and Veranius to advance the military cause, the mere fact that Tacitus himself credits Gallus at least with fort foundation argues otherwise. It is a curious fact that Suetonius[14] alleges that at the time of Veranius' death in A.D. 58 – that is, before Boudicca's rebellion – Nero appears to have contemplated a complete withdrawal from Britain; indeed, perhaps in anticipation of such a decision, one wealthy and influential Roman, the philosopher, Seneca, started to call in loans which he had made to British leaders.[15] However, it is argued[16] that the calibre of Veranius and his successor, Suetonius Paullinus, points to a much more dynamic view on the emperor's part.

Suetonius Paullinus, a general experienced in mountain warfare, arrived in A.D. 59 to complete the conquest of north Wales; indeed he was in the throes of delivering what was widely expected to be the decisive stroke – the attack on the Druidic centres on Anglesey – when he was diverted by the serious rebellion of the Iceni and Trinovantes under Boudicca,[17] an event which throws into high relief all the problems experienced as the Roman administration of the province took hold. The conquest of Wales remained unfinished until the governorships of Frontinus and Agricola in the 70s.

It was not part of Roman policy to maintain a direct military control over an area for longer than was necessary; indeed, in Britain, two areas – the territory of the Iceni in East Anglia, and part of that of the Atrebates in Sussex – had been left under the cover of treaty relationships with local rulers, respectively Prasutagus and Cogidubnus. In addition, as we have seen, the Brigantes of northern England enjoyed a treaty under their queen, Cartimandua. Military rule or the control of strong pro-Roman leaders was necessary at first, as the early steps towards the creation of a Roman province were not necessarily easy on the local populations. It took time, as Dio Cassius says of Germany, before the locals were 'becoming accustomed to hold markets and meeting in peaceful assemblages ... and were becoming different without knowing it.'

Of necessity, land was confiscated for food production, veteran settlement and town building, taxes were imposed, which will, at first at least, have made people acutely aware of their subject status,[18] although it has to be remembered that the military markets will have brought opportunities also to local producers. In the case of the early organisation of Britain, two separate areas of difficulty highlight the problems. The conquest of Camulodunum was followed by events which clearly were not well managed. The decision to build a grandiose imperial-cult temple there was resented – in principle because it was a symbol of an alien domination,[19] and in practice because local people were required to surrender land and money for its construction, as well as having to provide labour for it. This was shortly followed by more widespread requisitions when it was decided to create a settlement (*colonia*) there for veterans for XIV *Gemina Martia Victrix*; this resulted in confiscations of land both inside and outside the town to provide the necessary building- and farming-plots for the veterans. On a smaller scale, such confiscation will have been widespread in the new province as soldiers were discharged from service and settled locally.

A quite separate dispute troubled the Iceni in A.D. 59 who had already revolted under the pressure of Ostorius Scapula's policy of 'taming the natives'. When Prasutagus, the 'king and friend of the Roman people', died, it was decided that the treaty relationship should not be extended to his widow, Boudicca. The territory was seized –

3. Bronze head of Claudius. This bronze head was found in the river Alder in Suffolk; it is thought that it may have stood in front of the Imperial Cult temple at Colchester, from where it was taken as booty by Boudicca's rebels, and offered to the local god who was represented by the river.

and in a particularly high-handed manner – by the chief financial officer in the province (*procurator Augusti*). Whilst his flight from the province shows his realisation that he had overstepped the mark, this did nothing to mollify the aggrieved Boudicca. She led a rebellion, which united the Iceni and Trinovantes, and resulted in the deaths (allegedly) of seventy thousand people in London, Colchester and St Albans as well as a great deal of physical devastation in those towns. In addition, IX *Hispana*, holed up possibly at Longthorpe (Peterborough) with its commander, Quintus Petillius Cerialis, received a severe mauling. The famous bronze head of the emperor, Claudius, apparently wrenched from the rest of the body, which had stood outside the temple at Colchester, was deposited in the river Alder in Suffolk, evidently as a thank offering to an Icenian god. Paullinus appears to have reacted with indifferent efficiency, though eventually he saved the day – but at the cost of failing to complete the conquest of Wales.

The whole episode was damaging and unsavoury; it demonstrated the pitfalls of Roman administration at its worst. The aftermath, however, was another story: Nero withdrew the governor,[20] replaced the *procurator*, and set up an enquiry to see what lessons needed to be learned.[21] The governors who followed – Petronius Turpilianus (A.D. 61–63) and Trebellius Maximus (A.D. 63–69) – were clearly under orders to revise their priorities in favour of healing the wounds and letting tempers cool. Tacitus did not find it exhilarating, but there is little doubt but that it was what the province needed. The confidence of local aristocracies in the benefits to them of Roman rule had to be restored. As Tacitus put it,[22] this was the time for the British to learn the pleasures of peace and civilisation.

It is a mark of the success of Roman governors in the 60s that, apart from the rumblings of the anti-Roman faction amongst the Brigantes, the province remained quiet, even during the convulsions of the 'year of the four emperors' (A.D. 68–69). The breathing space was, however, vital, for the next great test – the emergence of the Brigantes as the open enemies of Rome – was about to erupt.

3

The North:
Objectives and Realities

THE rebellion of Boudicca was a traumatic event: the progress of the Roman conquest in Wales was stopped in its tracks, and the emperor, Nero, not only established an enquiry into the causes of the rebellion, but also, according to Tacitus,[1] instituted a shift of policy in Britain to one which, temporarily at least, was less thrusting and concerned more with consolidation than with aggression.

In such circumstances, the treaty which existed between Rome and Cartimandua, the queen of the northern tribal group known as the Brigantes, will have been especially valuable. Originally designed to protect the northern flank of the advance into Wales, the treaty now served to secure a buffer on the northern boundary of the province. It is not known *when* Rome initiated with Cartimandua a treaty which effectively made her Rome's 'client monarch', but it may have been at or soon after the time of the Claudian invasion of A.D. 43. In any case, it already proved its worth when Cartimandua in A.D. 51 ran a considerable risk by handing over to Rome the southern chieftain, Caratacus, who had sought refuge with her.

However, it is reasonable to suppose that the Romans knew enough of the turbulent state of Brigantian factional politics to be cautious about this treaty – a caution which will have been emphasised by the recent experience with Boudicca and the Iceni. In the short term, the treaty secured Brigantian neutrality, whilst Cartimandua won Roman support against her factional enemies, of whom the most impressive was Venutius, the man to whom she was married, and who was described by Tacitus as second only to Caratacus as a British warrior leader.[2]

The Brigantes are said by Tacitus[3] to have been the most populous of all the tribes of Britain; their territory appears to have spread from the north Midlands to beyond the Tyne–Solway gap. Within this area only the Parisi of east Yorkshire appear as a *culturally* separate group, though it is not known how far they maintained a political identity. It is, however, worth noting that, when in the early A.D. 70s Roman

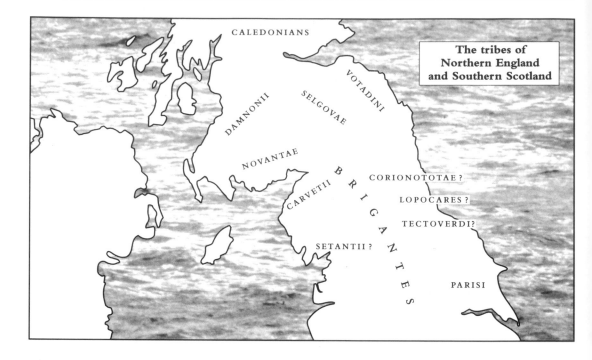

CALEDONIANS

**The tribes of
Northern England
and Southern Scotland**

VOTADINI

DAMNONII   SELGOVAE

NOVANTAE

CARVETII   B R I G A N T E S

CORIONOTOTAE?

LOPOCARES?

TECTOVERDI?

SETANTII?

PARISI

arms penetrated northern England, the Parisi appear to have been separated from the Brigantes by a line of fortifications, which included Brough-on-Humber and Malton.

Within the remaining territory it is unlikely that any Brigantian leader will have been able to exercise a unified control; the geography of the area argues strongly against it. Indeed, it is clear that the Pennines must have offered a significant political division, as the later Roman arrangements were able to base a political identity for the Brigantes in the east – at Aldborough (*Isurium*) – whilst leaving the west for rather longer under military control. Further, the existence within Brigantian territory of 'sub-groups', such as the Setantii and Carvetii, seems to suggest that whilst an allegiance may have been owed to Cartimandua as 'paramount monarch', individual warlords probably exercised local hegemonies. Indeed, the identification in the north west of recognisable groups of hillforts – as in southern and northern Cumbria[4] – appears to support such a contention.

The political centre of gravity amongst the Brigantes is hard to locate; most major hillforts in northern England have at one time or another been canvassed as Cartimandua's 'capital'. However, it remains a plausible line of argument[5] that in fact this centre lay east of the Pennines, with political power resting on the economic strength which lay in the good agricultural land of the Vale of York. Support for this may

Figure 2. Probable locations of the tribes of northern England and southern Scotland. The precise locations of many of these are hard, if not impossible, to pinpoint, though usually general locations can be worked out from a source such as the *Geographia* of Ptolemy of Alexandria. Boundaries between them were probably natural features, which will often have been the scenes of local warfare.

derive from the fact that, as we have seen, the Brigantes' Romanised centre was established at Aldborough, and from the presence nearby of the major pre-Roman fortifications at Stanwick. It may even be that the decision in A.D. 71 to establish a legionary fortress (for IX *Hispana*) at York was based on a recognition of the importance of the area in political and economic terms. There can be no doubting that over the years the civilian settlement which established itself outside the fortress became one of the major urban centres of the north.

In the 60s, the Roman frontier in Britain was drawn approximately from the Humber to the Dee, with legionary bases at Lincoln and Wroxeter, though an auxiliary fort probably already existed at Chester, which was crucial in facing both to the Brigantes and to the Ordovices of north Wales. It is evident that forts were being established during this period in the southern Pennines at sites such as Chesterton, Templeborough and possibly Middlewich also.[6]

It is clear from Tacitus' account[7] that during the 50s and 60s Brigantian politics were far from stable, and that relations between Cartimandua and Venutius, which were always strained, exploded on a number of occasions into direct confrontation; on one such occasion, Venutius is said to have brought in supporters from outside the tribe – presumably from north Wales. Under the terms of the treaty Rome was committed to helping Cartimandua, and Tacitus talks of military encounters between Roman troops and those of Venutius. The establishment of the forts of the southern Pennines was probably a result of this; but it is evident that military action may have been carried further north.

Whilst there is no sign of pre-Flavian forts north of Chester, finds of early Roman coins – particularly copies of Claudius' copper issues[8] – appear to indicate an early Roman presence. The distribution of these is concentrated in western coastal locations and along the major river estuaries. The absence of recognised permanent forts suggests that this military action did not lead to *occupation* at that stage, but some of the campaign camps (such as Mastiles Lane, on Malham Moor), which are notoriously difficult to date, may in fact belong to this period. It would appear that troops were transported from the Dee estuary, landed where necessary, and then returned to Chester when the job was complete.

Such tactics could obviously provide only a temporary respite; in any case, it was not likely that Venutius would easily abandon his attempt to take over the tribe. The undoing of the treaty was, however, precipitated, at least in part, by events outside Britain. In the spring of A.D. 68, Gaius Julius Vindex, the governor of the Gallic province of

Lugdunensis, launched a rebellion to topple Nero from power. The result was a period of almost two years of confusion throughout the empire, in which not only Nero, but also his three short-lived successors (Galba, Otho and Vitellius) met violent deaths. During this period, not only provincial governors and army commanders, but also the legionary and auxiliary troops as well, were absorbed in their support of the rival claimants to power. It is hardly surprising that in such circumstances Rome's enemies saw an opportunity ready for exploitation. For Venutius, smarting under the dishonour done him by his wife's re-marriage to his armour bearer, there would probably not be a better moment to destabilise Cartimandua. In Tacitus' cryptic words, 'Venutius won a kingdom; we had a war on our hands'.

The initial response rested with the governor, Vettius Bolanus (A.D. 69–71), who had been sent out by the emperor, Vitellius, to replace Trebellius Maximus who had left the province under pressure from the legionary commanders. The sympathies of the legions in Britain presented a complex picture: II *Augusta*, IX *Hispana* and XX *Valeria Victrix* had supported Vitellius in his campaign against Otho in the spring of A.D. 69, though none had taken any part in the fighting. A former British legion, XIV *Gemina Martia Victrix*, which had been removed by Nero in A.D. 67, had supported Otho in the fighting itself, and in the aftermath of Vitellius' victory, was returned to Britain. The fact that it did not regard itself as having been properly defeated in the war made its men uncomfortable colleagues of those in the other legions. The entry in the summer of A.D. 69 of Vespasian as a rival of Vitellius further complicated British legionary loyalties; Vespasian had commanded II *Augusta* at the time of the Claudian invasion, and his son, Titus, had served as a military tribune in a British legion – possibly IX *Hispana* when it was commanded by his brother-in-law, Petillius Cerialis.[9] XIV *Gemina Martia Victrix* probably transferred its loyalty from Otho to Vespasian, which in its turn left XX *Valeria Victrix* as the only legion remaining committed to the Vitellian cause; it was to win over this legion that in A.D. 70 Vespasian (who had become emperor in the last days of A.D. 69) sent out Agricola as its new commander. The fourteenth legion was during A.D. 70 or 71 replaced by a freshly raised legion, II *Adiutrix*.[10]

It is perhaps remarkable that in this confused situation, Bolanus was able to make any positive headway. However, the near-contemporary poet, Papinius Statius, indicates that Bolanus won glory in battle in Britain. We may reasonably assume that it was in such actions that the sting of the Brigantes was drawn and that Cartimandua was rescued,

4. Lead water pipe, Chester. The length of pipe belonged to the legionary fortress which was completed in the late 70s; it is one of the only two artefacts bearing the name of the governor, Agricola (A.D. 77–83). The full inscription, which dates to A.D. 79, reads: 'When the Emperor, Vespasian, and Titus, acclaimed IMPERATOR, were consuls for the ninth and seventh time respectively, and when Gnaeus Julius Agricola was Governor of Britain.'

taking no further documented part in events. The extent of Bolanus' campaigning is hard to ascertain,[11] for one of Statius' references credits him with victories against the Caledonians; unless [12] this simply implies seaborne activities in the far north – itself not an impossible proposition – it would appear that Bolanus is unlikely in the circumstances to have done more than to address the immediate problem, namely the rescue of Cartimandua. A more radical solution to the 'Brigantian problem' was clearly required.

Vespasian's victory over the corrupt and demoralised Vitellius in the last days of A.D. 69 finally resolved the civil war; it had lasted almost two years, and few parts of the empire had been left untouched by it. The founder of the new (Flavian) dynasty was entering upon no sinecure; Britain was in many ways typical of the problems that had to be faced – a partial breakdown in the security of the province, conjoined with the divided loyalties of the Roman troops. We have already seen that a positive step which was taken early on was the sending to Britain of the promising young senator, Gnaeus Julius Agricola, to become the new commander of XX *Valeria Victrix*, perhaps the least repentant of the British legions over its long-maintained loyalty to Vitellius. This legion, which was based probably at Wroxeter, was clearly to be of crucial importance in future operations both in north Wales and in the north of England.

Vespasian's problems were, however, by no means limited to Britain: the defeat of a Gallo-German rising initiated by the Batavian, Julius Civilis, was a priority, together with the subsequent reorganisation of the demoralised legions of the Germanies. The upheavals of A.D. 68–69 also left some broad and fundamental problems to be addressed; the legionary groupings within provinces needed to be broken up, and the formation of close liaisons between armies and their commanders had to be prevented by limiting the tenure of office of the latter to about three years. Not only this, but the Gallo-German rising indicated that the service conditions of the auxiliary troops required attention in order to integrate these more closely with the legionary section of the army. It was not, therefore, until A.D. 71 that Vespasian was ready to indicate a new policy for Britain by sending out as governor Quintus Petillius Cerialis, who was probably his son-in-law.[13] Cerialis was an experienced commander, though one whose record was not unchequered; his appointment presumably reflected Vespasian's understandable pre-occupation with domestic politics and the need to guarantee the army's loyalty. Most recently, Cerialis had been concerned in the defeat of the Gallo-German rising and the reorganisation of the Rhine garrison.

Cerialis had seen earlier service in Britain – as commander (*legatus*) of IX *Hispana* at the time of Boudicca's rebellion; his contribution to the crushing of the revolt did not represent an unalloyed success. Agricola had been a junior officer (*tribunus militum*) in the legion at the same time, and presumably the two men were seen by the new dynasty as a 'team', although Tacitus suggests[14] that Cerialis may not have been altogether the easiest commander for whom to work.

Tacitus does not describe in any detail the tactics or operations of Cerialis and Agricola in the early 70s, but it is a reasonable inference that two battlegroups were formed – one led by Cerialis himself, probably with his old legion, IX *Hispana*, operating out of Lincoln, and working on the eastern side of the Pennines; the other was spearheaded by XX *Valeria Victrix*, commanded by Agricola, and working out of Wroxeter,[15] conducting a parallel advance west of the Pennines. It is assumed – and likely – that construction work was commenced in this period on two forward legionary fortresses – at York, perhaps close to Cartimandua's former centre, and at Chester, where an auxiliary fort probably already existed. It should, however, be noted that, in the absence of literary or epigraphic references, archaeological evidence cannot satisfactorily distinguish between the work of Bolanus and that of Cerialis. It is in any case normal to ascribe to Cerialis the creation of the fort at Brough-on-Humber and the vexillation fortress at Malton; these may have been elements of a *limes* which separated the Parisi from the Brigantes.[16]

Cerialis is usually credited with the defeat of Venutius and his associates, who perhaps included the Carvetii and the Setantii, at the large site at Stanwick[17] on the eastern entrance to Stainmore, although the chronology of the site is complex, and more than one governor may have been involved in its reduction.[18] From there, Cerialis might have reached Corbridge by way of Binchester and Ebchester, and even penetrated southern Scotland. It is probable, however, that he crossed Stainmore and that the marching camps at Rey Cross and Crackenthorpe belong to this period.[19]

5. (OPPOSITE)
Campaign camp, Rey Cross-on-Stainmore. Temporary camps such as this mark the progress of the Roman army on campaign; it is thought that this example belonged to the campaigns of Cerialis and Agricola in the early 70s. The camp consisted essentially of a rampart and ditch enclosing a space in which the campaigning army pitched its tents: it had no gateways, but simply defended entrances. Such sites rarely survive well except on land that is agriculturally marginal.

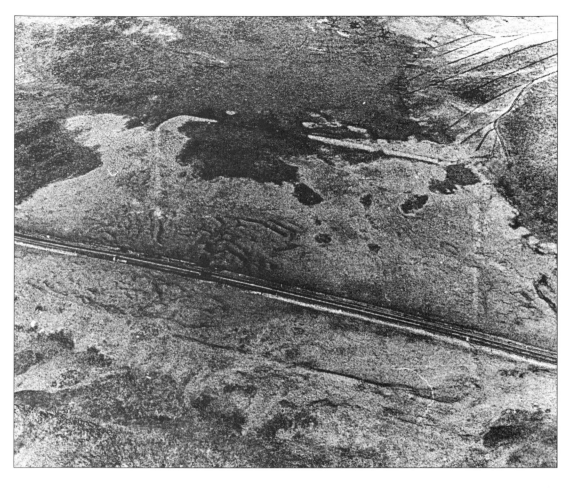

Agricola may have proceeded by land and sea on the western side of the Pennines; the earliest fort at Ribchester almost certainly belongs to the early 70s, and there is a strong chance, on artefactual evidence, that Lancaster does too. Precision regarding routes of penetration is hard to achieve, particularly since so few of the temporary campaign camps have been located. It is likely, however, that two routes were important during the period of conquest; first, that represented by King Street, which led from Littlechester (in Derbyshire), via Middlewich, crossing the Mersey a little to the east of the later industrial site of Wilderspool, and the Ribble near Walton-le-Dale; from there the destination of this route was presumably Lancaster. Secondly, there was the road, which later formed the main northward artery west of the Pennines, running from Chester, through Manchester, Ribchester and Burrow-in-Lonsdale, and thence along the Lune valley to Brougham. This latter route probably did not precede the development of Chester as a legionary fortress in the later 70s. Cerialis and Agricola may have met up in the neighbourhood of Brougham, and together proceeded to Carlisle, where a fort – or perhaps a vexillation fortress – was established in the early 70s.[20]

This series of campaigns reduced the Brigantes to obedience, sufficiently overawed to be safely left whilst Cerialis' successor, Julius Frontinus, returned in the mid-70s to the problems of Wales. Formal annexation of the Brigantes could wait until later in the decade; in the meantime, with no charismatic leader of the stature of Cartimandua or Venutius available, local warlords could be left to work off their tensions on each other, with all hope of coherent action destroyed. Policing of the territory was based upon the two northward-running roads, linked by transverse fortified routes, such as those above Rochdale (Blackstone Edge), through the Aire Gap, and across Stainmore. It is not clear whether we can place at this early stage a forerunner of the road, known since medieval times as the Stanegate, which was later to link Corbridge with Carlisle and Kirkbride.

Whilst the general strategy of 'divide and rule', or, as Virgil would have put it, 'warring down the proud, and sparing the suppliant' was employed in the aftermath of Cerialis' campaigns,there is evidence, as we have seen, of the introduction of physical means of separation; the line of fortifications running northwards from Brough-on-Humber is an example of it. Signs of a similar approach can be detected in

6. Watchtower, The Punchbowl Inn, Stainmore. This is one of a number of such structures that have been located on the Stainmore Pass: they appear to have been supported on four posts, and defended by a circular ditch (as at Burgh I, Plate 12).

7. Timber gateway, Carlisle fort. The remarkably well-preserved timbers of the south gateway of the earliest fort at Carlisle were dated to A.D. 72, indicating that the fort was established during the campaigning of Cerialis and Agricola. The picture shows two carriageways separated by a central spine: the carriageway on the right had been deeply rutted by cartwheels.

north-west Cumbria, where the discovery of an auxiliary fort at Blenner-hasset[21] prompts the suggestion that the fertile land of the Solway Plain[22] was protected from marauders from the hills by the fortification of a line from Carlisle to the coast, probably at or near Maryport – a precursor, in other words, of the road that was later to link the two sites through the fort at Red Dial (Old Carlisle). Although Maryport has yet to yield characteristically early pottery,[23] pieces dateable to the early 70s have been recovered from Blennerhasset, and, as we have seen, there is no longer any doubt that Carlisle was established at this early date. Thus early Roman treatment of the Brigantes displays two examples in which awareness of the political and economic geography of the area led to the inception of effective frontier- (or policing -) lines.

Traditionally, the formal conquest of the Brigantes has been credited to Gnaeus Julius Agricola, who was governor probably between A.D. 77 and 83 – an unusually long term in that period. In one campaigning season (his second) Agricola appears to have swept right through Brigantian territory – and beyond. Agricola's biographer, his son-in-law, the historian Cornelius Tacitus, lavishly praises Agricola's qualities of leadership and diplomacy, but seems to imply that there was no need for a great deal of fighting on this campaign; he was able apparently to play groups off against one another – perhaps groups such as the Carvetii and Setantii in the north west, and others such as the Tecto-verdi, Lopocares and Corionototae who have tentatively been assigned territory in the north east[24] – indicating that the major military blows had already been struck in this area. It is evident in any case that, by the end of the second campaigning season, Brigantian territory was sufficiently secure for Agricola's subsequent campaigns to concern themselves exclusively with Scotland, and to allow him to leave considerable areas of Brigantian territory – for example, the Lake District – temporarily outside the policing network of the Roman army.

The development of the site at Carlisle, begun under Cerialis, was continued, and a major supply base (or vexillation fortress) was built on the Red House site at Corbridge.[25] The certain existence by the end of the 70s of these two major sites clearly suggests the need for a physical link between them; if the Stanegate road had not existed since the time of Cerialis, then we may assume its inception under Agricola. There is, however, no unequivocal dating evidence for the construction of the road; the known milestones belong to the third and fourth centuries, and the dating difficulties that attach to individual sites along the Stanegate are considerable (see below in chapter 4).

8. Rampart corduroy, Ribchester fort. These well-preserved timbers were part of a 'corduroy' or 'raft', which was laid as the foundation of a turf rampart wall. It appears that this work dates to the early 70s.

Such a road will have been crucial to communication and policing; however, given Agricola's determination to complete the conquest of Britain, the road would not appear in the late 70s to have played a part in frontier thinking. That was to come later, as imperatives in Britain and the empire changed. Although those changes, which were to cause such rancour in Tacitus, were not long in coming, the Stanegate was in no sense *yet* seen as a frontier; Agricola's mind was set a long way from halting this far south.[26]

Agricola's third campaign extended the double line of advance into Scotland, reaching the Forth and the Clyde (*Bodotria* and *Clota*), two estuaries which unusually merit Tacitus' identification by the use of the actual names. It is likely, too, that this campaign proceeded beyond the isthmus as far as the river Tay – if that is the correct identification of the name, *Taus*, given us by Tacitus.

At this point in Agricola's governorship, the uncertainty over the precise dating of his tenure becomes crucial – whether he arrived in Britain in A.D. 77 or 78,[27] though there is little hope on present evidence of satisfactorily resolving the matter. The question assumes importance because changes of emperor may well have had an effect upon imperial policy in Britain. Vespasian died in June, A.D. 79, was succeeded by his elder son, Titus, who himself died on 13th September A.D. 81, to be succeeded by his younger brother, Domitian. Thus Agricola's long tenure of the British governorship spanned the reigns of three emperors, during which time it is likely that the pendulum of imperial favour was swinging away from the goal of total conquest in Britain.

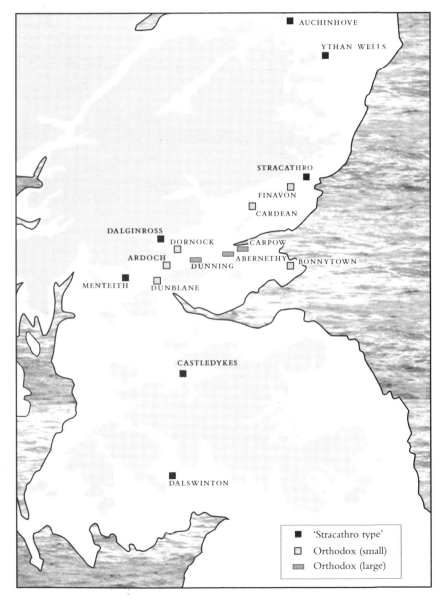

Figure 3. Agricolan 'campaign camps' in northern Scotland. Much remains unclear about Agricola's activities in northern Scotland, though the soundest evidence appears to be provided by the locations of the camps known as the 'Stracathro' type (see Plate 9).

33

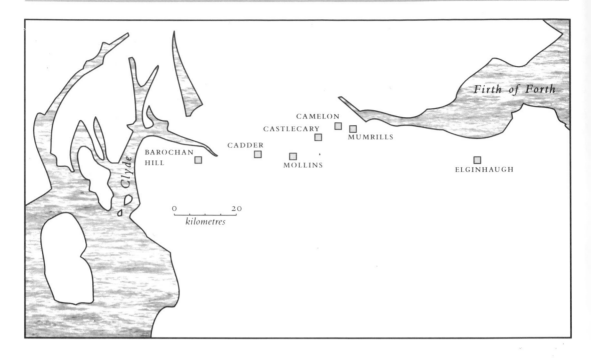

If Agricola arrived in Britain, as seems to be the implication of Tacitus, late in a campaigning season, then the likelihood is that the year was A.D. 77, in the first six months of which Agricola had been consul at the notably early age of thirty-seven – a sure sign of Vespasian's favour. On this timescale, Vespasian will have died during Agricola's third season in which, as we have seen, he advanced through southern Scotland, passing beyond the Forth–Clyde isthmus to the river Tay. It is evident that the fourth and fifth campaigns, which will have fallen in Titus' reign, did not involve activity to the north of the Forth and Clyde.

Tacitus describes the fourth campaign in the following terms: 'The fourth season was devoted to consolidating territory which had already been traversed; and if the courage of our soldiers and the glory of Rome had allowed it, a place for halting would have been found within Britain itself'.[28] He goes on to give a description of the estuaries of the Forth and the Clyde, indicating that the line between them was fortified in such a way as to protect territory to the south and effectively to shut the Caledonians out 'as if they were in another island'. It is evident, too, that there were those, whom Tacitus dismisses as 'cowards employing a specious wisdom', who were for holding the line of the Forth and the Clyde as the frontier of the province.

That Agricola fortified the Forth–Clyde line appears to be beyond doubt, but the locations of his fortifications have proved to be elusive. A long-held assumption was that there were Agricolan predecessors

Figure 4. Flavian forts of the Forth–Clyde isthmus. Although some of Agricola's contemporaries advised halting on the Forth–Clyde line, this was not Agricola's intention. However, it does appear that a transverse road was constructed, as further south on the Stanegate.

beneath forts of the Antonine Wall is generally based upon a false premise: the two phases of activity found at many forts of the Antonine Wall are now known to belong to the Antonine period, and not to represent an Antonine preceded by an Agricolan phase of construction (see below in chapter 7). Further, the recovery of artefactual evidence of the first century A.D., particularly coins, does not necessarily point to activity in the first century A.D.[29] On present evidence, the only obvious east–west linear arrangement in the area, belonging to the Flavian period, is that represented by the forts at Camelon, Mollins and Barochan.[30]

Agricola's fifth campaign, which included his contemplation of an invasion of Ireland, is again hard to locate, but appears to have been concerned with south-west Scotland; attempts to place it north of the Clyde are not convincing.[31] Almost certainly, the sea voyage with which Tacitus says that it commenced was in fact a voyage up the west coast from winter quarters in Chester. The result of this campaign will surely have been to secure all territory in Scotland south of the line of the Forth and the Clyde. If the earlier dating of Agricola's governorship is accepted, then the end of this campaign will have coincided with Titus' death and the accession of Domitian as Roman emperor.

If a 'policy debate' on the subject of Rome's objectives in Britain had been in progress through Titus' reign, the accession of his brother appears to have resolved it – temporarily at least; for Agricola's final two campaigns (in A.D. 82 and 83) were conducted in northern Scotland, culminating in a Roman victory at *Mons Graupius*. It can be assumed, however, that objectives in Britain will have continued to be weighed against imperatives elsewhere in the empire – particularly on the Rhine and the Danube, where signs of native restlessness had been evident since the late 60s. If more troops were needed in those areas, then Britain's garrison of four legions might begin to appear a luxury; thus whilst Agricola (and Tacitus) could afford to contemplate Roman military glory, those who would ultimately be held to account had to decide whether their objective was the conquest and formal annexation of the whole of Britain or whether they wished to secure a victory over the Caledonians which would relieve the military pressure in the north and provide a breathing space for the establishment of a frontier further to the south.

It has been suggested[32] that we should not expect *permanent* Agricolan forts north of the Forth–Clyde line, and that all permanent building as far north as Stracathro should be credited to Agricola's immediate successor, whose identity is unknown. The basis of this suggestion is

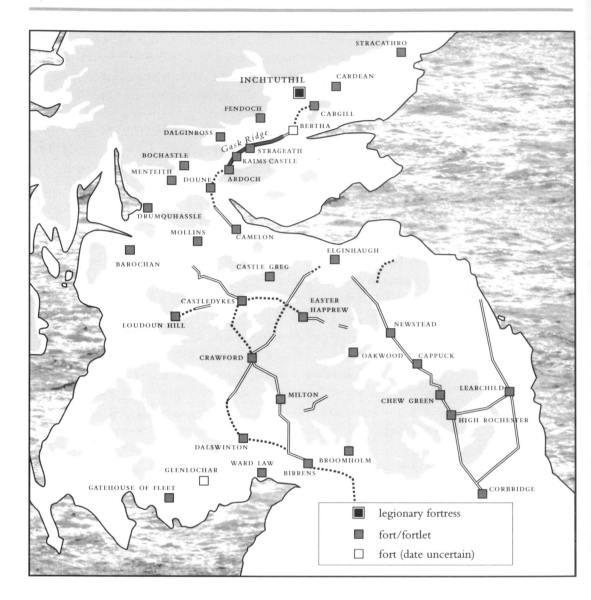

Tacitus' failure to mention fort building in these final campaigns. It should, however, be borne in mind that references by Roman historians to fort building are in any case little more than literary stereotypes, and that the significance of the presence or absence of such references should not be pushed too far. It is, of course, very difficult to distinguish different phases within so short a period on archaeological evidence, since most of it is not capable of such refinement of interpretation. On the other hand, the fact that the new legionary fortress at Inchtuthil was abandoned in A.D. 86 or 87, whilst still unfinished, suggests that it at least may not have begun construction until c. A.D. 84 or 85 – that

Figure 5. Flavian forts in Scotland. Agricola and his immediate successor do not appear to have established permanent forts north of Stracathro. Present evidence suggests that most, if not all, of these had been abandoned by c.A.D. 87.

is, after Agricola's departure. It is also worth making the point that the history of the forts running northwards from the Forth estuary appears somewhat more complex than those so-called 'glen blocking' forts which run from the Clyde estuary on the edge of the Highlands to Inchtuthil.

In these circumstances, we might ascribe the permanent forts of the eastern line, from Camelon to Bertha, to Agricola, and propose that the line from Barochan to Inchtuthil, whilst fought over by Agricola, was left to his successor to make permanent. There is some support for this in the fact that the site called by Ptolemy of Alexandria [33] *Victoria* (Victory) is probably to be identified with Dalginross; the fort in all likelihood gained its name from the defeat-turned-into-victory in Agricola's sixth campaign[34] which was evidently, from Tacitus' description, related to a marching camp rather than to a permanent fort.

The pattern of the sixth campaign appears in one sense to have continued the philosophy of the second and third – that is, by means of two northward advances; in this case we may assume that the pivotal points were Camelon (on the Forth) and Barochan (on the Clyde). The eastern line – Camelon, Doune, Ardoch, Kaims Castle, Strageath, Bertha, Cargill, Cardean, Inverquharity, and Stracathro – effectively separated the good agricultural land of the eastern coastal plain, (which may[35] have been the territory of Tacitus' *Boresti*-tribe), from the Highland massif. The grain of the lowlands was probably valuable to the Roman army and an object of envy to the farmers of the interior; in this way the interests of the Romans and of the coastal tribesmen will have coincided. An important feature of this eastern route is the Gask Ridge system of watchtowers (in Strathearn and Strathallan) – small timber towers set originally perhaps about half-a-mile apart – which were built either by Agricola or his successor,[36] and are very similar to contemporary structures on the Rhine-*limes*.

In the west, a line of forts was to lead from Barochan (on the Clyde), to Drumquhassle, Menteith (Malling), Bochastle, Dalginross, Fendoch, and Inchtuthil; we can assume that Agricola was responsible for the route and for the strategy that lay behind it, if not for the construction of the forts themselves. The decision to place a legionary fortress at Inchtuthil (for XX *Valeria Victrix*) indicates a contemporary assumption that the size of the British garrison would remain at four legions; the line from Barochan to Inchtuthil thus represented dispositions from which the Highlands could be penetrated, and eventually policed.

We are told by Tacitus[37] that a feature of Agricola's tactics which caused consternation amongst the Caledonians was the use of troops conveyed by sea as well as overland. This very ubiquity of Roman

troops was harassing; denied access down the glens, the Caledonians
had to choose between retreat and standing and fighting. Agricola
may have been running risks, too; the peculiar entrance ways of his
marching camps in northern Scotland – the double *clavicula* – seem to
show the need for extra protection for forces which were perhaps
spread too thinly for comfort. Further, Tacitus appears to imply –
through the medium of an oration put into the mouth of the Caledonian
chieftain, Calgacus – that Agricola was supplementing his army with
locally recruited auxiliaries – itself a strategy carrying high risks.

The final campaigning season was brought to a climax with the
decisive Roman victory at the battle of *Mons Graupius*; the precise

siting of this encounter remains elusive,[38] although the line of marching camps which follows the north-east coast up to the Moray Firth suggests that it was near here that Agricola's application of pressure paid off; the Caledonians had been chased enough; thus, they stood and fought – and lost.[39]

Agricola's success at *Mons Graupius* was the climax of his governorship; soon afterwards, however, he was recalled. Tacitus displays nothing but rancour over this decision, although Agricola's term of office had been twice as long as was usual at this time. For Tacitus, this was the ultimate 'sell out'; 'Britain was totally conquered and immediately allowed to slip'. Against the achievements of Agricola which recalled the conquerors of old, the emperor, Domitian, is claimed (wrongly) by Tacitus to have achieved success on the Rhine which was derisory by contrast.[40]

Tacitus' bitterness, of course, reflects both the general senatorial contempt for Domitian and the personal frustration at what he clearly regarded as the unacceptable treatment of his father-in-law. However, at least two of Agricola's predecessors may have been involved in crucial decisions in A.D. 83 concerning imperial imperatives; Julius Frontinus[41] was an adviser of the emperor on his campaigns against the German tribe of the Chatti, and indicates both the importance of this work and the success that attached to it. Secondly, Domitian's colleague in the consulship of A.D. 83 was Quintus Petillius Rufus, who may in fact have been Quintus Petillius Cerialis, the first Flavian governor of Britain whose full name was Quintus Petillius Cerialis Caesius Rufus.[42] Such evidence would indicate that Tacitus was probably well distanced from the generality of informed opinion, and might explain, for example, his generally cool attitude to Cerialis.

As we have seen, the sequence of events which followed Agricola's departure is not easy to reconstruct. Two inscriptions (*ILS* 1025; 9200) record the seconding of vexillations from the British legions for service in Domitian's German war; indeed, the former of these refers specifically to the services of Lucius Roscius Aelianus, a military tribune in IX *Hispana*, and it is worth remembering that it was the ninth legion which had found itself in difficulties, probably at Dalginross, during Agricola's sixth campaign. These troop removals, however, do not seem to have produced any immediate major policy reversal in Britain. Indeed, the coin evidence[43] suggests that it was not until *c*.A.D. 87 that major changes occurred. It was at this point in all probability that II *Adiutrix* was removed from Britain; with a garrison of only three legions, and important fortresses to be manned at York, Chester and Caerleon,

9. (OPPOSITE) Campaign camp, Dalginross. This is one of a number of campaign camps in Scotland which have an unusual entrance way, known as a 'double *clavicula*', where the rampart and ditch are drawn outwards to form a narrow entrance. This feature is not found on most campaign camps (e.g. Rey Cross, Plate 5), and such camps are thought to date to campaigning in the 80s.

the position of Inchtuthil as a legionary fortress was now untenable; construction work was stopped before the fortress was complete and the buildings demolished. The loss of the fourth legion meant that the plan to secure the Highlands was beyond the realistic capabilities of the British garrison.

However, between A.D. 83 and 87 the policy to which Agricola had been working remained essentially in tact. It is probable that the 'glen blocking' forts from the Clyde leading toward Inchtuthil, together with Inchtuthil itself, were being built during this period. Further, whilst the greater complexity of occupation of the Forth–Tay forts suggests that their building probably started earlier – perhaps during Agricola's third campaign – work no doubt was proceeding on the 'Gask Ridge frontier' during this period also. The Forth–Tay forts were probably given up at the same time as Inchtuthil and the 'glen blocking' forts, although it has been suggested[44] that they could have been retained a little longer.

It has always been assumed that the evacuation of the forts of northern Scotland related to the holding of a Forth–Clyde frontier for the remainder of the first century A.D. However, recent work on the Stanegate-*limes*[45] (see below in chapter 4) has suggested that the policy reversal of A.D. 87 was more radical, involving a more general withdrawal from Scotland, leaving only a few sites, such as Newstead and Dalswinton, as outliers to the new system. It is only at these more southerly forts that the coin series carry us beyond A.D. 87.[46] If this was the true extent of the post-Agricolan withdrawal from Scotland, then the harshness of Tacitus' judgement begins to fall into perspective; although troops were now available for major redeployment elsewhere in the north,[47] indicating that the new policy was not negative, it has to be admitted that a frontier of *Britannia* drawn between the Tyne and the Solway was a long way short of the aspirations of men like Agricola and Tacitus. To them, the objective had been total conquest; the reality was that it had been allowed immediately to slip. Others, no doubt, within senatorial circles shared their frustrations.

4

Flavian and Trajanic Frontiers

THE evolution of frontier systems in the north of Britain has been the subject of much discussion and modification of viewpoints, particularly with regard to the nature and chronology of such structures. It is now generally held that in northern Scotland, as in northern England, we have to find a place for the work of other governors besides Agricola[1] and that, although troops were being taken from the British garrison during the 80s, Roman policy remained essentially expansionist until the withdrawal of legion II *Adiutrix* around A.D. 86 or 87. Previous withdrawals, however, such as that of three thousand legionaries in the early 80s in connection with Domitian's German campaigning, did not so much alter the objectives as constrain what could be achieved at any particular time.

We have seen that during Agricola's governorship the line of the Forth and Clyde was proposed as a *terminus*, and that this was formalised by a series of forts. For Agricola and his successor, however, this was probably not seen as anything other than a base line, or 'jumping off' point, for continuing operations further north. It is unclear whether this was located precisely on the Forth–Clyde line – taking in sites such as Camelon, Castlecary, Mollins, Cadder and Barochan – or whether it ran a little to the north of this – through Doune, Bochastle, Malling and Drumquhassle. This had been extended by the 'Forth–Tay' frontier, which included Camelon, Doune, Ardoch, Strageath and Bertha along the strongly fortified routes of Strathallan and Strathearn; this effectively separated the coastal lowlands and their good agricultural land from the interior, protecting those to the east by denying access to marauders from the west. The line thus drawn from the Clyde to the Tay not only marked the recognition of the political importance of the Tay, but was extended in a line from Carpow – (if an early site underlies the Severan base) – to Bertha, Cargill and Inchtuthil, behind the earthwork known as the Cleaven Dyke.

The far larger troop withdrawals of the later 80s, however, necessitated a radical redefining of imperatives.[2] The scale of this is demonstrated by the deliberate demolition of the fortress at Inchtuthil, still unfinished, along with other permanent sites north of the isthmus. It has always

10. The Stanegate road, Vindolanda. This road, which formed the frontier of Roman Britain from the late 80s, is here seen running past the site of Vindolanda. The fort and civilian settlement (*vicus*) are seen as they were in the third and fourth centuries A.D. In the late 80s, the fort was much larger, and occupied much of the space later used by civilian buildings. The writing tablets came from waterlogged deposits between the late fort and *vicus*.

been assumed that this withdrawal stopped at the Agricolan line of forts between the Forth and the Clyde, thus retaining a full occupation of the southern Scottish Lowlands. However, an element of doubt that this was the strategy has existed for some considerable time in that major sites on the Tyne–Solway line – at Corbridge, Vindolanda and Carlisle – appeared to be the scenes of large-scale work also in the late 80s, prompting the suggestion[3] that work on a more southerly frontier had been commenced prior to a 'strategic withdrawal' from southern Scotland. This view, too, may well have been too conservative.

Aerial reconnaissance during the 1970s and 1980s has introduced important new information on the development of the Tyne–Solway line; first, it is now clear that fortifications continued westwards from Carlisle to the coast at Kirkbride in the form of forts and towers as well as linear features in the form of a road, running ditch and palisade. Secondly, it has been shown that the physical development of forts between Corbridge and Kirkbride is considerably more complex than was at one time suspected.

The *Stanegate* is the name which, since medieval times, has been applied to the road long known to have linked Corbridge and Carlisle.[4] Further, it is recognised that this road represented a stage in the development of the northern frontier, although it has been generally assumed that its active role was squeezed between the supposed withdrawal from

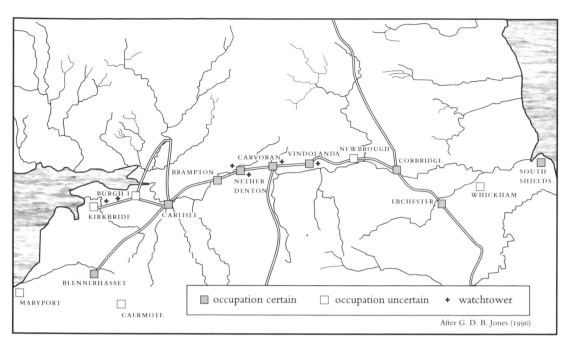

occupation certain occupation uncertain + watchtower

After G. D. B. Jones (1990)

Figure 6 (i). The Stanegate-*limes*. Present evidence, based largely upon aerial photography, suggests that in 'Phase 1' the troops brought back from Scotland were placed in large forts of 7–8 acres. In the second phase (*c*.A.D. 100), these forts were halved in size and the troops spread out amongst a larger number of smaller installations.

southern Scotland in *c*.A.D. 100 and the inception of the fort phase of Hadrian's Wall in *c*.A.D. 125, at which point most of the forts on the Stanegate were abandoned as redundant. It was further surmised that the 'Stanegate frontier' probably consisted of alternating auxiliary forts and fortlets, and that whilst some of the former probably dated back to Agricola's governorship, the system as a whole came into operation in the very earliest years of the second century A.D.

It is now possible to offer an alternative model of development; the early Flavian period saw the establishment of an auxiliary fort at Carlisle,[5] whilst during Agricola's governorship a vexillation fortress and supply base was built at Corbridge (Red House).[6] These two sites stood at pivotal points of the two northward arterial routes into Scotland, on either side of the Pennines. The early existence of a communications link between them is attested by the establishment in the mid-80s of the first of a number of superimposed fort phases at Vindolanda.[7]

We have little information from literary sources that is particularly helpful, although the Vindolanda tablets contain references that are pertinent. Tacitus, in a cryptic reference at the opening of his *Histories*, published *c*.A.D. 105,[8] talks of Britain being 'completely conquered, and immediately allowed to slip'; this reference applies to the Flavian period in general. The satiric poet, Juvenal, a near contemporary of Tacitus, implies warfare in Britain, and mentions a chieftain, named Arviragus;[9] unfortunately there is little detail, and, as often, events to which Juvenal alludes cannot be given a secure chronological context. Finally, Hadrian's biographer, Spartianus, in the *Writers of the Augustan History*, referring to the time of Hadrian's accession to power in A.D. 117, indicates serious disturbances in Britain, although providing no clue to their location.[10] The issuing of a 'subdued Britannia' coin by Hadrian in A.D. 119 appears to confirm the seriousness of the problem, and the need for immediate military action under the governor, Quintus Pompeius Falco.[11] Finally, Suetonius[12] mentions the insubordination of a governor of Britain, Sallustius Lucullus, although this presumably had more to do with the resentment felt against Domitian by members of the senatorial order than it did with the security situation in Britain. Lucullus may have been Agricola's successor, and will probably therefore have had to supervise the withdrawal from Scotland to which Tacitus so scathingly alludes.[13]

It is not surprising, in view of the development of Roman activities in northern Scotland in the 80s, that there should have been repercussions further south; for example, a writing tablet from Carlisle indicates the presence of legionaries in the fort in A.D. 83. Further, it is clear from a tablet from Vindolanda that in the first phase of that fort in the later 80s, the garrison unit (*Cohors I Tungrorum*) was severely under strength with a considerable number of its soldiers sick or absent on duty elsewhere – possibly at Corbridge.[14] These must have been disturbed times, and it is interesting to find on a Vindolanda tablet a spontaneous reaction to the British as *Brittunculi* ('horrid little Brits'), though it is unclear whether the comment is directed towards British opponents or to those who were being recruited into the Roman army.[15]

The evidence of Roman coins found on Scottish sites[16] makes it clear that the withdrawal from the north of Scotland occurred in *c.*A.D. 87, and was caused, at least in part, by the necessity to bring pressure to bear on European frontiers. The coin evidence also suggests that this evacuation went further than the line of the Forth and Clyde. However, it is less clear how we should interpret this evacuation; a second phase of Flavian activity has been recognised at a number of sites north of the Tyne–Solway line, in particular at Newstead and Dalswinton, and at Cappuck, Broomholm, High Rochester and Learchild. At the first two of these, the modification was substantial. Newstead was enlarged to 13 acres with a garrison of legionaries and auxiliaries, whilst Dalswinton was enlarged to over 10 acres, possibly with similar garrison implications.

This gives rise to the question as to whether a *limes* was drawn through southern Scotland with Newstead and Dalswinton as its pivotal points. However, in the light of present evidence from sites on the Stanegate, it seems more appropriate to assume[17] that these forts in southern Scotland were more truly outliers of a *limes* based upon the Tyne–Solway gap, although the very sizes of Newstead and Dalswinton leave doubts. It is possible that a compromise could be envisaged in which a short-lived frontier was strongly maintained, based upon Newstead and Dalswinton, until work was completed to establish a more convenient *limes* between the Tyne and the Solway.

The evidence from the Stanegate is of substantial modification occurring in the late 80s and early 90s, and based upon a number of large forts of seven to eight acres.[18] At Carlisle, enlargement is evident in the 80s, whilst further substantial enhancement in the early 90s has been noticed in the Lanes area of the City; at Vindolanda, the original fort of 3.5 acres was doubled in size, occupying an area beneath the later fort and *vicus*. The tablets indicate that this enlarged fort was intended for a double garrison, consisting of *Cohors VIIII Batavorum* serving alongside the original garrison of Tungrians. At Corbridge, the vexillation fortress (probably of 25–30 acres) was abandoned in favour of a new fort situated at about one mile to the east, which was evidently under construction in the late 80s. These reconstructions were apparently

11. The forts at Nether Denton on the Stanegate. This photograph shows the initial large fort which was subsequently reduced in size. This relationship, observed also at other sites on the Stanegate, provides the evidence for the development of the Stanegate-*limes*.

accompanied by the construction of at least three other forts of similarly large capacity at Nether Denton, Carvoran and probably Newbrough. The size of these forts along the Stanegate presumably hints at the large number of troops for whom new dispositions were having to be found, following the withdrawal from Scotland, and may reflect additions of cavalry to existing garrisons, a policy to which there is reference in the Vindolanda tablets.

It seems likely – although admittedly the evidence is not yet to hand to prove it – that at this stage the running barrier represented by the Stanegate was extended westwards from Carlisle to the coast at Kirk-bride, where harbour installations (of uncertain date) have been detected on the south bank of the river Waver, indicating the possible existence of a depot for the western half of the Stanegate system. It seems possible, too, that a similiar extension ran eastwards from Corbridge through Whickham (Washing Well), a fort at which two periods of occupation have been identified, to the coast at South Shields, where a pre-Hadrianic phase has been recognised.

Work in the 1970s and 1980s has gone a considerable way towards clarifying the complex developments along the 'western Stanegate'.[19] At a distance of one kilometre south of the village of Burgh-by-Sands a large fort of 7 acres has been located (Burgh I). It has been shown that three phases of development are contained within a period

12. The forts at 'Burgh I' on the western Stanegate. As at Nether Denton, a large fort was subsequently reduced in size.

13. The watchtower beneath the forts at 'Burgh I', during excavations in 1978. First observed as a cropmark, the watch-tower was the first structure on the site, and consisted of a four-posted tower, defended by an encir-cling ditch. After a short life, the site of the tower was le-velled, consolidated with cobbles and the rampart of the fort built over it.

14. The 'running ditch', Finglandrigg. The ditch, with a timber palisade, was part of the complex monitoring system put in place in the Solway Plain. It is here seen during excavation in 1994.

c.A.D. 90–130 – a four-posted timber watchtower built on a platform which was some nineteen metres in diameter and defended by a ditch. Subsequent to this came the fort of seven acres which was later reduced in size to a little over 3.5 acres. A little to the west lay another fort (Burgh III) which was built to enclose an area of 8.4 acres which was subsequently reduced to 5.3 acres. It is currently not clear whether this relates to the development of the Stanegate or to the construction of Hadrian's Wall. At Finglandrigg, further evidence of development has been recovered; in the first place, the Stanegate road itself has been located, with a ditch or ditch–and–palisade to the north of it. A circular site has been examined at Easton, which bears signs of similarity with the watchtower at Burgh I. To the west of Burgh, at Farnhill, a watchtower of the Burgh type was found to have had its ditch cut by an east–west running ditch and palisade.

It is likely, however, that the development on the Solway Plain of features such as these is more complex than has been thought; for running ditches, palisades and towers have been recognised also else-where in Solway. For example, a ditch and palisade, possibly with a road, runs westwards near Blencogo village in the direction (apparently) of Beckfoot. That this had more than one phase of use is demonstrated clearly by aerial photographs indicating at one point the re-use of a short section of the ditch as part of the demarcation/defence of a native farmstead. To the north of this, and heading apparently north-westwards in the direction of Kirkbride, is another length of ditch; the fact that this runs near, but not in direct association with, a small signal tower on Gamelsby Ridge again indicates complexity in develop-ment. This tower, supported on four posts, and enclosed by a ditch and palisade, is only eight metres in diameter across the ditch, and again recalls contemporary examples in Germany. It remains unclear whether these represent separate works or are parts of the same, but developing, system. Whatever the total extent and complexity of these features, we may assume that they are parts of a developing scheme for the monitoring of movement on Solway at an early stage of its occupation.[20]

The reduction in size noted at Burgh I (and Burgh III, if indeed this site is contemporaneous) is matched by similar reductions (by approximately 50%) at Nether Denton, Carvoran and (probably) New-brough (Sitgate). At the same time, the enlarged forts at Vindolanda and Carlisle and the fort at Corbridge retained their sizes. There is a strong suggestion that by at least the time of the modifications of Stanegate sites, the control of the system was located at Carlisle; for a Vindolanda tablet[21] record the presence at Carlisle of a man named Annius Equester, who is described as a *centurio regionarius* (or a kind of 'District Commissioner').

The reductions in fort size presumably indicate a policy of spreading the available troops between more installations. It may thus be that we should date the smaller sites along the Stanegate to this period of its history, although certainty is not presently possible, in view of the lack of dateable material available from these sites.[22] The fort at Bramp-ton (Old Church) is approximately 3.5 acres in size, corresponding

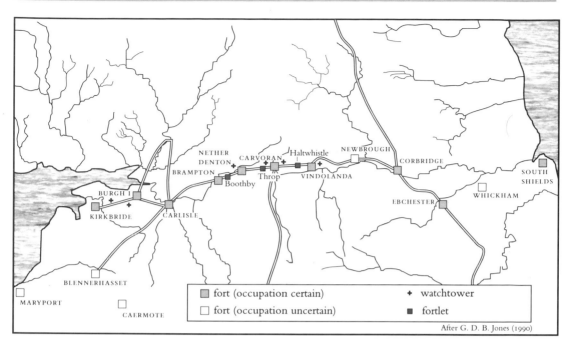

fort (occupation certain)   watchtower
fort (occupation uncertain)   fortlet

After G. D. B. Jones (1990)

reasonably closely to the size of 'reduced' forts on the Stanegate; the fort might, therefore, be contemporary with the second phase on the Stanegate; alternatively, a larger fort may await discovery in the area.

A number of smaller installations have been recognised, although again dating remains a serious problem; fortlets have been recognised at Boothby (between Brampton and Nether Denton), at Throp (between Nether Denton and Carvoran), and at Haltwistle Burn (between Carvoran and Vindolanda), where a complex of construction camps has been identified from the air. These are consistent in size, extending a little over 0.5 acres. In addition, there may be another at High Crosby (between Carlisle and Brampton), and Birley[23] speculates on possible sites for others to the east of Vindolanda. Finally, mention should be made of a number of watchtowers; Nether Denton is 'flanked' by towers at Pike Hill and Mains Rigg, though it remains unclear whether these structures do indeed relate to the Stanegate. East of Carvoran is a tower, which is normally referred to as '45a' (in the sequence of structures on Hadrian's Wall), though it does not appear to relate to Hadrian's Wall. Again, to the east of Vindolanda, at Barcombe Hill, there was a tower constructed of timber which evidently was intended to relate to the line of the Stanegate.

There is some evidence, then, to believe that early in the second century, the Stanegate underwent a complex modification. The *limes* then consisted of a road with regular forts, some of which were large, though most were approximately 3.5 acres in size. It is further likely that between each pair of forts were situated a fortlet and a watchtower. This will clearly have resulted in a more even distribution of manpower than was possible in the dispositions of the first phase. It remains unclear whether any further modifications were undertaken prior to the building of Hadrian's Wall, although there is a possibility that the fort at Nether Denton was replaced by a fortlet. It is also unclear what nature of commitment was retained to the north of the *limes* in its second phase, although it is possible that communications north of Carlisle and Corbridge were maintained.

The frontier will not, of course, have been exclusively military in nature; *vici* are certainly attested at Corbridge and Vindolanda, whilst excavations at Carlisle have indicated widespread non-military activity in the late first and early second centuries. At Nether Denton also, an extensive *vicus* developed, which survived the abandonment of the fort. Indeed, the continuing strength of the *vicus* at Nether Denton has been adduced to explain the apparent absence of a *vicus* at the nearby Hadrian's Wall fort of Birdoswald; if Nether Denton continued to thrive, then a *vicus* at Birdoswald would have been surplus to requirements.

Against what sort of historical background are we to view these frontier developments? We have already seen that Britain cannot be looked at in isolation from the rest of the Empire; it was inevitable that growing commitments elsewhere in the empire could not be met without some redeployment of troops, and it is clear that Britain lost troops in both the early and later 80s. The strain on resources imposed by difficulties on the Rhine and the Danube continued throughout the reign of Domitian. Further, it is hard to imagine that Trajan's forceful – and perhaps unnecessary – tackling of central Europe in his Dacian campaigns of A.D. 101–2 and 105–6 did not carry implications for troop deployments elsewhere, particularly since these campaigns culminated in the capture and organisation of Dacia as a Roman province with a permanent garrison of two legions. Further, within a few years of this, Trajan had embarked upon even more grandiose schemes in the east.

Of course, these commitments both imposed obligations and provided opportunities; for whilst some dreams had to be abandoned, troops were thus released not just for crises elsewhere in the empire, but also for redeployment within Britain;[24] the Stanegate-*limes* itself absorbed some – perhaps 6,500;[25] the opportunity could also be taken to consolidate the basic route of conquest established under Vespasian. New territory was brought within the policing network; forts were established in the Lake District – Watercrook (Kendal), Ambleside, Hardknott and

15. Fort at Hardknott Pass. This remotely situated fort was established early in the second century A.D. and was part of the policing network established in the Lake district; it occupied the midway point on the road which ran from Ambleside to the coast at Ravenglass. Its central range of buildings – headquarters, granaries and commander's house – is clearly visible.

Ravenglass, Troutbeck, Papcastle and Caermote – in a process which was continued through the later Flavian and Trajanic periods.

It is evident, too, that substantial and widespread modifications were undertaken at existing forts, although far more research is required before we can expect to understand fully the nature, chronology and purpose of these. Rebuilding in stone occurred at the legionary fortresses at Chester and York (*RIB* 464 and 665); some auxiliary forts were also rebuilt in the same way, though we should beware of necessarily seeing such activity as part of the same policy. Epigraphic evidence (*RIB* 604) places the rebuilding at Lancaster early in the second century, and it might be reasonable to assume that it was at this stage that early Flavian turf-and-timber forts would have naturally required refurbishment. It is likely, however, that this process will have come later at those turf-and-timber forts which were built in the A.D. 90s.

Modification may, in any case, have been a complex process; it may, as at Kirkham and Ribchester, have involved many phases of reworking of the defences; or it may have consisted of re-orientating a fort through 90 degrees, as happened at Lancaster where the main gate, originally on the eastern side of the fort, was moved to the northern side, again indicating changed priorities.[26] However, whilst we may be able to hypothesise on the nature of these new priorities, certainty is likely to remain elusive. Flexibility of garrison patterns in the later first and early second centuries is also implied by the enlargement of some forts, such as Lancaster, and the reduction in size of others, such as Castleshaw.[27] Again, it is not always evident when such modifications as these were undertaken; however, whilst we lack substantial evidence on garrison patterns, we can see sufficient to be able to question strongly the implication of Tacitus that the late Flavian period (and perhaps the Trajanic also) were times dominated by negative attitudes. Changing imperatives demanded flexibility, and there is strong evidence for that flexibility.

At the same time, it is clear that the infrastructure that supported the Roman policing network was itself enhanced; the development of *vici* outside most of the forts was clearly important in this, and many of the Vindolanda tablets suggest the ways in which forts were drawing on their hinterlands, presumably to the mutual benefit of the occupying forces and of the subject population. New roads were laid out, and we may be sure that to enable the forts to draw on the raw materials available in their areas, a network of smaller routes will have needed to be developed. Nor should we forget the importance of waterways; evidence from Ambleside, for example, with its large *vicus* and storage facilities within the fort, suggests the developing significance of Lake Windermere as a route of communication into the heart of the Lake District.

If garrisons were becoming more settled during this period, it is not surprising that the authorities sought also to improve the organisation of supplies; in the early years of occupation, military units evidently produced much of their own hardware. Small industrial sites, such as at Quernmore,[28] Scalesceugh and Brampton,[29] supplied their 'local forts' with utensils, tools and building materials. These, however, appear mostly to have been 'running down' in the second quarter of the second century A.D., as such supplies came to be organised in a more global manner. Large-scale contracts were evidently placed in the south of Britain and in the Nene Valley for pottery products, and there is evidence in the north, too, of a more organised approach.

A large industrial site developed in the Wilderspool and Stockton Heath areas of Warrington,[30] and another at Heronbridge (near Chester). Wilderspool's products have been recognised all over the frontier zone, and as far north as the Antonine Wall. It is evident that, contrary to early assessments, these were not sites run by the Roman army; whilst some of the original organisation and certainly the continuing markets for products rested with the army, the craftsmen were evidently

Romano-British. The breadth of products is strong witness to the local technology which was available to be tapped, and clearly the search for raw materials will have encouraged the further opening up of the military zone.

To facilitate the movement of such products the army operated its own depots; we have seen that the site at Corbridge (Red House) performed such a function for Agricola's campaigns in Scotland; indeed it was a role which Corbridge was to renew in the second century, as would South Shields in connection with the Severan attacks on northern Scotland in the early third century. In the north west, a major depot was developed, evidently in the late Flavian period, at Walton-le-Dale (Preston); this site was well placed to take advantage of the road network, and to make use of water transport along the river Ribble, which provided access to coastal shipping. This could give relatively easy access to a large number of sites by means of river estuaries, such as the Dee, the Mersey, the Lune and the Kent; further afield, routes could be plied to likely port sites, as at Ravenglass, Maryport and Kirkbride, and to Carlisle by means of the Solway estuary. It is possible, too, that contact would have been made with a site, now lost, at the southern end of Lake Windermere.[31] Although only a small area has been excavated at Walton-le-Dale, the identification of its large timber, 'shed-like', buildings has dispelled the long-held view that this was a fortlet.

We can thus see that the withdrawal from much of Scotland in the late 80s should be viewed in a positive light; military defeat had been inflicted upon the Caledonians, leaving the Roman authorities free to make decisions concerning the extent of actual occupation in the north which had regard to *all* imperatives. Withdrawal to the line of the Tyne and Solway was managed in a deliberate and unhurried fashion; it reflected the need for the redispositioning of troops in the empire's areas of difficulty, and offered the opportunity for the redeployment of troops in Britain in a way which positively enhanced the ability to guard and police the north.

As we have observed, it is possible to detect the evidence for the establishment of the Stanegate as a frontier in the later 80s and early 90s, and its modification, perhaps a decade later. The course of events which separated this modification from Hadrian's accession in A.D. 117 is, however, less clear. The conclusion of the Dacian Wars in A.D. 106 and the organisation of Dacia as an 'armed province' will have meant that there was little occasion to restore troops to Britain – even if that was any longer a desired objective. It has been shown, too,[32] how there was similarly little apparent desire to enhance arrangements on the *limes Germanicus*.

In any case, now that Trajan had stabilised the Danube frontier, he was free to turn his attention to another long-running 'imperial sore' – the relations with the kingdoms of Parthia and Armenia. The last four years of the reign saw an increasing commitment to the eastern theatre, with Trajan's solution becoming growingly 'global', looking towards large-scale conquest and the organisation of new provinces. It is not possible to tell how far (if at all) troops were taken from Britain to equip this expedition, unless the apparent reduction to a fortlet of the already-reduced fort at Nether Denton offers an insight. In any case, it appears that either real reductions in Britain or the Britons' perception of an emperor who was pre-occupied elsewhere led to difficulties.

16. Copper *as* of Hadrian. This coin, which depicts a 'dejected personification' of Britannia, was issued in A.D. 119, apparently to commemorate victories won on Hadrian's behalf by Quintus Pompeius Falco to restore a disturbed situation that had developed in the later years of Trajan's reign.

Spartianus' observation that at the time of Hadrian's accession, 'the Britons could no longer be held under Roman control'[33] provides a clear indication that imperial imperatives had to be reviewed by the new emperor. Further, the identification of a number of coin hoards belonging to the early years of the second century may provide another indication of unrest.[34] Trajan's governor, Quintus Pompeius Falco, was left in the province and was clearly responsible for a military victory in Britain, which was of sufficient significance to merit commemoration on the coinage of A.D. 119, both by a Victory issue and by a BRITANNIA issue.[35]

Finally, the fact that Hadrian's first imperial journey took in Britain, and may have been as early as A.D. 120[36] further points to the seriousness of the situation in Britain. That this trouble was located in the north is hinted at by the details of the depiction of *Britannia* on the coin of A.D. 119 and by the fact that the reclining river god, which features on a coin commemorating the first journey, has been taken as representing the river Tyne.[37] Clearly, action was required, though the fact that the siting of Hadrian's Wall represented no surrender of territory indicates that the situation was not beyond repair and that the trouble itself was probably not sustained beyond Falco's victory. Above all, Trajan's death brought imperial expansion to an end; the results of Hadrian's visit to Britain show that the new emperor's view of imperial security, whilst no less dynamic than that of his predecessor, was very different in its expression.

5

Hadrian's Wall

HADRIAN's Wall, with its forts, milecastles and turrets, and together with its associated surviving earthworks, provides Britain's most substantial extant monument of the Roman period. Set in some of the most dramatic scenery that England has to offer, it attracts countless visitors who inevitably ask a host of questions about it, but ultimately just enjoy it. Although urban growth in Newcastle and Carlisle has destroyed much of it in those areas, the Wall's central sector occupies unspoilt countryside which offers the visitor as much pleasure and fulfilment as the Wall itself. Inevitably, too, Hadrian's Wall has attracted much scholarly attention on to questions concerning its purpose, the nature of its structure, the way it operated, and how this may have changed over a period of nearly three centuries. Modern research is showing that, whilst the Wall was the result of a planning decision, we should be wary about becoming over-rigid in our interpretation of it and be prepared to see in its overall structure the results of responses to local needs at various times.

As we have seen, and as is made clear on the Jarrow inscription (*RIB* 1051), the decision to build the Wall intimately involved the emperor himself; almost certainly his presence in Britain in A.D. 121 was itself a response to difficulties that had been experienced in the north over the previous decade.[1] The precise seat of this trouble is not easily located, although the discovery of a number of early imperial coin hoards in the north west suggests that disturbance *may* have been quite widespread.[2]

Nor did Britain provide the new emperor's only anxiety; when Hadrian acceded in A.D. 117, his predecessor's eastern conquests were crumbling, and there were suspicions that Hadrian's own succession was marred by intrigue; the murder of four ex-consuls at the beginning of the reign, for which Hadrian vigorously disclaimed any knowledge or responsibility, served both to sour the new emperor's relations with senators, and to emphasise the sharp difference between him and his predecessor. From the point of view of some senior senators who had thrived on Trajanic militarism, the preoccupations of the new emperor seemed both weak and damaging – even treacherous.[3]

Figure 7. Northern England and southern Scotland in the Roman period.

ANTONINE WALL		HADRIAN'S WALL	
1. Whitemoss	11. Croy Hill	22. Old Church	32. Carrawburgh
2. Old Kilpatrick	12. Westerwood	23. Castlesteads	33. Chesters
3. Duntochter	13. Castlecary	24. Nether Denton	34. Halton
4. Castle Hill	14. Seabegs	25. Birdoswald	35. Rudchester
5. New Kilpatrick	15. Rough Castle	26. Throp	36. Benwell
6. Balmuildy	16. Camelon	27. Carvoran	37. Newcastle
7. Cadder	17. Falkirk	28. Great Chesters	38. Wallsend
8. Kirkintilloch	18. Mumrills	29. Haltwhistle Burn	39. South Shields
9. Auchendavy	19. Inveravon	30. Chesterholm	
10. Bar Hill	20. Kinneil	31. Housesteads	
	21. Carriden		

17. Hadrian's Wall at Cawfields. This is one of the most dramatic stretches of the Wall, as it utilises the Great Whin Sill; the mile-castle at Cawfields (MC 42) is seen at the bottom of the picture, and the *vallum* is clearly visible running a little to the south of the Wall.

In a period of increasing economic difficulty and personal uncertainty, Hadrian wisely appreciated that the empire as a whole could not afford and did not need further expansion, particularly of the vigorous (and disruptive) nature undertaken by Trajan. Like some others before him, he felt that more attention should be paid to safeguarding the integrity of the existing empire and promoting its internal strength by development of its infrastructure and enhancement of opportunities and participation by local grandees. Although he did not openly snub the senate, he also felt, as is shown by his reform of the civil service, that the trend towards increasing opportunities for members of the equestrian order should be strengthened. Further, some may have seen his cultural preoccupations as unnatural for a Roman emperor.

The interpretation of weakness, however, was erroneous: for the policy of developing the empire's internal strength was positive, and was vigorously pursued. There is evidence of frontier work on the Rhine and the Danube, in the east in the area of the rivers Tigris and Euphrates, and on the northern flank of the Sahara; much of this work at the least enjoyed some Hadrianic input. Such a natural barrier was not, of course, available in Britain; it was therefore reasonable that the Hadrian decided to build upon what already existed along the Stanegate;

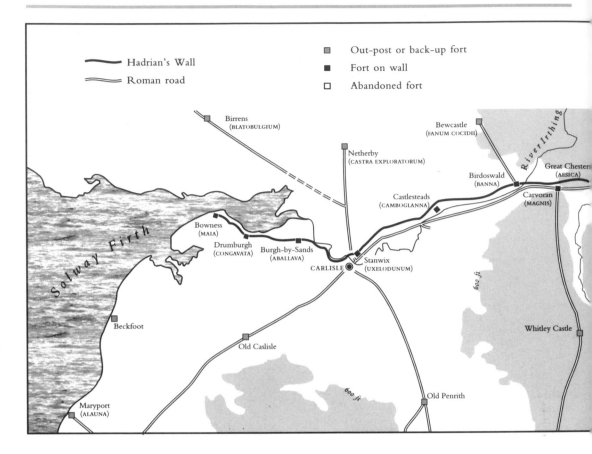

for Hadrian's Wall was essentially seen as an enhancement of the Trajanic frontier – a natural move in view of the fact that, whatever his policies elsewhere in the empire, Trajan had effectively reached the same decision with regard to Britain that Hadrian was to adopt on an empire-wide basis.

A positive policy initiative adopted by Hadrian was his decision to visit the armies in all the provinces; this was given a high profile through the coin issues which commemorated these visits. The fact that Britain figured early amongst the imperial visits indicates the seriousness with which Hadrian viewed the situation in the province that greeted him on his accession. That he was right to do so is confirmed by the letter, written in A.D. 162, by Cornelius Fronto to the emperor, Marcus Aurelius, in which it is said that in Britain and Judaea Hadrian suffered major losses of troops, which were remembered nearly half a century later. Somewhere, probably within the late Trajanic period, IX *Hispana* was transferred to Lower Germany; it was not, as the popular story has held, lost, though it may have suffered

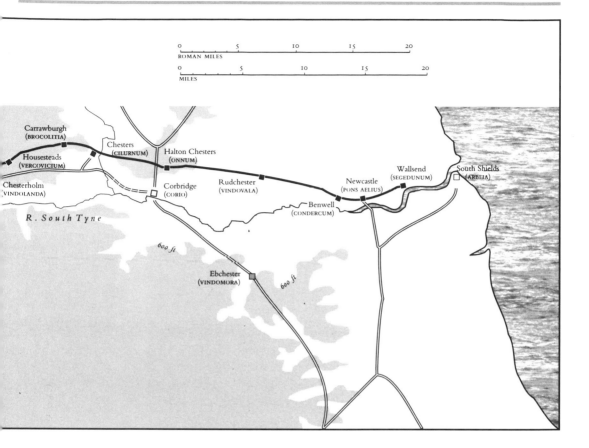

losses. It is not clear how long was the hiatus between its transference and the arrival of its replacement; if it was considerable, it might help to explain the unsettled conditions in the province.[4] In any case, VI *Victrix* was clearly handpicked for the particular job of frontier construction, since it will have had such experience in its previous posting on the Rhine.

Hadrian reached Britain in A.D. 121, and it has been suggested that he made straight for the northern frontier area and the heart of the province's difficulties by disembarking on the Tyne; an *aureus* of A.D. 120, showing a reclining river deity, has been thought to represent the Tyne (*Tina*).[5] VI *Victrix* may have arrived at the same time, together with a new governor, Aulus Platorius Nepos, replacing Trajan's governor, Pompeius Falco. We should, however, not imagine that Hadrian directed his attention exclusively to the frontier; whilst no doubt the strategy which lay behind the Wall's construction was his, he found time to strengthen the infrastructure, giving a greater measure of local control to tribal leaders; the civilian administration of the eastern

Brigantes, based at Aldborough (*Isurium Brigantum*), probably came into being at this time, and Hadrian's hand has been recognised in the establishment of a completely new town in the Fenlands – at Stonea, close to the site of the pre-Roman stronghold of the Iceni.[6]

Hadrian evidently had no fundamental quarrel with the line of the Stanegate frontier; it was after all, after the Forth–Clyde line, the obvious place at which to draw a linear frontier in Britain. Hadrian's Wall was, in the first instance at least, seen as an enhancement of, rather than as a replacement for, the Stanegate, and the first plan of the Wall zone included already-existing features of the earlier frontier. However, if Hadrian's view of the frontier was that in part its function should be to control movement, this could obviously be more effectively discharged if the frontier had a strong *visual* command of the territory in which it was set.

The Stanegate road lacked this advantage because of its close relationship with the valleys of the Tyne, Irthing and Eden rivers; the line selected for the Wall advanced northwards to occupy the northern crests of those valleys, and thus acquire a command of territory, over part at least of which the Romans will have exercised a kind of responsibility because it was still the territory of the Brigantes. Indeed, there is good reason to believe, because of the discovery at Birrens (Dumfriesshire) of a fine relief carving of *Dea Brigantia*, the tribe's tutelary deity Romanised into the classical form of a 'Winged Victory', that the so-called 'outpost forts' of Bewcastle, Birrens and Netherby in fact enclosed, protected and facilitated the policing of this area of Brigantian territory which had been isolated to the north of the frontier.

The initial plan was to build a linear barrier from Newcastle to Bowness-on-Solway, which was equipped with a small fortlet (milecastle) every Roman mile, and a pair of watchtowers (turrets) between each pair of milecastles. Thus, along the seventy-or-so miles of the frontier, there was a manned installation set at approximately every three hundred metres. To the north of the Wall, and separated from it by a cleared space (or berm), was a V-shaped ditch, which varied in width around an average of eight metres (twenty-seven feet) and was three metres (ten feet) in depth, with a square drainage channel (or 'ankle breaker') at the bottom. It is apparent, however, that where the geological conditions of an area caused difficulties in ditch digging or rendered it redundant, its excavation was not completed, and occasionally not even started.

The original length of Hadrian's Wall was to be seventy-six Roman miles (or seventy of our miles), – running from Newcastle, where a

18. Hadrian's Wall: Cawfields Milecastle. The milecastles were a feature of the first plan for Hadrian's Wall; in effect they were fortlets acting as defended gateways through the Wall. They had north and south gateways, with a barrack on each side of the roadway which ran through them. They were capable of housing about a dozen men.

new bridge was built and the site named *Pons Aelius* in honour of the emperor (whose full name was Publius *Aelius* Hadrianus). To the crossing of the river Irthing, the first forty-five miles were to be built of stone to a width of three metres (ten feet), whilst the remainder to the terminal point, just west of Bowness-on-Solway, was to be constructed of turves and with a basal width of six metres (twenty feet). The wall bridged three major rivers – the Tyne (at Chesters), the Irthing (at Willowford), and the Eden (at Carlisle); at the first two of these substantial remains of the bridge structures can still be made out. There was throughout good command to north and south, but nowhere more so than in the central sector where the Wall took advantage of the basaltic outcrop of the Great Whin Sill. By contrast, in the west, for the last few miles on the southern side of the Solway, the Wall was constructed only slightly above the high-water mark; it did not, of course, require striking physical command of the landscape to be able to police illicit crossing of the Solway.

The construction work was undertaken by parties from the three legions then based in Britain – II *Augusta*, VI *Victrix* and XX *Valeria Victrix*, together with help from the fleet (*classis Britannica*); there is

some indication of involvement on the part of
auxiliary troops, and local people may have
been used for heavy labouring and carting.[7]
The building work of the Wall, its installations
(apart from the forts), and the works along the
Cumberland coast, were planned together and
handled by the legionary work parties. Some
indication of how the work was divided is
given by the so-called 'centurial stones', on
which the contribution of a named century
within a numbered cohort is noted – the cohort being a sub-division of the legion, as the
century was of a cohort. However, there are
insufficient of these centurial stones to permit
a detailed discussion of work patterns on their
evidence alone. Further information comes
from a study of styles and techniques of building, as well as from the structure as a whole.
Recent work in the Burgh-by-Sands sector has
indicated that the building work of different
work parties, which has traditionally been recognised in the style of milecastle gateways,
milecastles of long and short axes, and turret
design, can probably also be seen in the
presence or absence of a cobble base to the
turf Wall.[8]

19. The Goddess,
Brigantia. This relief
carving depicts the
tutelary deity of the
Brigantes; she is in
the Romanised form
of a 'Winged Vic-
tory'. The carving
was found at Birrens,
suggesting that that
fort stood on the
boundary of Brigan-
tian territory. The
carving can be seen in
the National Museum
of Antiquities, in
Edinburgh.

As has been seen, Hadrian's Wall was conceived as an enhancement
of the Stanegate frontier, where in the first construction plan, the main
bodies of troops for garrison duties and police work were retained in
the existing forts. The nature of the first plan suggests that the principal
purposes were observation and the supervision of crossing in either
direction; for the milecastles were in reality fortified gateways. Those
crossing could be checked and, most importantly, where appropriate,
could be made to pay whatever dues attached to their purpose in
crossing.

Taxes were collected by different kinds of people, though all were
ultimately responsible to the emperor's financial official in the province,
the *Procurator Augusti*.[9] Much tax collection was done by officials in
the procurator's department but the leaders of the Romano-British
civitates were involved as part of their 'civic duties', and there was still
scope for the government to 'farm' to profit-making companies and

individuals the collection of some taxes – albeit under close scrutiny. Yet, corruption did exist; Tacitus tells us of 'dodges' organised by tax collectors to trick the taxpayer out of more money:[10] such practices were supposedly stopped by Agricola. Nonetheless, evidence exists to show that throughout the empire corruption continued, particularly in the form of bribes paid to ensure speedy and sympathetic consideration; for example, at the frontier, a payment might secure a token search of one's products – or no search at all. Much of this was in the process of being tightened up in the later second century with the appointment of a new type of official, a *beneficiarius consularis* (or 'governor's aide'), who appears to have had a range of duties, which included supervision of 'customs points'.

Probably the most significant piece of information to have come from a study of the Wall's structure is the evidence for a major revision in what is generally taken as the second *full* season of work – that is, A.D. 124. This evidence consists of sections where construction commenced for a wall of *full* width, but where the actual structure is only about six feet in thickness ('narrow' Wall); also, milecastles (such as 48a at Willowford) and turrets can be identified at which preparations were made for a wall of greater breadth than was actually built. It is most likely that the reasons for this were the decision to build twelve new forts on the Wall and to speed up the construction process. We can also see evidence of milecastles and turrets which had been started in their proper places, only to be overbuilt by the later forts.

In their physical relationship to the Wall, the forts fall into two obvious groups in terms of their configuration – those that were built to lie astride the wall, and those that utilised Hadrian's Wall as their own northern rampart, thus leaving only one gate open to the north. Some have interpreted this as a product of purpose – those lying astride the wall being intended for garrisons of cavalry, whilst the rest were for infantry. In some cases, the configuration was altered, so that at Birdoswald the turf-and-timber fort lay astride the Turf Wall, whilst the rebuilt Stone Wall was pushed northwards to join the fort at its north-east and north-west corners. An alternative explanation is that the difference in configuration *may* simply reflect a stage in development; since it may have been discovered that building forts astride the Wall was both unnecessary and uneconomical, it is possible that all those that were built in this way predate the remainder that were not; alternatively, as perhaps at Housesteads, the configuration may have been determined by the terrain.

In support of this, it should be said that those forts which are known to be later in date – Carrawburgh, Wallsend, the rebuilt Birdoswald – were all bonded into Hadrian's Wall at their own northern walls; the same practice was later to be adopted on the Antonine Wall. As we have seen in the case of Birdoswald, rebuilding offered an opportunity to alter the configuration. In all, the initial phase of fort construction appears to have continued until A.D. 138, when the old Stanegate fort at Carvoran was rebuilt; this fort was evidently sufficiently close to the wall to be considered to be part of it. It is to be assumed, however, that the majority of the forts on the Stanegate were rendered redundant by the changes of plan. Whilst no reason for the change is given in contemporary documentation, we may assume that it was done in the interests of security, convenience and efficiency; whilst it may reflect disturbances during and perhaps caused by the building of Hadrian's Wall, we should remember that in some areas Hadrian's Wall was separated by a considerable distance from the Stanegate – approximately seven miles, for example, between the terminal forts of Kirkbride and Bowness-on-Solway.

The final major feature to be constructed was the *vallum*, running the whole length of the Wall on it southern side.[11] This consists of a flat-bottomed ditch which was three metres (ten feet) in depth and six metres (twenty feet) in width at the top. A berm of thirty feet was cleared on each side of the ditch, bounded by mounds of earth which were neatly and deliberately revetted with stacked turves to retain the mounds' compactness. Thus from north to south, the ditch and mounds

Figure 9. A 'section' through Hadrian's Wall showing the principal structures.

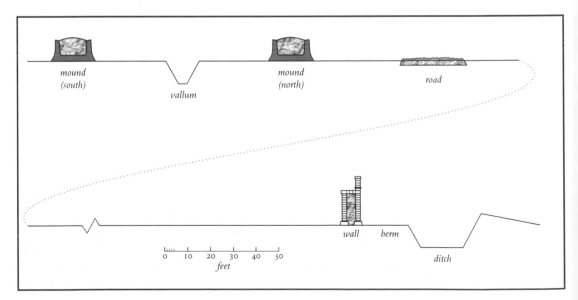

20. The Fort at Housesteads. The fort is the most completely excavated on Hadrian's Wall, and covers five acres, sufficient for a cohort of 1,000 men. In the north-east corner can be seen a pair of 'chalet barracks', belonging to a late refurbishment of the fort.

of the *vallum* present a feature that was thirty-seven metres (120 feet) in width.

The importance of the *vallum* is left in no doubt, for its construction was nowhere omitted – even in very uncongenial terrain. It was clearly constructed in conjunction with and as part of the fort phase of Hadrian's Wall, since it carefully skirted all of the forts, with the exceptions of Carrawburgh and Burgh-by-Sands; the former of these, although not much later than the others, was built over a filled-in stretch of *vallum*; it was evidently built as an afterthought, presumably to fill the otherwise long gap between its neighbours at Chesters and Housesteads. At Burgh-by-Sands, no evidence from the fort appears to pre-date the third century.[12]

The purpose of the *vallum* has been much debated; the idea that it reflects a pre-Hadrianic frontier phase is clearly not tenable in view of its physical relationship with the forts of Hadrian's Wall; nor would it make any sense whilst the main concentrations of troops remained in the Stanegate forts, since it would only have impeded movement between the Stanegate and the Wall. It is possible that, with the forts and their troops stationed on the Wall, the *vallum* offered a protection to them on their southern flank, indicating a closed zone and providing an obstacle which could hardly be crossed unintentionally. In this connection, it is worth noting that when the *vallum* was 'clean', the steeply sloping sides of the ditch will have provided a very difficult escape for unauthorised personnel. Alternatively, the *vallum* might conceivably represent a corridor for covert communication; the effect of the ditch and mounds will have been to allow troops to move anywhere along the line of the wall, unobserved from either north or south.

As we have seen, the western sector of the Wall – from the Irthing crossing to Bowness-on-Solway – was built of turf; of turf, too, were the milecastles and forts of this section, although the turrets were of stone, even on the Turf Wall. The reason for building in turf has been much discussed, and no totally convincing explanation as yet exists. It seems unrealistic to support the contention that there were inadequate supplies of building stone available, unless, of course, the security situation in the western sector at the time of construction was so sensitive that communications between the wall and quarry sites could not be guaranteed. It is possible that a particular problem was posed in the short term by an absence of limestone for the preparation of mortar. Neither of these suggestions, however, precluded the construction of the turrets in stone.

If we cannot derive a satisfactory explanation from negative arguments, we should turn to those that are positive: why was it advantageous to build the western section in turf? It should first be remembered that until the first two decades of the second century, the bulk of military construction had been carried out in turf rather than in stone; it was therefore a material that was tried and tested, and in which the military hierarchy will have felt confidence. There is no way in which such a finished product would have been less effective; its only problem, as with forts of turf and timber, will have been the need to introduce a major programme of refurbishment after about twenty years of life.

The use of turf in the western sector might indicate a need for speed of construction, and this in its turn might point to the west being the area which was most troubled by the disturbances alluded to by Spartianus. A further possible indicator of the validity of this hypothesis may lie in the extraordinary stone construction now visible in the southern guard chamber of the west gate of the stone fort at Birdoswald. This extremely fine masonry is hard to explain simply within the context of that gateway, but might be suitably explained if it is seen as a surviving fragment of a stone structure which pre-dated the fort – perhaps a trophy erected to commemorate Falco's victory of A.D. 118.

Commencement of construction of a policing wall might therefore reasonably have pre-dated (even if only by a little) Hadrian's visit to Britain. The local commanders started to build in material which they regarded as normal; the emperor, however, himself an architect of some note and with an eye to the psychological effect of the frontier and to his own reputation, perhaps had a preference for building in stone and thus ordered the construction to be recommenced at the eastern end. It may indeed always have been his intention to replace the turf wall when the time was right. There is still no sound evidence for the dating of this; theories vary from late in Hadrian's reign, to the period following the abandonment of the Antonine Wall, to a date early in the third century. It is not inconceivable that when Antoninus Pius came to reflect on this piece of 'unfinished business' he came to the view that for reasons to be explored later (in chapter 7) a completely new approach to the frontier was to be preferred. There is certainly no evidence from the structures of the turf wall which places the reconstruction unequivocally in Hadrian's reign.

Indeed, the chronology and development of the turf wall and its replacement may be much less uniform than was once supposed.[13]

21. Turf Wall, Apple-tree. Hadrian's Wall was constructed in turf westwards from the Irthing crossing; the section through it shows clearly the horizontal dark lines of turf, bound together with a grey clay.

Excavations at variety of sites, such as Castlesteads (which is detached from the Wall), Newcastle, Wallsend and Milecastle 39 (Castle Nick), suggest the existence of complex chronologies that were not uniform; there is evidence, too, that the stone fort at Birdoswald was built at a considerable time after the Wall itself was replaced in stone at this point. However, whilst the stone fort at Birdoswald was rebuilt on the same site as its turf predecessor, there is some evidence to suggest a more complex sequence at Bowness-on-Solway; here aerial photographic evidence points to the possibility that the turf-and-timber fort was situated a little to the west of the stone fort. This in its turn raises a question concerning the purpose of the large postholes located in 1973 beneath the features of the western gate of the stone fort. These were at the time interpreted as relating to the gate's timber predecessor, but a sounder explanation might be that they belonged to a watchtower (of the type located at Burgh I on the Stanegate) which pre-dated both the turf-and-timber and the stone forts. At the least, it appears unwise to assume that we can necessarily formulate a model based upon limited evidence, and impose it as a sequence common to the whole of the western sector. Modifications had to be introduced also to reflect experience, such as the fitting of sluices to the Irthing bridge at Willowford, which is thought to have followed flooding in the mid-second century A.D.

22. The fort at Bewcastle. This fort unusually has the configuration of an irregular pentagon, as it fortifies a hilltop. It is one of those that probably enclosed Brigantian territory left exposed to the north of the Wall. Its Roman name was probably *Fanum Cocidi* ('the Shrine of Cocidius', a representation of whom can be seen in plate 49).

What strategy lay behind the building of Hadrian's Wall? What can it tell us of the political situation that existed in the early years of the second century? As we have seen, the change of plan which led to the building of a narrower wall and to the placing of the forts on the Wall clearly indicates a review of security, convenience or strategy – or a combination of them. So long as the main concentrations of troops remained on the Stanegate (that is, up to *c*.A.D. 125), it is easy to see the Wall as a line for surveillance and the control of movement. The interpretation of milecastles as fortified gateways indicates clearly that they were put in the role of supervising movement rather than pre-venting it; many will have had personal or professional reasons for passing through the Wall in either direction. Only those whose activities aroused suspicion will have been stopped.

Such duties were carried out by the small groups of soldiers housed in the milecastles and turrets, from which there was easy access both to the north and to the south, and laterally along the wall itself. It is assumed on present evidence that the milecastles, depending on their individual size, will have housed from eight to thirty-two men, whilst the turrets perhaps required six each. Lateral patrolling was an activity peculiarly appropriate to Hadrian's Wall, if it was equipped, as the Rudge Cup appears to suggest, with an elevated and protected walkway – a feature not universal on all Roman frontiers, but recalling a facility available in individual forts. There is no evidence, however, to suggest,[14] that we should view the Wall as an elevated fighting platform, as even on the broad sections the movements required for such an activity will have been severely restricted. Nonetheless, the height will have provided a good, all-round, visibility, including the ability to see to the bottom of the northern ditch.

If trouble erupted at any spot, immediate help will have been available, but *not* in substantial strength. Major reinforcements will have had to come from the main garrisons on the Stanegate; thus communi-cations between the Wall and the Stanegate were of crucial importance. We cannot be certain why it was decided to bring the garrisons on to the Wall itself; it might indicate that the security situation around the Wall caused problems, or it might suggest that the actual building of the Wall, as had happened years before with the building of the *colonia* at Colchester, had inflamed sensibilities and exacerbated difficulties; this is not unreasonable when we remember that the Wall will have disturbed social and agricultural communications, and, in the west, as we have seen, actually left a section of the Brigantes adrift on the northern side. Alternatively, the decision to man the Wall in strength and abandon the Stanegate may have been due to nothing more sinister than a need for enhanced convenience. Indeed, the retention of Carvoran within the Wall system argues that convenience was a crucial factor.

The Wall well symbolises the imperatives of Hadrian's frontier policy. His predecessor's imperial policy has been interpreted as offering signs of megalomania; in reality, it was driven by similar requirements to that of Hadrian. Trajan wished to secure conditions of peace and stability in the empire and saw territorial acquisition and the consequent ability to police old enemies as the means to this end. In the end, Trajan was faced with a 'worst-case scenario'; the troops required to achieve this were probably sufficient if war was not conducted simultaneously on more than one front. By the end of his reign, however, Trajan was faced with completing and securing his new eastern conquests, with stabilising his recent success in Dacia, and with 'holding the line' elsewhere. In A.D. 117, these needs could not all be handled with a finite supply of troops.

Hadrian, too, wanted stability on the frontiers, with the opportunity to develop prosperity inside them. His policy, as his biographer states, was to separate the Romans from the barbarians by means of visible boundaries which were never, however, intended to stop traffic. He bought his stability by allowing former enemies to settle inside the frontiers – a policy castigated by critics as the 'barbarisation of the empire'. He gave such people a stake in the empire by forming out of them contingents of 'irregular' troops (*numeri* and *cunei*, *pedites* and *equites*), thus hoping to make policing relevant and effective. In this way, it was hoped that a certain homogeneity would settle over both sides of a frontier area, and that Romanisation would provide the true security.

Because of this, the area to the immediate north was treated much as that to the south of Hadrian's Wall, with a network of roads and policing forts. With regard to Hadrian's Wall, as we have seen, a particular political reason might explain the dispositions at Bewcastle, Birrens and Netherby. The fact that it does not provide the whole explanation can be seen from the maintenance of dispositions to the north of Hadrian's Wall in the eastern sector – along the continuation of Dere Street, as at Risingham and High Rochester – though the dating of these cannot yet be regarded as secure; on present evidence, they appear to relate to a later stage in the development of the northern frontier. We should in any case remember that outliers had been maintained in southern Scotland, when the Stanegate frontier was first inaugurated; such forts might have been crucial in maintaining communications with the Scottish Votadini.

It would appear, too, that the estuaries of the Tyne and Solway were regarded as to a degree insecure; in Hadrian's reign, in the east the Wall was extended to a new terminal fort at Wallsend, and a further fort placed on the coast at South Shields; in the west, a far more complex system was put in hand, and to that we shall now turn.

6

The Fortifications of
the Cumberland Coast

THE choice of a title for the present chapter is difficult; amongst the many problems that surround the interpretation of the structures on the north and west coasts of Cumbria is that relating to their purpose. The title chosen is one that is intended to avoid begging this or other extant questions.

Hadrian's Wall itself terminated at Bowness-on-Solway; it has, however, long been recognised that fortifications continued along the Cumberland coast, for there have for centuries been records of finds associated with what are now recognised as auxiliary forts at Beckfoot, Maryport, Burrow Walls (Workington), Moresby and Ravenglass.[1] The detailed histories of these forts vary considerably; Beckfoot, Moresby and Ravenglass, although not precisely contemporaneous, appear to have been Hadrianic foundations, whilst Burrow Walls appears on the present evidence to be later,[2] and Maryport is probably earlier.[3] Occupation at all of them seems to have been carried into the fourth century.

It is, however, for little more than a century that work has proceeded in recognising elements of a much tighter scheme of fortification, consisting of milefortlets (like the milecastles of Hadrian's Wall) and towers (like the turrets of Hadrian's Wall); these were spaced in such a way that the milefortlets will have been one Roman mile (1620 yards or 1481 metres) apart; the equidistant placing of two towers between each pair of milefortlets will have meant that the structures were separated from each other by 540 yards (or 494 metres). These spacings, however, were not absolutely rigid throughout the system;[4] the precise positions of sites may well have been governed by the requirements of signalling, in particular the intervisibility of sites with a fort, or with another site which was so linked to a fort.[5]

The initial recognition of stone towers was due in 1880 to two independent researchers – R. S. Ferguson and Joseph Robinson of Maryport, both of whom were responsible also for clarifying the anatomy of the fort at Beckfoot.[6] Four isolated towers were found –

Pasture House (3A), Herd Hill North (3B), Wolsty Bank (13B) and Risehow Colliery (26B). No milefortlets were found, though their existence was surmised by R.G. Collingwood in a paper (1929), which argued for a coherent system of 'signal stations' along the coast.

A major advance came in the 1940s with the excavation of a milefortlet at Castlesteads (Cardurnock; MF 5) and a survey of that area of coastline which revealed more structural evidence.[7] Further sites were brought to light from the air by the Cambridge University Aerial Photography Unit during the drought conditions of 1949. Since then, the unflagging fieldwork and excavation of Richard Bellhouse has greatly enhanced our knowledge of the system, aided since the 1970s by further aerial reconnaissance and excavation by teams from Manchester and Lancaster Universities.[8] The most recent synthesis and site enumeration is that of Richard Bellhouse (1989), who has also produced a memoir (1992) of Joseph Robinson, who truly deserves to be regarded as the 'father' of modern research on the subject.

The structures are enumerated from Biglands House Farm (MF 1), which is situated one mile to the west of Bowness-on-Solway; the enumeration continues to Tower 26B (Risehow Colliery), although the stretch from Tower 5A to Tower 8B is totally putative, in that it allows for the existence of the system around the inlet called *Moricambe*

23. The fort at Beckfoot. This heavily defended fort was built in Hadrian's reign as part of the coastal system. Its street system can clearly be seen, as can two external ditches and two palisades.

although there is in fact no evidence that sites ever existed on this stretch. Nor was the Stanegate fort at Kirkbride apparently in service beyond the middle years of Hadrian's reign.[9]

Few of the milefortlets have received extensive excavation, and ironically the first that did (Castlesteads/Cardurnock) has proved to be untypical in a number of ways; first it is a good deal larger than all others that are known, enclosing an area of 1130 square metres in its Hadrianic form – in other words, approximately three times the area of others which vary between c.270 square metres and c.370 square metres. The explanation for this probably derives from its position as the terminal milefortlet of the Cardurnock sequence, and it appears that ditches here ran out on to the shore. Secondly, unlike the other milefortlets for which information exists, it had only one gateway, which faced north – that is, away from *Moricambe*, although it has another unique feature in the form of a four-posted timber tower built into the fortlet's south-west corner, which would presumably have afforded visibility over the inlet. Again it differs from most other sites, as presently understood, in that is was reoccupied in the fourth century. It is not unlikely that on the other side of the inlet, Skinburness (MF 9) was a similarly large structure and assumed an equivalent 'terminal' role.

24. The Milefortlet at Biglands. This is the first milefortlet of the coastal system, situated at a mile to the west of the terminal of Hadrian's Wall at Bowness-on-Solway. It was built of turf and timber and was defended by a single ditch and palisade. It is approached from the east by a pair of parallel running ditches which formed a cordon in which the fortlet was situated. Like many of the excavated coastal installations, the milefortlet had three phases of occupation, all within the second century A.D.

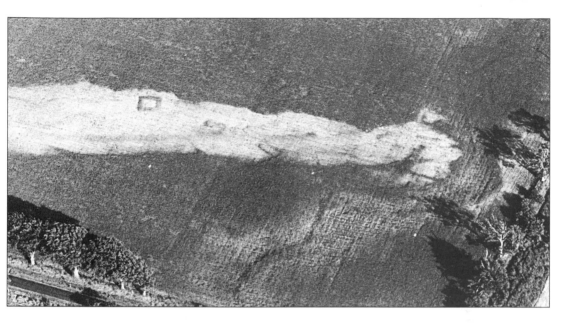

25. Tower 2B, Campfield. The square cropmark is caused by the stone watchtower which formed the third phase of activity at the site.

None of the milefortlets are of stone construction: the ramparts of Biglands (MF 1) were built of turves whose individual sizes varied considerably.[10] Turf construction has been noted at a number of other sites, although at Swarthy Hill (MF 21), the rampart appears to have consisted of an earth-fill between two 'walls' of stacked turves. As has been observed widely, the fortlet at Biglands had three building phases, all apparently within the second century; rampart width differed in each phase, and in the later two a timber revetment was added to the front of the rampart. The third phase represented a considerable reduction in size. We should, however, beware of assuming total uniformity in chronology; the milefortlet at Swarthy Hill (MF 21) apparently had only one period of occupation – in the reign of Hadrian.[11]

It is assumed that most of the milefortlets had two gateways, front and rear; some that are claimed to have had only one appear to have been wrongly interpreted on the basis of aerial photographs. At Biglands, the first two phases had six-post gateways, whilst the third phase was merely a passage through the rampart. The fortlet at Biglands was surrounded by a single ditch, which was V-shaped in profile and with a square 'sump' or 'ankle breaker' at the bottom. The three constructional phases were not represented in the ditch, which appeared merely to have been cleared out and re-used.

The interior arrangements of the fortlet were unimpressive with buildings of timber and turf on either side of a central roadway, presumably offering barrack accommodation and cooking facilities for a patrolling garrison of around a dozen men.

Elements of a considerable number of the stone-built watchtowers have been located, although only one – at Campfield (2B) – has been the subject of a large-scale area excavation.[12] This has shown that the tower, which was approximately 4.5 metres square, was preceded by two earlier timber towers, beneath and alongside the later stone tower. The three-phase arrangement, which is evident also at Tower 4B (Cardurnock), mirrors that identified at Biglands and at a number of other milefortlets. The sequence of development recorded at Campfield is parallel to that known in the Taunus section of the German frontier and elsewhere.[13]

Since the mid-1970s, aerial photography has located the presence of running linear features on the coast; the interpretation of these has proved to be controversial, particularly with regard to their dating. It is generally recognised that on the eastern approach to milefortlet I (Biglands) lies a pair of parallel ditches. Their relationship with the milefortlet appears to be shown by the fact that the ditches are heading for junctions with the northern and southern elements of the ditch around the milefortlet. In other words, the milefortlet was protected within a double ditch cordon. Work on a pair of ditches in the Cardurnock area demonstrated two significant points with regard to their dating: first, they appeared to *pre-date* the milefortlet (MF 5), and secondly, they were themselves sealed by a rubbish deposit which was dated to the third quarter of the second century A.D.

Aerial photography and excavation have also revealed the existence of palisades in both the Cardurnock and Silloth areas. Although dating of the latter *may* be regarded as uncertain, the former appear to cohere with the ditch construction in the area. The nature of the Silloth palisades show that stakes were held at regular intervals in a matrix of grey clay; the presence of the remains of nails suggests that these posts supported a fence. The whole recalls a statement in the *Life of Hadrian* in *The Writers of the Augustan History*[14] that Hadrian used lines of stakes in various parts of the empire as a means of keeping out the barbarians.

Figure 10. The Cumberland coast. Although many small sites (milefortlets and towers) have been lost by coastal erosion, it appears that in Hadrianic times there were two sectors, from Bowness-on-Solway to Cardurnock, and from Skinburness to Risehow. There is no evidence of installations between Cardurnock and Skinburness.

26. Rampart turves, Biglands Milefortlet. The individual turves with which the rampart was constructed can here be seen in plan. On excavation, the impression given was of a rather shoddily constructed fortlet.

Although the passage is normally taken to refer to Germany, there seems to be no reason why we should not also relate it to the fortifications of the Cumberland coast.

Thus, the structural evidence, fragmentary though it still is, indicates a system of fortifications, similar to those of Hadrian's Wall itself, and linked by linear features, such as palisades and ditches – and presumably a road also; this, although recorded as long ago as in Stukeley's observations, and apparently confirmed by work in the nineteenth century, has remained elusive in the more recent research.

The major interpretative matters affecting the Cumberland coast system, besides that of the nature of the structures themselves, are the questions of the extent, dating and purpose of the fortifications.

First, extent; we need here to make a distinction between the extent of a coherent system of fortifications and of occasional structures on the coast. As we have seen, there are three auxiliary forts south of Maryport – Burrow Walls, Moresby and Ravenglass; of these Moresby has a definite Hadrianic origin, whilst Ravenglass appears to be Hadrianic on grounds of artefactual evidence. Burrow Walls is more equivocal and may be later. Certainly, Ravenglass appears to have been occupied continuously into the late fourth century,[15] and Moresby has produced dating evidence through to the fourth century.

The discovery from the air of possible coastal sites – as at Harrington,[16] – and of Roman material at places such as Braystones, Beckermet and Eskmeals,[17] together with the discovery of a ditched enclosure beneath the fort at Ravenglass,[18] has led to suggestions that a coherent coastal system ran to Ravenglass, or even beyond. It has, however, to be said that no structural evidence accompanied the finds between St Bees Head and Ravenglass; further, the 'site' at Eskmeals is now known not to have been of Roman origin. The ditched enclosure at Ravenglass, whilst it was obviously earlier than the fort, remains of uncertain date and nature.

The assumption that the chief purpose of the system was for the transmission of signals seemed to make St Bees Head a suitable terminus. If, however, this was not the purpose, then the changing nature of the coastline south of Maryport, together with the structural evidence, would argue against the existence of a coherent system beyond Joseph Robinson's tower (26B) discovered in 1880 at Risehow Colliery. The type of landfall, against which the system may have been directed, would have been less feasible beyond this point, as cliffs provided more of a natural barrier.

Thus, the coastal system appears to have consisted of two sections on either side of *Moricambe* – from Skinburness (MF9) to a point south of Maryport, where it may be right that there was a terminal milefortlet at Flimby, and from Bowness-on-Solway to Cardurnock (MF5). It is not clear whether there were any structures in the mile between Bowness and Biglands (MF 1), though a case has been made for 'tower OB'.[19] It is, however, worth noting that the excavation of the western gateway of the stone fort at Bowness-on-Solway[20] revealed four large postholes beneath the gateway, which were interpreted as elements of the gatehouse of the turf-and-timber phase of the fort; it is possible, as we have seen, that these were in fact the posts of a watchtower.

Secondly, the chronology; we have noted that the chronology of the forts shows individuality, and that at least one of them – at Maryport – probably preceded the system, being established at least as early as the Trajanic period. We have also seen that the forts were evidently occupied in the fourth century; three – at Ravenglass, Maryport and Bowness-on-Solway – were substantially rebuilt after the trouble of A.D. 367;[21] further, Maryport has produced some very late coin evidence.[22] Some of the structures of the coastal defences have produced evidence of activity in the fourth century, including the milefortlet at Cardurnock[23] and MF 12 and 20, together with Towers 13A and 16A;[24] Tower 2B has yielded evidence of activity in the third century. It is clear that, in any case, substantial attention was paid to the defences of the west coast in the fourth century, with Saxon shore type forts being constructed at Cardiff, Caernarfon, Caer Gybi and Lancaster. It is not unlikely that, as on the east coast, some new coastal towers were put

27. Altar of Marcus Maenius Agrippa. The altar is one of those dedicated to *Jupiter Optimus Maximus* ('the Greatest and Best') at the beginning of a year by Maenius Agrippa, the tribune in charge of the garrison at Maryport. The facts that Agrippa was a friend of Hadrian's, and enjoyed a rank higher than usually associated with command of an auxiliary unit suggest that Maryport may have been the head-quarters of the coastal system. The altar was one of a number of fine stones which had been ritually buried in Roman times, and which were recovered by members of the Senhouse family. They are now housed in the new Senhouse Roman Museum at Maryport. The inscription reads: 'For Jupiter, Greatest and Best, and for the Emperor's Divine Spirit, Marcus Maenius Agrippa, the Tribune, set up this altar.'

in place on the west coast, too; the discovery of a gold *solidus* of Theodosius I (A.D. 383–388)[25] beneath Muncaster Castle suggests the possibility.[26]

A considerable number of the coastal sites have demonstrated a strong chronological consistency – three separate phases of occupation within the second century; whilst the evidence is strongest in the milefortlets, three occupational phases have been observed in some towers and in the linear features in the Cardurnock peninsular.[27] The sites at which large-scale excavation has taken place offer the best opportunity for pinpointing the three phases; the dating at Biglands (MF I) remains the most secure,[28] where the evidence suggests that the three phases were separated by the two phases of occupation on the Antonine Wall (see below in Chapter 7). Thus, the first phase is placed in *c*.A.D. 120–140, the second phase in *c*.A.D. 155–159, and the third from *c*.A.D. 165 (when the Antonine Wall was finally abandoned) to an unspecified date, but almost certainly within the second century.

As we have seen, there is some evidence from Cardurnock to suggest that some of the structures at least were built later than the linear features. It is uncertain how the new fort at Beckfoot related chronologically to the rest of the system – whether it was contemporary with it or replaced milefortlet 14, of which it has to be said that no evidence has been found. There is some attraction in dating the linear features and some structures to the same time as the building of Hadrian's Wall, whilst the fort at Beckfoot and at least the milefortlet at Cardurnock may be seen as contemporary with the 'fort phase' of Hadrian's Wall.

The third question – concerning the purpose of the coastal fortifications – is perhaps the most elusive. It is clear that we cannot accept the 'signalling' role assigned to the system by Collingwood, but that we should instead relate the purpose of the coastal fortifications more closely to that of Hadrian's Wall itself. Clearly, a military purpose might have been envisaged in the event of the turning of the western flank of Hadrian's Wall. The political stance of the tribes of south-west

Scotland might have made this a more real fear in the west than it was in the east, where only the fort at South Shields guarded the southern bank of the Tyne beyond the terminal fort at Wallsend.

We should, of course, recall that the hinterland of the coastal fortifications was, on the evidence of aerial photography, densely populated; indeed, the prosperity of the Solway Plain may have been significant both in the role of supplying the Roman frontier army and as a source of wealth for Carvetian 'magnates' who were to become crucial to the operation of the limited local self-administration eventually developed into the *civitas Carvetiorum*. The coastal fortifications, then, may well have played a role in protecting this developing prosperity from the threat of rustling and marauding from across the Solway; the fortified road from Carlisle to Maryport, through Red Dial, may well have offered a similar protection from the upland Brigantians of the Lakeland hills. Nor was this the first occasion upon which protection had been afforded; in the early days of conquest, the road from Carlisle to Maryport, through Blennerhasset, and later the western Stanegate had offered the means to police and protect the area.

28. Palisade, Silloth. The palisade is seen in the form of a row of double postholes; large numbers of nails were found nearby, indicating that the posts supported a continuous fence.

However, the relationship between the coastal fortifications and Hadrian's Wall suggests another possible purpose. The Wall controlled the passage of trade in either direction and facilitated the collection of the appropriate taxes. The coastal fortifications may, therefore, have ensured that trade between north-west England and south-west Scotland was properly regulated, and any possible tax evasion obviated. The existence of these mechanisms will, of course, have encouraged economic intercourse between the two areas, since otherwise traders would have had the inconvenience of having to make a journey to Bowness-on-Solway, if not to Carlisle, for proper regulation.

Finally, the troop commitment; we may reckon on 1,500 soldiers being required to man the forts at Beckfoot, Maryport and Moresby; the milefortlets may have required 250 and the towers 200, though this latter 450 may have been drawn from the 1,500. Decisions concerning the use of the available troops will probably have been made at Maryport and Bowness-on-Solway, whose commanders perhaps exercised jurisdiction over their adjacent sectors. In the case of Maryport, at least, the numerous inscriptions tell us that the fort commander carried the elevated rank of tribune; further, at least one of the holders of the office, Marcus Maenius Agrippa, was a friend of Hadrian himself.[29]

Yet, despite their obvious importance, the coastal fortifications were just as vulnerable to the changing whims of imperial policy as was Hadrian's Wall itself.

7

A Renewed Offensive:
The Antonine Wall

HADRIAN died in A.D. 138, at the age of 62; for an emperor who had achieved so much for the empire's stability, there was surprisingly little grief. The Roman senate and its members maintained a deep distaste for an emperor who, they suspected, had been responsible not only for the murder of some of their colleagues, but also for a deliberate downgrading of their august body. Some of them may have hoped that his death would lead to a rebirth of Trajanic militarism, with all of the opportunities which that would bring for personal glory and advancement.

Titus Aurelius Fulvus Boionius Arrius Antoninus was not Hadrian's first choice as successor; coming to power at the age of fifty-two he had been chosen only in A.D. 138, following the death of Lucius Aelius Caesar (born Lucius Ceionius Commodus) shortly before Hadrian's own death. In a manner that recalled Augustus' own dynasticism, Hadrian sought to tie up the succession in the next generation, requiring Antoninus to adopt as his sons the youthful Marcus Annius Verus (better known as Marcus Aurelius) and Lucius Aelius' son, who is known to history as Lucius Verus. Marcus Aurelius married Antoninus' daughter, Faustina, and Lucius Verus later married Marcus Aurelius' daughter, Annia Lucilla. Like Tiberius Caesar more than a century before, Antoninus looked very much like a dynastic stop-gap.

Antoninus' family, although long-resident in Rome, had originated in Gaul; in senatorial circles, the family was eminently respectable, and Antoninus, who had been consul in A.D. 120 and proconsul of Asia in the mid-130s, was known as a sound and honest administrator. His career, however, lacked any prominent military post. He was, perhaps, an obvious second choice, who was very soon put to the test, as Hadrian's declining health necessitated Antoninus taking up the effective reins of government immediately.

Antoninus' position in Rome seems a little equivocal: on the face of it, his lack of military experience will not have gone unnoticed amongst those with a taste for military adventure. Again, there were some in senatorial circles who thought that they had a stronger claim to power than Antoninus. Yet against a background of such misgivings, Antoninus was able to give a striking display of strong-mindedness, which earned him his famous sobriquet of *Pius*; *pietas* was a 'virtue' which described the devotedness with which a man honoured the gods and his family. Antoninus displayed his *pietas* by winning from an unwilling senate the honour of posthumous deification for his adoptive father. Yet, the mere existence of criticism, even rivalry, put Antoninus into a risky position; earlier events had shown how such dissatisfactions could assume serious proportions particularly if elements of the army were to become involved. In this sense, it is possible that Antoninus had a similarity with Claudius, almost exactly a century before, in that there was a need to make a positive appeal to the legions.

Why, then, after all the hard work that had brought Hadrian's Wall to fruition did Antoninus so soon abandon it, re-occupy southern Scotland and construct a new wall between the Forth and the Clyde? Antoninus' biographer, Julius Capitolinus, is not particularly specific: 'He conquered the Britons through his legate, Lollius Urbicus, setting up another wall, this time of turf, when the barbarians had been driven back'. If this can be taken at face value it suggests the quelling of disturbances; Antoninus' coinage was certainly making claims for military victory in A.D. 143.

Another reference is to be found in Pausanias' *Description of Greece*,[1] which was written in the late second century. Pausanias indicates that Antoninus was not a 'proactive warmaker', and refers to Britain as one of the places where military action had to be taken. Unfortunately, however, Pausanias' notice of this trouble is confused and confusing; he relates how Antoninus punished the Brigantes by depriving them of territory following their attack on the 'Genounian region'.[2] The problem here is that no such region is known in Britain, and attempts, often highly ingenious, to explain and locate it have never carried full conviction.

An easier explanation is that the incident does not refer to Britain at all: there was a tribe named the Briganti (or Brigantes) who lived in the Alpine province of Raetia, and significantly they had neighbours called the *Genauni*. It would seem that Pausanias has made a mistake of location. This does not, however, solve our problem; for Pausanias has referred to Antoninus *making war in Britain*, and increasingly it appears that he has suffered from a deep confusion. The Brigantes of Britain provoked Antoninus' retaliation, but Pausanias has obfuscated their fault by confusing them with the activities of another tribe of the same name.

Thus, we are left in uncertainty as to what the British Brigantes had actually done. Suggestions that there had been rebellious outbreaks in the tribal 'heartland', or that they had been attacking their southern neighbours (the *Coritani* or the *Cornovii*) seem inappropriate explanations of an imperial response which was located in southern Scotland. Again, we should not forget that some of the Brigantes were isolated on the northern side of Hadrian's Wall; it is not inconceivable that they were interfering with their neighbours. It is here worth noting that the military dispositions of the Antonine occupation of southern Scotland are especially strong in the south west, with a concentration of fortlets in Annandale and Nithsdale.

Of the tribes of southern Scotland who were closest to Rome, we should mention the Votadini of the east; the tribe might even have had a treaty which would, if the tribe had been attacked, have justified and necessitated intervention on their behalf. Further, the land of the Votadini was amongst the most fertile in northern Britain, and grain from there was probably already helping to supply the Roman army. That situation would have justified attention, including the 'depriving of the Brigantes of their territory' and the inclusion of the territory of the Votadini within the province, to ensure their protection.

There seems little now to support the idea, once canvassed, that an objective of the Antonine reoccupation of Scotland was to acquire fresh manpower for the Roman army; this would also, by removing younger men of military age, have reduced the threat of disturbances in the area. However, there is little or no sign of depopulation in southern Scotland, and, in any case, the majority of known British units in the Roman army pre-existed the reign of Antoninus.

We can thus see a number of local contexts in which military intervention was justified – even to the point of initiating a full annexation of southern Scotland to facilitate policing of the area. Yet, Capitolinus' reference to 'driving off' barbarians, coupled with the building of the new wall, still appears to suggest that there may have been interference from elsewhere. The *Caledonii* will, of course, by now have recovered from their defeat at the hands of Agricola; these people, perhaps now calling themselves *Maeatae* (or part of a group that did), may have been in a position to plunder and disrupt further south. Indeed, it is worth remembering that when, early in the third century, Septimius Severus tried to initiate a solution to the Scottish problem, he totally by-passed southern Scotland, and campaigned, as

Agricola had done in A.D. 82 and 83, north of the Forth–Clyde line. In such circumstances, it could be argued that the new frontier brought Roman troops closer to where the trouble lay, and demonstrated that to an extent Hadrian's Wall had become an anachronism. Against such a 'global' theory, it has to be asked why, if imperatives had shifted so obviously and dramatically, was it satisfactory within twenty years to abandon the Antonine Wall and southern Scotland, and resume occupation of Hadrian's Wall.

A final point may be made about Antoninus himself; we have seen that he enjoyed the reputation of not being a warmonger; the fact that he claimed public credit for success in Britain when he did not for military success elsewhere, suggests that his own reputation was firmly attached to this project. As has been suggested, it may have been due to a desire to make his mark firmly with the legionary army. We can, however, be reasonably certain that his purpose was not to impress the supposedly disgruntled generals of Trajan, for they did not benefit from this resumed military activity; indeed, the governor of Britain, Q. Lollius Urbicus, who masterminded the invasion, was a Hadrianic protégé. His appointment, together with Antoninus' broad imperial policy, serves to emphasise that we should view this period in the empire as representing essentially a continuation of Hadrianic policy rather than a reversion to an older style of militarism.

In a number of ways the new invasion of Scotland echoed aspects of Agricola's third campaign of A.D. 79 – the re-opening of the land routes in southern Scotland, the reoccupation of Newstead and a number of other Agricolan sites in southern Scotland, and the rebuilding of Corbridge apparently in the form of a depot, which is attested on a building inscription of A.D. 139, recording the presence there of II *Augusta* (from Caerleon). This strongly suggests the development of a military 'build up' by that time. There does not appear to have been a similar enhancement of activity at Carlisle, which suggests that Corbridge was selected as a base for the *whole* operation and that on this occasion the Clyde estuary may have been reached overland from Corbridge. Carlisle may in fact have been concerned with a separate part of the enterprise, namely the refortifying of Annandale and Nithsdale.

Tracing the routes of advance provides difficulties, since in southern Scotland there are marching camps which potentially derive from a number of different phases of campaigning. In the case of the Antonine advance, the soundest criterion for the identification of relevant marching camps appears to be that of their relationship to an *existing* road system. It is the fact that this has proved to be relatively straightforward in the east but much less so in the west that has prompted the suggestion of the wider-ranging role of Corbridge. Although the occupation and policing of the reoccupied southern Scotland carries many reminiscences of Agricola's occupation of this area – particularly with regard to the forts held – there are significant differences; we have already noted the extra attention which was paid to the south west; the key Agricolan site at Dalswinton played no part in the Antonine scheme; instead the significant forts were at the Agricolan site of Glenlochar and a new site at Carzield. These were backed up by a considerable number of small forts or fortlets (as at Barburgh Mill).[3] Indeed a striking difference between this and earlier occupations lay in the greater use made of fortlets, indicating that a relatively small number of troops was being disposed very economically.

The Antonine Wall is thirty-seven miles in length, and spans the narrowest neck of land in Britain, on a line which, as we have seen, had already been identified in the later first century A.D. as a possible *terminus* of Roman activities. Agricola's line of forts, however, ran somewhat to the north of the shortest line, and the post-Agricolan withdrawal from Scotland made no use of it at all.

The *limes* itself has proved to be more resistant to informed discussion than has Hadrian's Wall, partly because of the relatively large amount of damage done to it by the major conurbations of Edinburgh and Glasgow, and partly because its almost complete reliance on turf and timber as basic construction materials has left it generally more vulnerable to the ravages of time. The Wall itself and its associated installations have been revealed only slowly, and it is only in recent years that we have begun to recover and understand the nature and purposes of the range of forts, fortlets and other sites on the Wall, and to grasp the significance of their relationships.

The *limes* and its associated sites are reckoned to run to Old Kilpatrick on the Clyde from Carriden on the Forth, although the eastern terminal fort does not appear formally to have been reached by the Wall; in effect, it guarded the end of the '*limes*-zone' and was apparently matched by Bishopton on the southern shore of the Clyde. In all, there are likely to have been eighteen forts on the Wall (including those at Carriden and Bishopton) and ten fortlets; of these, seven occupied intermediate positions between forts, whilst the other three were sited in close proximity to a fort, perhaps indicating that an original fortlet was subsequently considered to be capable of providing a level of cover sufficient for an intermediate position. Of the intermediate fortlets, that at Watling Lodge may be regarded as a 'special case', since it was covered immediately to the north of the wall by the rebuilt Agricolan fort at Camelon, which was itself the first of a series (along with Ardoch, Strageath and Bertha) of 'outpost forts' lying along the road leading to the river Tay, and thus serving to isolate the Fife peninsula. The southern shore of the Forth had two forts east of the Wall's termination, placed at about a half-day's march apart, at Cramond and Inveresk. It has been pointed out that these forts were situated at river mouths and may thus have been adjacent to harbour facilities.[4] This will have emphasised communication both with the Tyne and with the grain supplies of Fifeshire. In addition, these forts lay on the crucial road from Corbridge by way of Newstead. If the purpose was to enhance the protection offered to the Wall's eastern flank, a similar purpose was probably served in the west by the sites on the southern shore of the Clyde – the fort at Bishopton and the fortlets at Lurg Moor and Outerwards.

It is possible that eventually the fortlets will be seen to have been regular features along the whole of the Wall; at present, however, only a small number is known. These differ in size and shape from each other, some being more elongated along their north–south axes; whilst their purpose may be similar to that of the milecastles of Hadrian's Wall, the fortlets of the Antonine Wall differ in one significant respect – being defended by one or more ditches. The internal buildings of the fortlets are suggestive of the barracks in the milecastles of Hadrian's Wall.

There is a small number of even slighter sites – usually termed 'enclosures' and 'expansions' – which have been thought to provide for a function similar to that of the turrets of Hadrian's Wall. However, the three enclosures around the fortlet at Wilderness Plantation appear to be extremely slight in structural terms, consisting of a small ditch and rampart enclosing a space which, in excavated examples, have revealed no clue to their purpose. The expansions, of which six are known, are turf platforms built upon foundations of cobble, and attached to the southern face of the Wall. There is no evidence that timber watchtowers were built on these, and a long-held explanation that they were beacon stances remains preferable to other notions.

It seems clear that, as on Hadrian's Wall, the planning of the Antonine Wall was an evolving process; further, the rate at which in recent years new sites have been discovered leaves some doubt as to whether the planning process can as yet be regarded as fully understood. On present evidence, it appears that the Antonine Wall took its plan from the second planning phase of Hadrian's Wall. Indeed, we should probably regard it as natural that 'on the ground' this would reflect the attitude of local commanders.

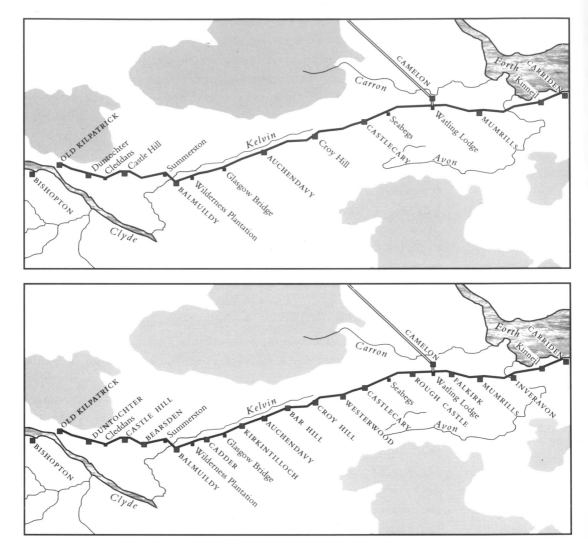

The Wall itself ran for thirty-seven miles, following the southern shore of the Forth, the valleys of the Carron and the Kelvin, and from there to join the northern shore of the Clyde. On its northern side, it was fronted by a V-shaped ditch, which varied in depth between two and four metres, and was between six and twelve metres in width. The width of the berm between the Wall and the ditch varied from nine to twelve metres, the wider berm corresponding with the incidence of the narrower ditch. Only at Croy Hill did the arrangements depart from this; there the lie of the land left the fort on a crag and the ditch some thirty metres distant on lower ground. The earth from the ditch was put on the northern lip making an extra mound (or *glacis*), which effectively enhanced the depth of the ditch.

Beyond the ditch, at Rough Castle, lay an area of closely-set pits (*lilia*), into which were inserted upturned sharpened stakes; the whole was then covered with branches and bracken. Such 'man traps' may have been more commonly used than is often supposed. It is clear that the momentum of any attack from the north would have been severely disrupted by such a feature – the main purpose of any combination of extra-mural obstacles.

The Wall itself was built of blocks of turf or clay, but laid upon a foundation of cobbles, some fourteen feet (4.5 metres) wide and revetted with stone kerbs; at intervals this base was pierced by a drainage channel. Such is the degradation of the structure that it is hardly possible now to be certain as to its height and configuration; however, it is felt that it was battered on both sides, rising to a height of between three-and-a-half and four metres with a patrol walk on top protected by a wattle fence. The absence of postholes descending through the turf structure of the Wall would appear to preclude the possibility of a more substantial protection on the top of the rampart – unless, of course, the height of the Wall was much greater than is generally supposed. In any case, it has to be said that there is no satisfactory archaeological evidence either for a wooden rampart protection or indeed for the 'duck boards' which would have been a prerequisite for a patrol way.

The planning of the Wall is thought to display two stages; the first was for six forts, set at a distance of approximately eight miles apart and each capable of housing a complete auxiliary unit. These primary forts were situated at Carriden (4 acres), Mumrills (6.5 acres), Castlecary (3.5 acres), Auchendavy (approx. 2.8 acres), Balmuildy (4 acres), and Old Kilpatrick (4.2 acres). The spacing of these indicates the adoption of the same principles as on Hadrian's Wall. Of these, two (Castlecary and Balmuildy) were constructed of stone; indeed, Balmuildy was equipped with stone 'wings' as if the builders expected it eventually to join with a stone wall. Further, Balmuildy is the only fort to have produced inscriptions bearing the name of a governor – Lollius Urbicus – which again indicates an early stage in construction. It is believed that as part of this first phase fortlets were placed at intervals of one Roman mile; of these – perhaps 29 or 30 in all – nine are known – at Kinneil, Watling Lodge, Seabegs, Croy Hill, Glasgow Bridge, Wilderness Plantation, Summerston, Cleddans and Duntocher. These were clearly planned as one with the Wall, and have the same configuration as the milescastles of Hadrian's Wall; their chief point of difference from their Hadrianic predecessors lay in the fact that most of them were defended by one or two ditches on their eastern, southern and

Figure 11 (OPPOSITE) The Antonine Wall. These plans indicate that initially it was expected that the Antonine Wall would resemble Hadrian's Wall, with a small number of large forts and intervening smaller installations. The final plan showed considerable modification, with forts much more closely spaced.

western sides. Like the forts, they had the protection of the Antonine Wall and its ditch on their northern sides.

The chief modification of the plan for the Wall was the addition of extra forts – possibly as many as twelve or thirteen. These forts, of which eight are known, were generally much smaller than the primary forts – as small as 0.5 acres at Duntocher – and some were not capable of housing a complete auxiliary unit; indeed, some appear to demonstrate this further by the lack of a headquarters (*principia*), indicating that the headquarters staff of the soldiers in garrison were housed elsewhere. It may be assumed, therefore, that the smaller forts were garrisoned by detachments of units which were housed elsewhere in the system. As with the primary forts, these too were orientated to look north, and many appear to have been joined to the Antonine Wall when it had already been constructed, though that at Bar Hill[5] lies at a short distance to the south of the Wall. At Duntocher, the already existing fortlet was apparently subsumed into the new fort, whilst at Croy Hill the new fort was constructed about fifty metres to the east of the existing fortlet. These forts were equipped with up to three external ditches on their three exposed sides; it may be noted that all forts of the Antonine Wall followed the pattern established with

29. Antonine Wall ditch, Watling Lodge. This is the best-preserved section of the ditch on the north side of the Antonine Wall; the vestigial remains of the Wall itself can be seen as a slight running 'hump' on the inner (left-hand) side of the ditch.

30. Rough Castle, Antonine Wall. The fort at Rough Castle is one of the best preserved on the Antonine Wall; it was protected by two ditches and the Wall made up its north rampart. To the east of the fort is a defended annexe, which housed, amongst other things, a bath-house. To the north of the Antonine Wall and its ditch can be seen an area of pits (*lilia*), which formed a kind of mantrap; each pit contained a sharpened, upturned stake and was concealed with brushwood.

the later forts of Hadrian's Wall in that none sat astride the Wall. It seems clear that forts were seen from the outset as an integral feature of the Antonine Wall, whereas, as we have seen, their presence on Hadrian's Wall *may* have been primarily governed by emerging considerations of convenience.

Some of the forts of the Antonine Wall were equipped with annexes, which housed *essential* extra-mural buildings such as bath-houses and facilities for stores. These were not intended as defended enclosures for civilians; indeed, their military purpose is shown clearly at Rough Castle where the fort's ditch system was extended to include the annexe. The forts were linked by a road (the Military Way), which both went through the forts, forming in some cases the *via principalis*, and was equipped with 'by-pass loops' to avoid unnecessary congestion within the forts. With the exception of the stone-built forts, the turf ramparts of the rest were, like the Antonine Wall itself, built upon bases of kerbed rubble. The chief internal buildings were generally of stone, whilst the barracks were constructed of timber.

The garrisons of the forts are not fully understood; as on Hadrian's Wall, and as is demonstrated by the highly ornate distance slabs, the construction work on the Antonine Wall was carried out by detachments of the three British legions (II *Augusta*, VI *Victrix* and XX *Valeria Victrix*). Whilst some legionaries may have been employed as garrisons – as they certainly were in the hinterland at Newstead[6] – the main bodies of troops on the Antonine Wall were auxiliaries. Most appear to have been infantry, for only at Mumrills is there unequivocal evidence of a cavalry garrison, whilst at Bearsden the configuration of a barrack block led the excavator to suggest that cavalry may have been involved in garrison duty at that fort, too.[7] These troops were intended to police the surrounding area and respond to problems; they were not meant as a static force to defend the Antonine Wall.

Whether the Antonine Wall was intended as a way of bringing the frontier closer to the real enemies of Roman Britain, or whether it was intended to bring the tribes of southern Scotland more effectively into the network of policing, it is clear that Hadrian's Wall will have become to a large extent redundant; in any case, there can hardly have been sufficient troops in Britain to man both walls, since the Antonine Wall will have required some six or seven thousand troops in addition to the approximately fifteen thousand who were disposed along Hadrian's Wall and the Cumberland coast. The *precise* status, however, of Hadrian's Wall and its installations during the Antonine period is less clear.

We can be certain that the milecastles and turrets went out of service; at the former, the gates appear to have been removed so that there was no impediment to traffic. Whilst there was apparently no attempt to dismantle the Wall itself, lengths of the *vallum* were effectively 'neutered' by the destruction of the mounds at regular intervals and the infilling of the ditch with the mound material, thus providing regular causeways. The position of the forts is less clear; whilst most on artefactual evidence were evidently abandoned, since there is no substantial overlap of samian pottery at the two Walls,[8] it is possible that a few may have retained a function in the overall distribution of forts in the hinterland of the new frontier; it is worth noting that a military diploma, dating to A.D. 146, has been found at Chesters. Presumably, however, most elements of the Hadrianic frontier were abandoned, as soon as its successor was in place.

The evidence from the Cumberland coastal sites is clearer; here, as we have seen, there were three phases of occupation of the fortlets,[9] the towers[10] and the linear features,[11] with clear periods of abandonment between them. It seems likely that the first phase of coastal defences came to an end with the re-occupation of Scotland; if their purpose was concerned with supervision and taxation, then they would have

31. The fort at Ardoch. This fort was first established during Agricola's governorship, and was one of a small number to the north of the Antonine Wall that was kept manned. The Antonine fort was remarkable for its quintuple ditch system.

now become redundant. Of the forts, however, it is clear that Maryport remained in commission.[12]

It is also likely that some forts in northern England were abandoned, if for no other reason than to provide troops for garrisoning re-occupied Scottish sites. Whilst at many the artefactual evidence is not sufficiently well understood for certainty, it is likely that, for example, Binchester and Ebchester (in Co. Durham) and Lancaster and Watercrook were without garrisons during the early Antonine period.

The later history of the Antonine Wall has proved to be controversial – not only the date of the final abandonment, but also the question of a short break in occupation in the second half of the 150s. With regard to the latter, it has long been assumed that evidence of destruction at Antonine sites in Scotland, together with the issuing in A.D. 154–5 of a 'dejected *Britannia*' coin,[13] indicates that in the mid-150s the Romans were pushed unceremoniously out of Scotland as a result of an attack by their enemies from the north of the Antonine Wall. It has, however, to be said that destruction by fire does not provide unequivocal testimony to enemy action; indeed, it is doubtful in the extreme whether such action would in any case have resulted in the comprehensive destruction seen on Scottish sites. This is far better explained as resulting from deliberate demolition by the Roman army itself – a point emphasised by the discovery at Bearsden of a discarded claw hammer and nails.

Some difficulties arise over the interpretation of these events because of the nature of the dating evidence. First, the *Britannia* coin: it was, as we have seen, issued in A.D. 154–5. It would thus appear likely that the trouble which it implies should not be dated later than A.D. 153. The nature of the trouble is probably, without further evidence, beyond recovery; we have seen that an invasion from the north appears to be unlikely. Nor is there any particular evidence which supports the location of the difficulties in southern Scotland. Indeed, in the re-occupation of southern Scotland in *c.*A.D. 158, no area of the south reflects increased vigilance. There may have been disturbance amongst the Brigantes of northern England; however, the types of evidence usually introduced to support this notion are not particularly helpful, although it has been suggested that the presence at Ribchester of reinforcements from Germany in the early 160s may point to a background of disturbance amongst the Brigantes (*RIB* 589).[14] The allusion by Pausanias to trouble amongst the Brigantes is much more likely, as we have seen, to refer to the beginning of Antoninus' reign, whereas the evidence of coin hoards which is sometimes introduced to support the idea is, if valid at all, much more supportive, as Robertson shows,[15] of disturbances later than this – in the reign of Marcus Aurelius.

We are left, therefore, with disturbances which are hard to pinpoint, although it is possible that the inscription from Newcastle (*RIB* 1322) referring to reinforcements from the Germanies during the governorship of Julius Verus for the legions in Britain suggests some 'stock taking'. It is possible that these troops represented the return of some that had been sent from Britain to the Rhine in the early 150s.[16] Further, it is possible that this 'stock taking' included, with or without the direct permission of the emperor, a withdrawal to Hadrian's Wall apparently in A.D. 157–8. Since rebuilding work at Birrens can be given a similar date it may indicate that the abandonment of the Antonine Wall was viewed in much the same light as the post-Agricolan withdrawal in A.D. 87; the new frontier – that is, Hadrian's Wall – was 'protected' by the maintenance of outliers in southern Scotland.

Yet, very shortly after this, there appears to have been a re-occupation of southern Scottish sites, of sites on the Antonine Wall, and of those to the north of it; had Antoninus Pius changed his mind, or had he

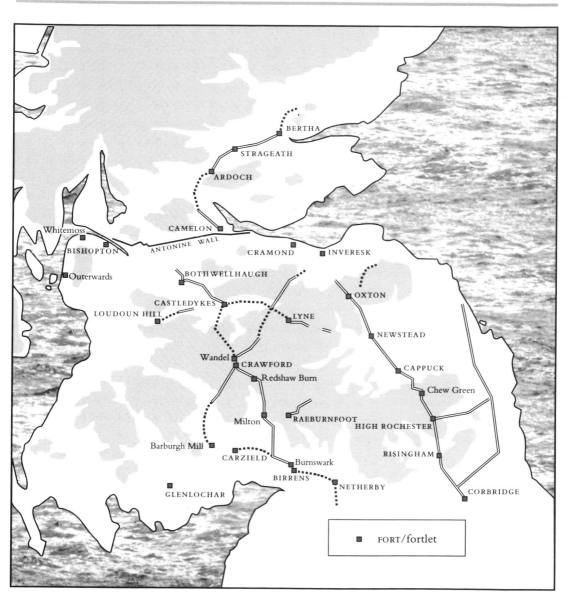

1L7MXF8H/eQ3NOLJvB4...

Figure 12. Scotland in the Antonine period. Many, though not all, of these sites represented refurbishment of old Agricolan forts. The Antonine advance relied effectively on a strategy similar to that of Agricola in A.D. 79.

countermanded actions which Julius Verus had taken on his own initiative? The fact that Verus was replaced as governor in A.D. 158, although not (it has to be said) after an unduly short tenure, may not be insignificant.

The re-occupation showed differences from the first Antonine occupation of southern Scotland; garrisons were certainly changed, and the density of Roman sites was thinned – particularly noticeably in south-west Scotland. Also, it may be that the reoccupation of the Antonine Wall itself was selective, as Bearsden did not display a second phase of occupation. Attractive as it might sound, the dating evidence does not quite appear to fit the theory that the Antonine Wall was abandoned late in the reign of Antoninus Pius, only to be re-occupied, perhaps as a punitive measure, on the orders of Marcus Aurelius on his accession in A.D. 161.

The final abandonment of the Antonine Wall and southern Scotland has occasioned similar difficulties of dating and interpretation. Essentially, three quite different dates have been canvassed for the final abandonment of the Antonine Wall:[17] an inscription from the Wall fort of Castlecary (*RIB* 2148) has been thought to indicate occupation down to the closing years of the second century – or even beyond. In the absence of similar material from other Antonine Wall forts, this might best be explained as indicative of a temporary re-use of that fort by a patrolling group. Secondly, a date in the early 180s has been canvassed on the basis of a hoard of *denarii* from Briglands (Kinrosshire),[18] the latest coins of which belong to the reign of Commodus (A.D. 180–192). Although it has been argued that the existence of such a hoard pre-supposes a military occupation of the Antonine Wall, it has to be pointed out that such a use of this hoard has no more validity than if we were to try and employ the Falkirk hoard[19] to prove occupation of the Antonine Wall into the middle of the third century. If an immediate source of the coins is required, it should be borne in mind that the abandonment of southern Scotland was probably organised more gradually than that of the Antonine Wall itself.

The strongest evidence, however, is that derived from the pottery found at forts of the Antonine Wall.[20] The study of the samian ware reveals that the main series terminates in the mid-160s; this corresponds well with the dating derived from those coins from forts of the Antonine Wall which represent *casual losses*.[21] Further, we should note the considerable amount of evidence of rebuilding at Roman sites on Hadrian's Wall and its hinterland during the governorship of Calpurnius Agricola (A.D. 163–6).[22]

It is evident, therefore, that early in his reign, Marcus Aurelius decided that the use of the Antonine Wall had run its course. There is no evidence that this decision was occasioned by pressure from northern Scotland; indeed, as noted above, it appears that the withdrawal from sites between the walls may have extended into the 180s. In any case, it is clear (as we shall see in chapter 8) that problems continued around Hadrian's Wall for the remainder of the second century. The pressure which precipitated Marcus' decision was almost certainly *external* to Britain. The philosopher emperor was involved in warfare throughout almost the whole of his reign – on the Rhine, on the

Danube, and in the east. In addition, his problems were exacerbated by growing financial disorder and by the depopulation of areas in western Europe occasioned by the effect of plague brought back by armies returning from eastern wars.

This was a concatenation of misfortune which will have made the occupation of southern Scotland appear a luxury, although the reference of Dio Cassius[23] to the sending of 5,500 Sarmatians to Britain as reinforcements in A.D. 175, indicates that the strong commitment to Britain remained. Indeed, the fighting in northern Britain, which appears to have occupied a number of the governors in the last four decades of the second century, gives practical expression to this. The Romans remained committed to peace on the northern frontier; indeed it was that commitment which led in the early third century to the final imperial involvement in Scotland — in the form of an army led by the emperor, Septimius Severus, himself.

8

Frontier Hostilities:
The Intervention of
Septimius Severus

THE chief obstacle to our understanding of events in northern Britain following the evacuation of the Antonine Wall lies in the shortcomings of the available written accounts; they are patchy chronologically, and extremely elusive of detail.

There are, for example, two references in the *Life of Marcus*[1] to threats of war in Britain – one at the beginning of the reign, the other apparently coinciding approximately with the death in A.D. 169 of Marcus' co-emperor, Lucius Verus. The first looks authentic as information is given that Sextus Calpurnius Agricola (governor, A.D. 163–6) was sent to deal with it; the second lacks any detail, and its wording is strongly suggestive of its being a mistaken repetition of the earlier reference. Again, in the *Life of Commodus*, the author refers to Commodus' assumption of the title *Britannicus*,[2] implying that it was undeserved; no information is given of events to which it might have related, although the coinage confirms that the title was assumed by Commodus in A.D. 184.

Dio Cassius, as we have seen, records the sending to Britain in A.D. 175 of 5,500 Sarmatian Iazyges; we have little indication of how these reinforcements were used, although a unit of them did serve at Ribchester, and finds at Papcastle of characteristically eastern European metalwork suggests that some may have been there too. Dio also describes as the 'greatest war' of Commodus' reign that which was conducted by the governor, Ulpius Marcellus (A.D. 181–4);[3] this may be the same occasion as that described by Commodus' biographer (13,5) as the Britons' 'rejection' of that emperor. Dio records that the Britons had crossed 'the Wall' and destroyed an important Roman army and its general, and that Ulpius Marcellus was sent after them, destroying them totally; Dio gives little detail, however, and the bulk of his short account is given over to a laudatory sketch of Ulpius Marcellus himself.[4]

Epigraphic evidence adds a little to our picture, though most of it is difficult to date with precision; an inscription from Kirksteads – a little to the west of Carlisle – which probably dates to the reign of Marcus Aurelius (*RIB* 2034), commemorates Roman successes across the Wall; a dedication from Carlisle (*RIB* 946), which dates probably to the reign of Commodus, records the slaughter by Roman soldiers of a band of barbarians. Another inscription, probably from later in the second century (*RIB* 1142), from Corbridge records the annihilation of a group of Corionototae, a tribal name otherwise unknown, but perhaps a sub-group of the Brigantes centred on the Corbridge area, which, on the evidence of Vindolanda tablets, appears to have been called *Corio*. Finally, a tombstone from Ambleside recalls, with unusual frankness, the deaths of a father and son, both serving in the army, at the hands of the enemy *inside their fort*. This inscription,[5] which is not specifically dated, appears to belong to the late second or early third centuries.

Between them, this small group of inscriptions provides sufficient evidence of continuing disturbances and instability in the frontier area in the second half of the second century A.D. To it, we may add those inscriptions, which indicate rebuilding work on Hadrian's Wall or in the hinterland;[6] those which might point to local defeats suffered by units of the Roman army or to the repositioning of units, are spread across the later second and early third centuries, and thus argue for continuing, probably localised, problems rather than for a cataclysmic defeat. It is clear, too, that whilst these difficulties were often dealt with by localised or more broadly based retaliation, recourse was also had to the payment of subsidies to real and potential enemies. That something of this sort had been done in the later second century – perhaps after the victory of Ulpius Marcellus – seems clear from a reference in Dio, under the year A.D. 197,[7] that the Caledonians had 'broken their promises'.

Although we hear of no more disturbances amongst the British tribes during Commodus' reign, it is clear that the Roman army in Britain was far from stable; two Roman officers – Priscus (a legate) and Publius Helvius Pertinax (governor) – were approached by their troops with a view to making bids for power. They refused, but the requests indicate a discontented army in Britain, perhaps as a result of the stern disciplinary attitude, which Dio enthusiastically notes as a hall-mark of Ulpius Marcellus; we should note, too, that severe disciplinarianism was the chief weapon by which Pertinax retained his troops' loyalty to Commodus.

The empire was, however, once again plunged into turmoil in A.D. 192 by the assassination of Commodus on the last day of that year. Pertinax succeeded him, but his reign was shortlived; the real struggle was fought out between the governors of three of the most significant provinces – Pescennius Niger (Syria), Septimius Severus (Pannonia) and Clodius Albinus (Britain) – carrying on intermittently until early in A.D. 197. It has often been argued that Albinus recklessly denuded the province of troops in order to pursue his imperial ambitions; hence, the idea that the northern frontier suffered a cataclysm in A.D. 197. However, whilst it is likely that the distraction of the Roman army will, as in A.D. 68–69, have offered an opportunity to Rome's enemies, there is no evidence to suggest that Hadrian's Wall was attacked on a broad front and demolished.

It is more likely that in such a period some of the results of Roman diplomacy came undone – as they had in A.D. 69. Virius Lupus, the governor sent by Severus to replace the defeated Albinus, found, as we have seen, that the Caledonians had broken their promises, apparently by co-operating with the Maeatae. Since it was clear that the resources were not at that time available to mount a major expedition

32. The fort at Birdoswald. This fort was built in stone, probably early in the third century A.D. The original turf-and-timber fort lay astride the Turf Wall, but when the Turf Wall was replaced in stone, the Wall was re-aligned on to the north wall of the fort at Birdoswald.

in Britain, Lupus had to content himself with applying diplomacy to the Maeatae, and paying over subsidies, by which he managed apparently to secure the return of some Romans who had been captured. It has been suggested that some of the coin hoards found in Scotland ending in coins of the later second and early third centuries may provide a reflection of such payments.[8]

Lupus, together with his two successors, Pudens and Senecio (A.D. 202–8), appears to have put in hand a substantial programme of rebuilding on Hadrian's Wall and the hinterland. There is no indication that this should be seen as rectifying war damage; rather it appears to have been a reflection of Septimius Severus' determination that, whilst he did not look to a reconquest of the whole or part of Scotland, he would ensure that Hadrian's Wall provided an effective barrier against the Maeatae and the Caledonians. At the same time, the attention paid to the hinterland may also show an appreciation of the need to back the linear frontier by defence in depth.[9] Although a relatively large crop of inscriptions from the first half of the third century provides clues to Roman strategy, we are hampered by the facts that few military sites in the north have been comprehensively studied and that the artefactual evidence is less well understood than it is for earlier periods.[10]

Severus himself, accompanied by members of his family, came to Britain to campaign in A.D. 208.[11] The *real* purpose of this is unclear; for although Herodian reports that the emperor's visit was prompted by a report from the governor that the province was in a rebellious state, Dio implies that Severus' worry was that peace in the province may have enervated the legions. The true reasons may, as in the cases

33. The stone granaries, Birdoswald. The fort granaries are easily recognisable by the buttresses on the outside walls; these supported the walls of the building against the weight of the heavy roof.

of Claudius and Antoninus Pius, have had more to do with the emperor than with Britain; for it is made clear that Severus wanted to win military glory for himself, and wished to try to bring to heel his sons, Caracalla and Geta.

A major point at issue in the later second and early third centuries are the identities and locations of the two tribes with whom the Romans were most commonly in contact (peaceful or hostile) – the *Caledonii* and the *Maeatae*. Dio is at once helpful and confusing; he says that they are both 'group names', subsuming small entities, and that the Caledonians lived beyond the Maeatae. However, he talks of the Maeatae as living close to the Wall, without indicating which one. The reference must, however, almost certainly be to the Antonine Wall (although long defunct by Dio's time of writing), since evidence shows that the tribal names of southern Scotland were not subsumed into the larger group name. It may, therefore, be simplest to place both tribes beyond the Forth–Clyde line, with the Maeatae inhabiting the land between the Forth and the Tay, and with the Caledonians beyond them. This would leave the Caledonians in much the same territory as they had been when they were defeated by Agricola. We have seen that a purpose of Agricola's fort dispositions and particularly of the Gask Ridge *limes* had been to separate these two and play them off against each other. It is tolerably clear from the references in our sources

34. The stores building, Corbridge, which shows Corbridge in its supply role for Hadrian's Wall, and perhaps specifically for Septimius Severus' campaigns in Scotland.

35. (OPPOSITE) The fort at South Shields. The original fort at South Shields was built probably in the Trajanic period as the eastern terminal of the Stanegate-*limes*. It subsequently formed an eastern outlier of Hadrian's Wall, guarding the Tyne estuary. The whole fort was converted into granaries in the Severan period to supply by sea the campaigns of Septimius Severus in northern Scotland.

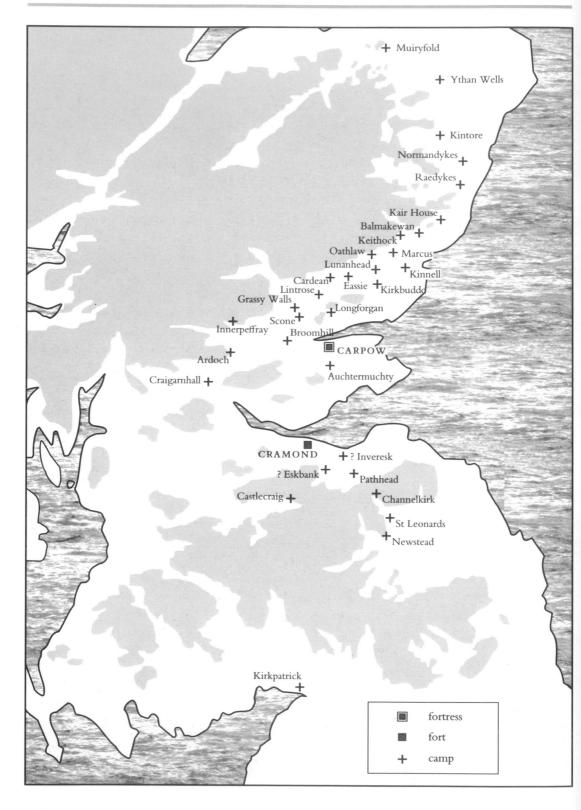

Muiryfold

Ythan Wells

Kintore

Normandykes

Raedykes

Kair House

Balmakewan

Keithock

Oathlaw

Lunanhead

Marcus

Kinnell

Cardean

Lintrose

Eassie

Kirkbuddo

Grassy Walls

Longforgan

Scone

Innerpeffray

Broomhill

CARPOW

Ardoch

Auchtermuchty

Craigarnhall

CRAMOND

? Inveresk

? Eskbank

Pathhead

Castlecraig

Channelkirk

St Leonards

Newstead

Kirkpatrick

■	fortress
■	fort
+	camp

36. Denarius of Septimius Severus. This is one of a number of coins issued to commemorate his victories in Britain; it shows a 'winged victory' and the legend VICTORIAE BRIT ('Commemorating Victory in Britain').

Figure 13. (OPPOSITE) Severan sites in Scotland. The fact that the majority of sites of this period were campaign camps suggests that Severus did not have the permanent re-occupation of Scotland in mind; rather he was repeating, on a larger scale, the campaigning of Agricola's last year in office, probably with a similar objective. The different sizes of these camps indicates that the British garrison was divided into campaign groups of varying size.

to promises, agreements and subsidies that this had remained the policy up to Severus' time.

The nature of the campaigns[12] is not clearly laid out in the sources, whose writers prefer to concentrate on the difficulties of the terrain.[12] That Severus intended both to impress and to be effective is in no doubt in view of the size of the expedition (*RIB* 591),[13] the fact that large sums of money were brought to Britain and the frequent references to aspects of the expedition on the coinage.[14] The imperial entourage based itself at York: Severus himself and Caracalla appear to have masterminded the military side of affairs, whilst Geta was left in charge of the province itself, during which time he appears, amongst other things, to have been responsible for the martyrdom of St Alban.

The nature of the expedition appears to have been a two-pronged attack – by land along Dere Street, and by sea up the east coast; rebuilding at Corbridge (on Dere Street) and at South Shields on the southern bank of the Tyne estuary appears to have been related to supplying the expedition – and possibly the re-occupation of Scotland, if that was intended; the large-scale provision of granaries at South Shields appears to point in that direction.[15]

The tactics of the British tribes appear to have been as they had been with Agricola – to draw the Roman army further and further north into more hostile terrain and stretching its supply lines; only two permanent forts were established in these campaigns – at Cramond on the Forth and the legionary base at Carpow on the Tay; these will obviously have been of major importance in supplying the expedition as it moved further north, and both, of course, could be supplied by sea as well as overland – hence the vital importance of both Corbridge and South Shields.

The large number of other Severan sites in Scotland are marching camps of four different sizes (165, 130, 110 and 63 acres); all of the very large camps – presumably for the full expedition – lie on Dere Street, between Corbridge and the Forth. Those of 63 and 130 acres lie from the Forth to beyond the Tay, whilst those of 110 acres lie between Raedykes and the Moray Firth. These clearly reflect the splitting of the army into operational groups of different sizes and it would appear that two seasons of campaigning were involved (in A.D. 209 and 210). It was in all probability Severus' intention during this period to annex the territory covered. Campaigning was hard, as is indicated in the sources by the number of Roman losses – put by Dio at 50,000 (surely excessively) – and by the impression of the constant pressure of hard work.

In the end, in A.D. 210 a peace was agreed in the presence of both armies; by it, the British ceded territory and captives to Rome, and Severus and Caracalla retired, celebrating victory on the coinage and assuming the title, *Britannicus*. Before the year was out, however, both tribes were once again in revolt, and Severus, now too ill to participate, sent Caracalla to lead the army. Severus died at York early in A.D. 211, and Caracalla, realising that he now had new battles of a political nature to fight, made peace with the British, paid subsidies and abandoned all sites and territory north of Hadrian's Wall; Britain held no further interest for him.

Thus, the last attempt to annex Scotland to the province had ended, with apparently no more success than on earlier occasions. However, as we shall see, although Caracalla may have been despised for purchasing peace with the barbarians, the peace he bought lasted through most of the third century.

9

The Evolution of the Frontiers
in the Third and Fourth Centuries

As we have seen, Hadrian's Wall was reoccupied almost in full after the abandonment of the Antonine Wall in *c*.A.D. 163. Further, we need to remember that the abandonment of the Antonine Wall does not imply the total evacuation of southern Scotland. Indeed, it is evident that through the period up to Severus' campaigns, the frontier zone was evolving in important ways.

First, it appears that until *c*.A.D. 180, forts were held as far north as Newstead and Birrens, and possibly outpost garrisons may even have made some use of certain Antonine Wall forts. Even after A.D. 180, there was no question of abandoning the remaining outliers of Hadrian's Wall; Netherby, Bewcastle, Risingham and High Rochester were kept in active condition, and, to judge from the name given in the Antonine Itinerary to Netherby – CASTRA EXPLORATORUM (or 'fort of the scouts') – these forts had an important role in patrolling and intelligence gathering capacities. It is likely that it was the trouble to which Ulpius Marcellus was sent to respond which led to this reappraisal of positions. It has further been noticed that the garrisons ascribed to the outpost forts were too large for their capacity alone, and that detachments from such units must have been spread more widely, but in small groups.

Secondly, the garrisons of Hadrian's Wall were themselves re-organised; the principal effect of the changes was to introduce more cavalry on to the wall, and therefore greater flexibility in patrolling; the number of cavalry units was enhanced, as was the number of units comprising a mixture of cavalry and infantry. As a result, more than two-thirds of the Wall forts now housed at least some cavalry. It is not unlikely that these changes, too, were introduced during the regime of Ulpius Marcellus. Some garrisons were supplemented by the addition of irregular units (see above on p. 70); this will also have emphasised the developing flexibility.

We can also see evidence of structural changes: following the experience of the Antonine Wall, a military way was introduced linking the forts of Hadrian's Wall, and usually sited between the Wall itself and the *vallum*. Many of the turrets appear to have been demolished, and the Wall made up on their sites. At some milecastles, gates were closed or in some cases narrowed from a vehicular to a pedestrian width. In all, it appears that the Wall itself was becoming less significant than those of its installations that remained. The effect of these changes and the reoccupation of sites in northern England will have been to heighten the perceived strategy of defence in depth.

As we have seen, the sites of the Cumberland coast, apart from the forts, entered a third phase of occupation after the abandonment of the Antonine Wall. How long this continued is less clear; indeed, the pattern may not have been homogeneous, though many do not seem to have lasted beyond *c.*A.D. 180, which may indicate again the 'reforming hand' of Ulpius Marcellus. However, caution is necessary in view of the fact that the two towers which have yielded coins have produced issues of the second half of the third century. It may be significant that of the milefortlets studied only Cardurnock (MF 5) displays extended occupation; as has been pointed out, it is large enough to have stood as a fortlet in its own right.[1]

37. This milestone, erected in the reign of the Gallic rebel emperor Postumus (A.D. 259–268), is one of a small number of inscriptions providing evidence that the Carvetii were given the status of a partly self-governing *civitas*. (RPC CAR = R(es) P(ublica) C(ivitas) CAR(vetiorum).)

Following the settlement of Caracalla with the Caledonians and the Maeatae, there was nearly a century which appears to have been little disturbed by warfare, although there was by no means a uniform pattern of occupation of military sites in northern Britain. Our knowledge is not helped by the paucity of source material, and by the lack of clarity of what there is. The *Notitia Dignitatum*, a document detailing military dispositions throughout the empire and *compiled* apparently in the early fifth century A.D., provides an uncertain picture of the situation in Britain, as the information which it gives may not all relate to the same period. At face value, however, it suggests that the line of Hadrian's Wall was held by normal auxiliary units which had been at the forts at earlier periods, whilst the forts of the hinterland were manned largely by irregular units. It is not known whether these were really contemporaneous, or whether the *Notitia* has conflated information belonging

38. The fort and *vicus*, Vindolanda. The excavated buildings of the *vicus* include the bathhouse, a *mansio* (hotel), strip houses and workshops, flanking the road that led out of the fort's west gate.

to different periods. Even if the references are contemporaneous, it is far from clear at what levels of manning these units of the Roman army were kept.[2]

Inscriptions suggest that over the first few decades following Caracalla's settlement, there was a busy programme of rebuilding at Roman forts in the north, though it is not clear how far this represented routine refurbishment or rebuilding after a period of abandonment. As Breeze has pointed out,[3] during a period in which there was little or no warfare the training of military units will have had to be kept up; evidence for this has been located at Woden Law (Roxburghshire) and at Burnswark (Dumfriesshire), both former hillforts. The true picture of occupation on Hadrian's Wall in the third century is hard to establish; at Housesteads, occupation was apparently fully maintained, whilst at Wallsend and Birdoswald there is evidence at least for the reduction of garrisons – if not total abandonment.[4] Coin evidence points to the abandonment of Castlesteads by the middle of the third century, whilst the fort at Carlisle seems to have been abandoned, too. Nor should we assume that such abandonments followed a uniform pattern, for they were still taking place in the later third or early fourth centuries – as at South Shields.

We should not, of course, assume that these fluctuations and changes in the pattern of military occupation led to instability amongst the rest of Romano-British society in the frontier zone. Indeed, surviving evidence points in a quite contrary direction; for example, at some stage in the middle of the third century, a degree of local self-government was given to the people of northern Cumbria with the establishment of the *civitas* ('self-governing canton') of the Carvetii, apparently a sub-group of the Brigantes.[5] Such a decision presupposes not only political stability in the area, but also the existence of considerable wealth on the part of local grandees, who will have been called upon to provide financial support for such a venture. Carlisle, which was presumably the tribal centre, developed buildings which were consonant with this promoted status.[6]

Epigraphic evidence points to other, apparently non-military, administrative units; for example, a *curia* ('assembly') of the Textoverdi (or Tectoverdi) is indicated in the Tyne valley (*RIB* 1695), and references to *vicani* ('townspeople') at Vindolanda (*RIB* 1700) and at Old Carlisle (*RIB* 899) may indicate some form of urban organisation. From Old Penrith comes a record of Flavius Martius who is described (*RIB* 933) as a senator of the Carvetii. It is, in any case, clear that towns/markets developed and flourished in the frontier zone, as at Chesters, Housesteads and Vindolanda;[7] at Corbridge, although the site probably remained within military jurisdiction, a town developed covering thirty acres within its walled area. It is possible, too, that Romanised forms of urban organisation remained in the third century north of the frontier – for instance, at old Roman fort sites such as Carriden on the Antonine Wall[8] or at native sites such as Traprain Law.[9]

The burden of this evidence is that, perhaps with thinning numbers of soldiers in garrison, more admininistrative and local government responsibility was being entrusted to the Romano-British themselves. Their ability to carry this function will itself have derived from the prosperity – commercial, industrial and agricultural – which was a developing feature of the Romanising of northern Britain.[10] Some villas appeared in the north east, as at Holme House, Piercebridge,[11] though in general Romano-British farms, in terms of their appearance at least, remained anchored in their British heritage – unless, of course, the increasing number of sub-rectangular huts is indicative of Roman influence.[12] It is clear, however, that farming was pursued densely and that some sites – for example, at Ewe Close in the upper Lune Valley – became extensive, commanding large tracts of land. Indeed, aerial reconnaissance has shown considerable developments in areas such as the Solway Plain, and in the Eden and Lune Valleys.[13]

Such sites were undoubtedly catering for the markets which were provided by the Roman forts and by their associated settlements; a wide range of food products will have been demanded which were supplied by the arable farmers of the valley floors and by stock managers on the higher fells. No doubt, some of these were already processing their 'raw materials', whilst others will have sold their goods on to the towns for processing. Again, both in town and country, local people will have been exploiting other natural resources, perhaps enjoying in some cases special military protection, as may have happened in the case of the heavily defended fort at Whitley Castle.

It was, of course, crucial for Romanised sites that they continued to relate to markets; this clearly meant diversification of outlets. Thus whilst demilitarisation of the fort at Vindolanda led apparently to a rapid collapse of the *vicus* in the 270s, at other sites, such as South Shields, civilian settlers were apparently able to retain a commercial momentum even when the army moved away. In this, of course, they were following a route which in the early years of occupation had determined success or failure for many towns in the south of Britain.

How long these conditions of peace and prosperity were maintained in the frontier zone is hard to say, though we need to remember that for the empire as a whole the mid-third century was a disturbed time; economic and political instability took their toll, and between A.D. 259 and 273, Britain joined other western provinces in the breakaway movement, known as the *Imperium Galliarum* ('Independent Empire of the Gauls'). The economic problems are manifested in the near collapse of the coinage and the appearance of huge numbers of locally produced 'radiate copies'. The genesis of many of these problems lay in the military reforms of Septimius Severus, which made promotion through the ranks the effective way of achieving status. The anarchy of the middle of the century and the financial irresponsibility to which it led were the ultimate manifestations of this.

Despite the depths to which the empire had sunk recovery began in the 270s, and Britain was restored to the control of the central government by the defeat of the Tetrici in A.D. 273. In A.D. 284, Diocletian came to power, and initiated reform; in A.D. 285, he split the empire with Maximian into eastern and western halves. The 'principle of fragmentation' encouraged Carausius, an officer of Maximian's based at Boulogne, to believe that he, too, could have a share – as is demonstrated by his coin issue showing three imperial heads with the legend CARAVSIVS ET FRATRES SVI ('Carausius and his Brothers'). The refusal of Diocletian and Maximian to recognise Carausius as their brother turned him into a usurper; from A.D. 287 to 296, under first Carausius and then Allectus, Britain again split away from the control of the central government.[14]

Britain was restored to the empire in A.D. 296 by Constantius I ('Chlorus'), the father of Constantine. By this time, Diocletian was in the midst of a major programme of constitutional and administrative reform. The empire, already divided into two, was further split into four (the 'tetrarchy'); a ruling college was established in which there were two senior men (*Augusti*-Diocletian and Maximian) and two junior figures (*Caesares*-Constantius and Galerius). Britain fell within the part administered by Constantius.

39. Radiate of Carausius. Unusually, the coin unusually has three heads on the obverse side – Carausius' own, and those of Diocletian and Maximian, whom Carausius referred to as his 'brothers'. Their failure to acknowledge this left Carausius in a state of rebellion in Britain.

Several other changes affected the provinces; in the first place, provinces were split up, making 120 over the whole empire: Britain, which had been made into two provinces by Severus (*Britannia Inferior* (north); *Britannia Superior* (south)) now became four; *Britannia Secunda*, which consisted of everything north of a line drawn between the Humber and the Dee, had its administrative capital at York. The south east and Midlands became *Flavia Caesariensis* (north) and *Maxima Caesariensis* (south), whilst Wales and the west country were formed into *Britannia Prima*. Each had its own governor, but together they formed a *diocese* under the control of a *vicarius*, who was responsible to Constantius through a praetorian prefect.

The army was also reformed; legions were split into smaller entities, and more irregulars – *numeri*, *cunei*, *milites*, *pedites*, *equites* – were brought in. With smaller units mobility was enhanced, vigour and freshness increased, and frontier enemies given the clear impression that the Roman army was more ubiquitous than it had seemed earlier in the third century. Some *alae* and *cohortes* were retained, but generally these were not seen as matching up to the new need for rapid and flexible response. In the north, the *exploratores* ('scouts') who had been disposed to the north of Hadrian's Wall, were re-titled *areani*, but maintained the same function. Troops were also kept at the centre first with the imperial entourages, and later under officers called *magistri*, and could be used as mobile field armies accompanying emperors or other delegated generals on campaign. The army's command structure was also revised, the *Notitia Dignitatum* listing three separate military commands in Britain – the *dux Britanniarum* ('duke of the Britains') who was responsible for the northern frontier zone, the *comes litoris Saxonici* ('count of the Saxon shore') whose responsibility was the maritime frontier of the east and south coasts, and the *comes Britanniarum* ('count of the Britains'), who had control of a mobile field army and who may have been a later addition to, or replacement for, the command structure. The development of these reforms and others concerning the financial system by Diocletian and Constantine, together with reform of the coinage represented a period of major initiative to get the empire back on its feet, and to improve security both inside and outside its frontiers.

During the fourth century, all of Britain's external boundaries came under pressure at one time or another; as a result, the make-up of populations in those areas began to alter in character; the various invaders generally did not wish to destroy, but rather to settle and share in the empire's prosperity (*foederati*) and, if that was not possible, to grab some of it for themselves; Hnaudifridus' detachment at Housesteads might have constituted such a group, and the hall-like building of the later fourth century, which was constructed on the site of the granaries at Birdoswald, might represent further such evidence. The frontiers of principal activity, however, were those in the north and along the eastern and southern coasts, and the west coast also received attention.

It is not clear when trouble first broke out on the northern frontier, although the sacking of parts of the fort at Bewcastle, apparently in the 280s, may be a first sign of it.[15] Not too much store, however, can be set by the non-recovery of coin hoards – often cited as a sign of military danger; in the cases of many of the hoards which terminate with coins of the later third and early fourth centuries, the real cause was most probably *financial* rather than political or military instability.[16] It is possible that Diocletian's assumption in A.D. 284 and 285 of the titles *Britannicus Maximus* may have had something to do with resumed hostilities. The background to this is not clearly apparent; but the idea that troops were being taken from the north to meet the new maritime threat in the south is countered to some extent at least by the construction from new of a fort at Piercebridge and the apparent remanning of the fort at Lancaster, both in the 260s. There were clearly troops to spare for these contributions to the development of defence in depth in the northern frontier zone.

As we have seen, however, it was not apparently considered necessary to maintain large northern garrisons in the last decades of the third century. The thin nature of many garrisons is demonstrated by a general lack of coins of Carausius and Allectus as site finds in the north. But this thinness of garrison levels is much more likely to be a reflection of overall planning than to have been caused by a specific decision by

Figure 14. Coastal defences of the third and fourth centuries. The Saxon shore forts appear to have been constructed within the period c.A.D. 240–310, whilst the west coast defences consisted of new sites established in c.A.D. 320–330, and refurbishments of existing sites. The towers of the Yorkshire coast appear to be later than c.A.D. 370.

Allectus to denude northern garrisons in an effort to resist an invasion from Constantius in the south. Further, the dilapidation noted in many northern forts, prior to refurbishment in the early fourth century, appears to offer confirmation of this view.

It is in the context of the late third century A.D. that we first find mention made of the Picts, whose name is a Latin word meaning 'painted'. A reference in a Panegyric of Constantius I[17] talks of the Picts and the Hiberni and their barbaric fighting methods. The Picts of the late third century A.D. evidently lived beyond the Forth–Clyde line; again, they represented a large grouping of local tribes. The late historian, Ammianus Marcellinus,[18] describes the Picts as an amalgamation of the *Verturiones* and the *Dicalydones*, the latter evidently the *Caledones* of earlier times. It is likely that in broad terms the tribal arrangements which had been in place in southern Scotland in the early third century were still intact.

The *Imperium Britanniarum* was dissolved in A.D. 296, and the British provinces became once more a part of the central imperial structure. The submission of Britain was, as the Arras medallion shows, received by Constantius in person; it is not clear, however, whether he took measures against the Picts on that occasion, or whether this occurred on a subsequent visit in A.D. 305–6. That the Picts were defeated in A.D. 306 is clear; less so, however, the question of whether a re-furbishment of northern military installations was set in train then, or ten years previously. An inscription from the fort at Birdoswald (*RIB* 1912) specifies major work on the commander's house (*praetorium*), the headquarters (*principia*), and the bath-house; work of such a sub-stantial and fundamental nature would suggest either enemy action or a period of neglect. Work is also confirmed by an inscription from Housesteads (*RIB* 1613); although in this case, the nature of the work is not specified, it is hard to resist the idea that it included the remodelling of the barracks, noted in recent excavations. In this, the old style of barracks was replaced by an arrangement in which there was a centurion's quarters and a number of rooms (or 'chalets') for the men. This modifi-cation has been observed at three other wall forts (Birdoswald, Greatchesters and Wallsend) and at Risingham and High Rochester.[19]

At around the same period, we can point to the rebuilding of the fort at Vindolanda (probably after a period of demilitarisation), and possibly also at Low Borrow Bridge in the Lune Valley, which was thought to show constructional parallels with Vindolanda.[20] Some repair work is also evident on milecastles and turrets of Hadrian's Wall, though it should be added that few of the latter type of structure appear to have been occupied in the fourth century. Some reconstruction work appears also to have been carried out on Hadrian's Wall itself to the west of Birdoswald, though it remains unclear how important the Wall itself was in the fourth century. Some of the structures of the Cumberland coast have produced evidence of activity in the fourth century, though at what point is less clear; these are milefortlets 5 (Cardurnock), 12 (Blitterlees) and 20 (Low Mire), and Tower 26A (Cote How). The coastal forts remained operational; indeed, a new one was added – at Burrow Walls.[21]

Our evidence for activity in the frontier zone in the remainder of the first half of the fourth century is slight; Constantine I assumed the titles *Britannicus Maximus* in A.D. 314, and his son, Constans, mounted an expedition to Britain in A.D. 342–3, which was of sufficient significance

to detain him through the winter; it is thought that the latter event may have been connected with a reorganisation of frontier scouts.[22] It appears likely that Picts and Scots had treaties with Rome during this period; Ammianus refers, however, to them laying waste to areas near the frontier in A.D. 360,[23] and such activity may have penetrated into the province, if we are to place weight on a group of coin hoards from Corbridge, terminating in the 340s.

We have seen that the early part of the fourth century showed signs of difficulties experienced on the west coast of the province; although never distinguished as a separate command, the west coast received, apparently in the second quarter of the fourth century, a series of completely new fortifications after the style of the Saxon Shore forts – at Cardiff, Caernarfon, Caer Gybi and Lancaster; that these were aimed at the Hiberni and Scotti (whom the *Panegyric of Constantius* picked out as allies of the Picts) seems in little doubt. The new structures indicated a new imperative of frontier defence – large 'castle-like' forts from which attackers could be repelled, and capable, it would appear, of housing civilians as well as soldiers. At Lancaster, recent (1992) excavations have suggested that the *vicus* may have 'died' in *c*.A.D. 340–50, perhaps as civilians were taken inside the protection of

40. Housesteads fort: 'chalet barracks'. These irregularly arranged barracks with open fronts are characteristic of fourth-century re-construction in the forts of Hadrian's Wall. The change in type *may* indicate a more flexible use than had been the case in earlier forts.

41. The 'Wery Wall', Lancaster. This shape-less stump of masonry in the background has been known for cen-turies; its name means simply 'defensive wall'. Excavation in the 1970s showed that it was the core of a polygonal bastion that probably stood on the northern corner of a new fort, constructed in c.A.D. 320–330. It obliterated a bath-house, the remains of which can be seen in the foreground.

42. The late fort at Caer Gybi (Holy-head). This bastioned enclosure provides an idea of the nature of the fort of which Lan-caster's 'Wery Wall' (plate 41) was a part. It is still unclear whether the structure at Caer Gybi was a four-sided fort or a three-sided enclosure defending a dis-embarkation point.

the new fort. It is also possible that the defenders at Lancaster were provided with intelligence from the sea by an irregular unit of boatmen, whose vessels (*barcae*) were especially suitable for action in the shallow waters of Morecambe Bay.[24] It may well be that the west coast, particularly in Wales, saw federate settlement from across the Irish Sea.[25] The chronology of the development of west-coast defences is not clear, though the fort at Ravenglass was certainly one of those rebuilt after

43. Portchester Castle, wall and bastions. This 'Saxon shore' fort was constructed in c.A.D. 300. Its 'castle like' architecture indicates a development of the late Roman fort from 'police station' to defended strongpoint. The purpose of the bastions was evidently the mounting of pieces of heavy artillery. Two-thirds of the surviving masonry is Roman, the remainder Norman.

the disaster of A.D. 367,[26] and the discovery of a *solidus* of Theodosius beneath the tower of Muncaster Castle (above Ravenglass), together with other finds of late coins in coastal locations, prompts the suggestion that coastal towers may have been built in the north west,[27] as they were in the north east after the disaster of A.D. 367.

Of the enemies of Roman Britain, perhaps the most prominent were the Saxons from the border territory of the modern states of Germany and Denmark; their raids, which had started in the third century, were of sufficient severity to prompt not only the building of a series of 'castle like' forts from the Wash to Southampton Water, but also in the military reorganisation of the early fourth century the establishment of a separate command under the 'count of the Saxon shore';[28] this reference in the *Notitia Dignitatum* provides the evidence that this area of Britain's coastline was given the name, 'Saxon shore'.

The significance of the command and the name applied to the area have been much debated; was the 'Saxon shore' the coastline which was merely *attacked* by Saxon raiders, or could the name contain an indication that the area was *settled* by Saxon *foederati*? Were the new forts on this portion of coastline intended to deter Saxon raiders or could they conceivably have been built by the usurper, Carausius, to keep his 'British empire' from being re-absorbed by Rome?

Although the chronological evidence is by no means clear cut, it appears that Saxon raiding on the coast of south-east Britain began in the first half of the third century, and that the earliest forts – at Brancaster and Reculver – may have been built then; signs of destruction at some coastal towns may point to the effects of the raids and why they began to cause concern. It appears that the British coastline was not viewed in isolation either by the Saxons or by the Romans, and that a programme of new fort building was set in train along the coasts of the Low Countries and of northern France. Indeed, the 'Saxon shore' was probably viewed as a command with two geographical areas of responsibility.

Whilst the early forts were like their predecessors of the second century, those that came later – in the later third and early fourth centuries – displayed major innovations that appear to have been copied from the new style of town walls that were being constructed in Gaul in the second half of the third century. The chief characteristics of the new forts, as demonstrated (for example) at Portchester Castle in Hampshire, are their high, thick walls, their heavily defended narrow entrances, and the bastions on the exterior of the walls at intervals or on the corners (or both). At the same time, the rigidity of the 'playing card' shape, so frequently associated with earlier forts, loosened. The new forts often had angular corners, and, as at Pevensey, might desert the rectilinear plan altogether in favour of taking the best defensive position on a particular piece of ground. The new forts also tended to be considerably larger than their predecessors.

The logic of the new format seems to derive from a changed view of a fort's role and purpose. In the earlier period, forts housed soldiers whose main job was patrolling; thus, it was important to have clear access ways to allow the rapid deployment of troops into the surrounding countryside; a Roman military unit did not expect to be attacked *inside* its own fort. The imperative now was the strategic positioning of the fort – often on a river estuary – where those inside could attack raiders by means of artillery mounted on the bastions. These would also provide excellent lookout posts. Ultimately, however, the defenders would be inside a fort – perhaps rather as in a medieval castle – gaining protection from attack. It is unclear who would be inside, as the sizes of many military units of the later third and fourth centuries are difficult to establish; even the size of legion II *Augusta*, stationed at Richborough which was presumably the headquarters of the command, is imponderable in the light of Diocletian's reorganisations. The interiors of the forts provide few clues to the identity of their inhabitants, and it may be, in view of the size of many of the forts, that both military and civilian inhabitants were housed in them.

The chronology of the development of the coastal system remains unclear; as we have seen, some of the earliest forts were probably in position in the first half of the third century; Carausius is often credited with a major contribution, though this has proved to be impossible to determine from archaeological evidence. It would, however, be appropriate, in view of his maritime experience, to assign Carausius at least a prominent part in the development, though it appears that the system was not complete until the early years of the fourth century. It is probable, therefore, that both Constantius I and Constantine I played their parts; indeed, the fort at Pevensey has been seen as an addition as late as the reign of Constans in the A.D. 340s.

By the middle of the fourth century, therefore, it is appropriate to think of three separate frontier arrangements in Britain – Hadrian's Wall and the forts of its hinterland, together with some features of the Cumberland coastal defences, to deal with Picts and Caledonians, the new forts (and perhaps watchtowers) of the west coast to guard against the Scotti from Ireland, and the forts of the 'Saxon shore' to handle Saxons and Franks. Potentially, there were great difficulties and dangers here, though Constantinian *Panegyrics* paint Britain as a land of great resources from which both Constantius I and his grandson, Julian, were able to transfer supplies in order to revitalise damaged sites and military units in western Europe. The dangers were, no doubt, enhanced if significant settlement in these frontier areas had been permitted to Rome's enemies, though the threat was perhaps held at bay by the fact that the new settlers would presumably not be anxious to share their 'good luck' with newer settlers. The Roman historian, Ammianus, however, writes of Britain's morale being low at this time 'due to past disasters'.[29]

Pressure was evidently beginning to increase; despite the fact that the Picts and Caledonians apparently had treaties with Rome, they are said by Ammianus[30] to have been raiding near the frontiers in A.D. 360, though it remains unclear precisely which localities are meant; they may have been raiding amongst the tribes of southern Scotland, or crossing the line of the Wall – (though it is quite likely that by this stage the individual forts were more important than the linear barrier itself) – or even outflanking the Tyne and Solway estuaries and raiding on the north-east and north-west coasts. Troops available in Britain were evidently unable to cope, and elements of a field army were sent under Lupicinus (*magister armorum*) to deal with the situation.

After yet more problems in the mid-360s, a major explosion occurred in A.D. 367, in what Ammianus described as 'the conspiracy of the barbarians',[31] in which all of the enemies of Roman Britain attacked at once, evidently aided by the treachery of the *areani* ('scouts'). We are told that the count of the Saxon shore was killed and the *dux Britanniarum* severely embarrassed, though recent research has urged caution in ascribing too much destruction to this single incident.[32] It has, indeed, been suggested that the northern frontier itself may have been bypassed, as the attackers went for richer pickings further south.

The emperor, Valentinian I, sent Theodosius with a small field army to clear Britain of raiders and to make good the damage; he is said to have repaired 'cities and strongholds', though again we have to be careful about ascribing all repair work to him because it has a notional date in the later fourth century. Some of it probably does belong to Theodosius, though it has been argued that much of the 'gate blocking' in evidence at northern forts belongs to earlier periods. Plausibly, however, a new form of late Roman construction, based upon heavily packed postholes rather than on horizontal sleeper beams, and noted at Ravenglass, Maryport and Bowness-on-Solway,[33] should be dated to this period.

It is also at this stage that a new British provincial name, *Valentia*, appears. It has been suggested that it was applied to a new province, formed out of north-west England and north Wales, with the aim of producing a coherent defence for the west coast.[34] However, perhaps more plausible than this or any other specific locality is the suggestion that the name derives from that of the reigning emperor (Valentinian) and was applied honorifically to the whole of Britain to celebrate the recovery.[35] Also belonging to this period was the construction of a new series of watchtowers on the north-east coast – from Huntcliffe to Filey, though possibly running further north.[36] It is clear that the significance of these sites – and perhaps of others in the west – was to give early warning of seaborne raiders. Indeed, their concentration in the north might suggest that seaborne raids from Scotland were as much of a threat as those from Europe.

That some re-building and reassessment took place in the north seems clear; there are signs of work at Birdoswald, Housesteads and Vindolanda, whilst at Rudchester and Haltonchesters a similar construction technique can be seen as that (noted above) at Ravenglass, Maryport and Bowness-on-Solway. Only at Vindolanda has any indication of extra-mural settlement been noted dating to the second half of the fourth century – and that after an interval of nearly a century – though such evidence *may* have been missed elsewhere. It remains possible that the forts now housed a farmer militia and the families of such men; the terraces visible at Housesteads may reflect cultivation practices of such a group. It is also clear that, where this had not already happened,[37] the 'outpost forts' were abandoned, and this confirms Ammianus' observation that the *areani* were now disbanded[38] – presumably because of their treachery. That the remnants of the army and the Romano-British who had come to rely on them now looked towards defence in depth can be seen from the evident contemporary importance of the routes from York to Corbridge, from York to Carlisle, and from Chester to Carlisle; on the latter, the two new fortlets – at Wreay Hall and Barrock Fell – were built possibly at this time, if not earlier.

The last decades of the fourth century remain difficult to disentangle; although dating of the command of *dux Britanniarum* in the *Notitia Dignitatum* remains hazardous, it would appear that, if it relates to the latter years of the fourth century, the forts of the hinterland remained manned, and that defence in depth was still a real strategy. It may also be in this period that a field army was stationed in Britain under the command of a new officer, the *comes Britanniarum*.

In the early 380s, it appears that Magnus Maximus waged war against the Picts and Scots, and finds of his coins at Corbridge and at South Shields, both with a history of use as supply depots, may indicate that he was actively intervening in southern Scotland, both by land and sea,[39] and he may have temporarily established some measure of control over southern Scotland. However, Maximus was primarily concerned with the establishment of authority in western Europe, and is often said to have removed troops from Britain to facilitate this. Although the abandonment at this time of a number of northern forts has been postulated, it is hard to be conclusive. It may in any case be that forts were losing an exclusively military role and were becoming more like self-supporting villages – though this, too, is difficult to prove. Further, the fact that coins continued to arrive in Britain – albeit in decreasing

44. 'Hall' building, Birdoswald fort. This large building (of Saxon type) was constructed on top of the granaries in the late fourth century. Its outline has been depicted in the present arrangement by tree trunks placed on the locations of original post pads, which were found during excavation.

numbers – into the earliest years of the fifth century suggests that some element of organisation remained for paying an army which probably in any case was by now receiving the bulk of its remuneration in kind.

Magnus Maximus' endeavours ended in the disaster at Arles in A.D. 388, and this, together with a disaster at Aquileia in the same year, was probably a signal for the resumption of raiding on Britain's frontiers. It may not be unconnected with this that Saxon metalwork has been found at Corbridge, whilst at Birdoswald a 'hall-like' structure was erected on top of the northern granary. The last recorded intervention in Britain of any significance by a representative of the central government was that of Stilicho in the late 390s and early 400s, though the extent and location of his work is hard to pinpoint.[40] The court poet, Claudian,[41] indicates that he saw action against Irish, Picts and Saxons, though he does not appear to have re-established any kind of hold on southern Scotland. It is possible that he had a hand in the establishment of 'protectorate kingdoms' in Wales, allowing settlement on the part of people from across the Irish Sea. Around this time, too, the British Saxon-shore command appears to have been separated from its continental parts. The idea, however, that Stilicho commissioned building work on the Saxon shore, supposedly evidenced by a piece of stamped brick from Pevensey, falls now that the brick in question has been established as a forgery of the twentieth century! Stilicho is recorded, however, as having removed more troops from Britain.

The fact, however, that Britain was still regarded as part of the Roman empire indicates that the frontiers were still essentially in tact, and capable of defence. The first decades of the fifth century brought that into question; although the current rejection of Honorius' well-known rescript of A.D. 410 as applying to Britain removes a precise date from the chronology of Roman Britain, it is clear from the sixth-century historian, Zosimus, that the first quarter of the century saw the death-throes of Britain as an institutional part of the Roman empire. The anarchy that is evident in the establishment of a series of 'usurpers' between A.D. 406 and 411 saw the removal from power and influence of those who sought to maintain the link with Rome. Whilst those who sought an independent power for themselves, such as Vortigern, may have rejected the government in Rome, they were still champions of Romano-British culture; the efforts of townspeople across the old province, and even in the northern frontier area (as is demonstrated in Carlisle), to retain their Romano-British identity provides the ultimate proof that within its frontiers Britain had become effectively Romanised. To that degree, we can count the frontier of Roman Britain as having made a significant and lasting contribution.

45. Blocked gateway, Birdoswald fort. It was characteristic that late in the occupation whole (or parts of) gateways were blocked up to make the forts less penetrable. At Birdoswald, the northern carriageway of the east gate was blocked, and the south carriageway of the west gate.

10

Britain Within Its Frontiers

A S WE HAVE SEEN, a Roman frontier served a number of purposes: not least amongst these was the creation of the security essential to the establishment of a Romanised way of life.[1]

Across the country was a network of roads, many of them laid out in the first place for military purposes, but then used and added to by civilians to carry on a variety of social and economic purposes. As the military emphasis moved northwards in the later first century A.D., so the character of administration in the south of Britain became more civilian in nature. The British tribes, many of which had opposed the conqueror, now became channels through which local administration could be exercised. The towns, many of which had started life as *vici* supporting and supported by Roman forts, took on an administrative role within the tribes, but ultimately depended upon continuing commercial success.

The descendants of tribal aristocracies, which themselves had emerged in the late Iron Age through economic success, could be 'trained' to take on a leading role in local government; the presence in York, probably in the A.D. 80s, of a schoolmaster, Demetrius of Tarsus (*RIB* 662–3), indicates how the Romans may have gone about winning the minds of these descendants of aristocracy. Ultimately, however, they could be lured by a long-successful Roman formula – namely that the acceptance of burdens meant the winning of privileges.

Even before the arrival of the Romans, Britain was on record as producing, amongst other things, an exportable surplus of grain; this represented the source of wealth for many aristocratic families. Clearly, the market for grain, for other agricultural produce, and for manufactured goods, increased as forts were established and *vici* grew adjacent to them. The towns became the marketplaces, where people from town and country could buy and sell what they wished. In this way, town and country in Roman Britain became interdependent; in the peace and stability that Romanisation produced both flourished. The evidence of some town-houses and some country villas demonstrates the degree of what could be achieved, and there is every reason to believe that the beneficiaries were the Romanised British; whilst there might be

some investment from overseas, we should discount the idea of a large immigrant civilian population. Further, Latin *Panegyrics* of the fourth century show that this prosperity was retained until well into that century.

The frontiers, of course, were by definition within the military zone of the province; whilst it is clear that there could not be the same degree of civilian input into administration, opportunities of various kinds existed for economic advancement, and as time went on this could for some mean advancement in status, too; the establishment of civilian administrations amongst the Brigantes and the Carvetii demonstrates this adequately.

We should not, of course, think of Roman frontiers as 'thin lines', marking the boundary between what was Roman and what was not; the lines were themselves parts of frontier zones, in which those who lived 'outside' the frontiers themselves were still drawn firmly into a political and economic network.[2] Tribes, such as the Votadini of Northumberland, might have treaties with Rome, and might trade their goods with the Roman province; their menfolk might join the Roman army, and the tribes would receive subsidies from Rome. Many of the coin hoards located in southern Scotland may represent such subsidies, and the great treasure from Traprain Law shows that the practice was probably retained until very late.[3] Where people both

46. The fort and *vicus* at Old Carlisle. This photograph shows the fort clearly as a platform; the heart of the *vicus*, instead of flanking one or more of the fort's exit roads, developed along the adjacent road from Carlisle to Maryport.

47. 'Strip' house, Vindolanda. These buildings, with their gable ends facing the street, were common in the *vici* of Roman Britain; they provided a shop on the street frontage, with living accommodation behind.

north and south of a boundary line were effectively parts of the Roman network, then the boundary itself became little more than a point where dues were collected.

In the early years of conquest, we may assume that locally at least the impact of the occupiers would have been considerable.[4] Carlisle, for example,[5] has shown evidence of pre-Roman ploughing beneath Roman sites; the Roman habit of fortifying and securing communications through river valleys will have denied local access to areas of what must have been the best agricultural land. At least one farm is known to have been 'trapped' between Hadrian's Wall and the *vallum*, causing in all likelihood uncompensated ejection of the original inhabitants from the military zone.[6] Evidence has come from a number of forts on the Stanegate and on Hadrian's Wall both of ploughing and of farmstead structures beneath the forts themselves.[7] Such events will clearly have proved disruptive, causing individuals to feel resentment; perhaps more serious, at least temporarily, was the separation of a considerable area of Brigantian territory to the north of Hadrian's Wall.

We may assume that further disruption will have been caused by decisions regarding land use within the *territorium* of each fort. The amount of land so involved is hard to quantify, though the number of

military installations in use in the north – Higham[8] calculates forty in the late Hadrianic period – will indicate that a substantial block of land must have come under some sort of military supervision – used for grazing of fort animals, for the growing of fodder and bedding, for distribution to time-expired veterans, for civilian settlements and roads. Against such real and potential disruption, the compensating opportunities must have been quite considerable for local people.

An immediate point of contact for soldiers and natives was provided by the *vici*; these 'informal' towns grew up outside most forts – stretching as ribbon developments along one or more of the exit roads from a fort, or, as at Old Carlisle, along a nearby main road. Such 'towns' had no pre-planned size or shape, but appear to have grown according to need. Some of them, such as Old Penrith[9] and Ambleside,[10] became large and carry every indication of a long-term prosperity, whilst Carlisle and Corbridge clearly outstripped even these. One at least – Old Carlisle (*RIB* 899) – appears to have enjoyed a degree of self-government, whilst both Housesteads and Vindolanda provide signs of civilian organisation. It is clear that upon official recommendation the status of

48. Bath-house, Hardknott fort. This bathhouse is a small suite of rooms in a linear arrangement, with the furnace area and the hot room at the far end in this photograph. Its small size was due to the fact that this fort had no civilian settlement (*vicus*).

a *vicus* could be enhanced in recognition of achievement and physical growth.[11]

Achievement was presumably a measure of size, which in its turn will have been a measure of the success of *vicani* in catering for the needs of the adjacent fort. Social integration might develop, with serving soldiers forming relationships with local women, and raising families; over the years, these often became stable, and, after the reforms of Septimius Severus, could be translated into marriage. But the most obvious area of independence and integration of Roman and native lay in the fields of commerce and industry. Whilst it is clear that the Roman army could from the outset of occupation obtain some of what it needed from local sources, some products – such as samian ware – had to be imported from the continent, and others produced by the army itself. In a number of places in the north, we have record of 'industrial estates' where units of the Roman army manufactured a range of items for themselves – for example, at Holt,[12] Brampton,[13] Muncaster[14] and Quernmore.[15] Such sites appear to have flourished until the Hadrianic period, but were gradually rendered redundant, as the Romano-British economy itself became more organised and productive; large contracts for pottery vessels were put out in southern England, local fine wares (such as Nene Valley pottery) were developed, and it is evident that native craftsmen were drawn into more organised industrial complexes, as at Wilderspool,[16] and the distribution of their products handled presumably through military depots, such as that recognised at Walton-le-Dale (Preston).

Civilians were also attracted into the *vici* to provide for soldiers services of various kinds for which those soldiers could afford to pay; the well-paid troops in a fort thus acted as a magnet in economic terms. No doubt, some of these civilians may not have been British or, at least, not local to areas in which they worked; itinerant traders will have formed a significant part of any workforce.[17] Those from abroad had ready physical access through the ports that developed along river estuaries – Brough-on-Humber, South Shields, Newcastle-upon-Tyne, Carlisle, Maryport, Ravenglass, Lancaster, Walton-le-Dale, Chester, and not to mention Ptolemy's *Portus Setantiorum*.[18]

Typically, the *vici* consisted principally of long, narrow, 'strip' buildings, with their gable ends facing the streets – indicating presumably that street frontage space was at a premium; apart from a 'cleared zone' (or *cordon sanitaire*) in the area of the fort's defences, such buildings would push themselves right up to the fort. They consisted usually of a single storey, and appear often to have comprised a shop on the street

49. Iron-working hearths, Manchester. These hearths, which were housed probably in 'lean-to' sheds, were used for the reduction of iron ore; they were found in 1972 on what appeared to be an 'industrial estate'.

frontage itself, with living accommodation behind it for tenants or owners. It was normal to have to pass through one room to reach another (which was socially rather undistinguished), but in one case at Vindolanda, it is possible that two adjoining properties came under a single ownership, allowing the intervening alleyway to be used as an internal corridor giving independent access to the rooms of the building. No doubt, small-scale manufacturing or processing could be carried out at the rear of such premises; in the case of the so-called butcher's shop at Vindolanda, this probably included the slaughtering of animals that had been brought to the *vicus* alive.

Vici appear to have developed around almost all forts in the north – even in relatively remote areas; though there is currently no evidence for a *vicus* at Hardknott, an equally remote fort at Maiden Castle-on-Stainmore did apparently support a *vicus*. Here, platforms cut into the hillside on the fort's southern flank appear to have been constructed for rectangular *vicus* buildings. In many cases, buildings in the *vici* were constructed probably of timber in the first instance (as at Watercrook),[19] and subsequently rebuilt in stone or stone and timber. It is unlikely that a *vicus* would have survived the demilitarisation (permanent or temporary) of its adjacent fort; indeed, a special regional role would have been required if this were to happen.

A clue to such 'special' *vici* may exist in size or status; Corbridge clearly maintained an existence independent of the presence of a fort, though military connections remained strong. It is evident that the *vicus*

50. Cocidius plaque, Bewcastle. The silver votive plaque of the god, Cocidius, is crudely executed, and reminds us of the 'matchstick figures' found on local copies of Roman coins. It is likely that Bewcastle was a cult centre of this local god.

at Old Carlisle enjoyed a special status, which may be reflected in the fact that it appears to have enjoyed a closer physical relationship with the neighbouring road (from Carlisle to Maryport) than with the fort itself. Carlisle clearly developed a special position within the administration of the north west. Other large *vici*, which may have enjoyed a degree of physical independence from their neighbouring fort were Piercebridge, where the crossing of the river Tees by Dere Street may have given the site an especial importance, and (possibly) Ambleside; here a large *vicus* probably reflects the importance for its region of a site at the head of a major line of communication which is represented by Lake Windermere. It is worth noting that the size of the *vicus* may carry the same implication as the large size of the granaries within the fort − namely that the site enjoyed a major responsibility for supplying other sites in the area. One further special case may be provided by Ribchester − which, in the *Ravenna Cosmography*, is referred to as BRESNETENACUM VETERANORUM. The name would suggest a military reserve role in the area, and the special status of the site may be demonstrated by a 'rampart and ditch' defence which it appears to have enjoyed.[20] In most cases, however, it can be assumed that if the garrison moved on, so too did the camp followers; for local farmers would rarely be able to generate sufficient surplus to support a *vicus* on their own. To survive, a *vicus* needed a fort or other special conditions.

Meeting the needs of the garrison was, therefore, the chief function of a *vicus*; this would imply the provision of places for entertainment and relaxation and places where food and drink might be purchased. It would be reasonable to conclude that in the latter case, shop proprietors might purchase their goods from passing or regularly visiting tradesmen, or by having arrangements with local farmers to purchase the products of arable farming or animals − (mostly cattle) − for meat; deals might also be done with individuals to supply deer and wild boar − (which presuppose the continuing existence of suitable habitats) − as well as fish and foul.

Some manufacturing was also conducted in the *vici*; we have to assume that deals were struck between *vicani* and others for the supply of wool for textile manufacture, of hides for tanning and then making up into a variety of consumer products, including shoes. The potter, too, will have needed a regular supply of his raw material, as will the metal worker. These two will obviously have enjoyed a good business in the sale and repair of vessels of various kinds, of tools and jewelry, as well as a vibrant trade in religious and sepulchral objects; the superstitions of Roman and native provided a market which had to be supplied. How such manufacturers were organised is hard to say; some, no doubt, operated on a very individual basis, though at Manchester there was evidence of the concentration of such activity into an area – a kind of industrial estate.[21]

As we have seen, some of those who lived in, or perhaps more often, passed through the *vici* came from other parts of the Roman empire. Of course, many soldiers in the Roman army came from other provinces, particularly from those in western Europe; Lucius Julius Apollinaris, for example, whose tombstone was erected in Lancaster (*RIB* 606), is announced as a 'man of Trier', (that is, in Germany). Many such soldiers settled locally on their discharge from the army, thus bringing about a constant process of diversification in the urban and rural populations. We have noted the presence in York, probably during Agricola's governorship, of a schoolmaster, Demetrius of Tarsus. Similarly, Chester has produced evidence of two Greek doctors – Hermogenes (*RIB* 461) and Antiochus[22] – whilst from Burrow-in-Lonsdale a Latin inscription (*RIB* 609) is dedicated by one, Julius Saturninus, to the health goddess, Hygiaea – (that is, with the Greek form of the name). Personal names of Greeks are often Latinised beyond recognition; thus it is possible that the oculist, Publius Clodius, who worked

in the *vicus* at Watercrook, was also a Greek. Carlisle, too, has the tombstone of another Greek, Flavius Antigonus Papias. Whilst many from the eastern Mediterranean may have been involved in 'the professions', it is worth noting that the frequent discovery of Roman imperial coins of eastern origin, especially Alexandrian coinage, is indicative of a healthy trade in progress between Britain and the eastern Mediterranean; that trade will clearly have required visits at least to Britain by those organising such activities.

In view of the cosmopolitan make-up of populations of many of the *vici*, a wide variety of religious beliefs was undoubtedly catered for;[23] surviving inscriptions provide the evidence for this, even when temple buildings themselves remain unlocated. The practice of religion provided a strong bond between occupiers and occupied, since both cultures were polytheistic, and conceived of their deities as having the role of guardianship over particular activities in life. Thus Roman and British gods could be readily equated through function; Mars, the Roman war god, could, for example, be combined into a 'composite deity' with British gods such as Cocidius, Ocelus, and Camulos. These 'composite deities' were often worshipped in Romano-Celtic temples, buildings which may have owed something to Rome in terms of the structural materials used, but which were to all intents and purposes derived from plans of a pre-Roman type. It is likely that in many cases such temples were erected on sites whose religious significance went back into the pre-Roman period; thus the Celtic water nymph, Coventina, was Romanised, and a shrine erected over her sacred spring at Carrawburgh, on Hadrian's Wall.

The Roman army had gods who were of especial significance to itself – Jupiter, Mars, Hercules as well as the obligatory 'imperial cult'; but the soldiers could readily take on gods with *local* significance, such as the tutelary deities of tribes and towns – for example, Brigantia (depicted as a classical 'winged victory' in a carving from Birrens), and Carlisle – or other local gods such as the horned deity from Maryport or Jalonus, the god of the Lune valley. In one case, a Roman fort – Bewcastle – appears to have taken its name *(Fanum Cocidi)* from the fact that it was built on a site that was sacred to a god.

Gods also had 'civilian' functions; thus, the townspeople *(vicani)* of Vindolanda, many of whose livelihoods depended upon metal working, saw the smith-god, Vulcan, as having an especial significance to them *(RIB* 1700), and Corbridge has produced a figurine mould of a smith-god. Apollo, too, had a number of facets important to a *vicus* community; he was connected with health, with commerce, whilst both Ribchester

51. Marsyas statuette, Papcastle. This bronze statuette is approximately six inches high: Marsyas was a satyr who was rash enough to challenge Apollo, the god of music, to a music competition, promising that, if he lost, he would submit himself to being bound and flayed alive. He lost, and the statuette shows him bound, awaiting his fate. The statuette was excavated in 1984 from what may have been a temple of Apollo. The subject was also popular with artists of the Renaissance.

and Papcastle have produced references to the god with his musical connection: at Ribchester, there is a fine relief carving of Apollo-Maponus showing Apollo with his lyre (and incidentally referring to the existence in the *vicus* of a temple to the god), whilst Papcastle has produced a unique statuette of a bound Marsyas who dared to take on Apollo in a music contest – and lost. Could such dedications indicate the existence of guilds of musicians in these *vici*, who looked to Apollo's protection of their art?

The very superstitious nature of soldiers and civilians, who at every turn sought the protection of guardian deities, were themselves good for trade; both potters and metalworkers will have been in constant demand for the manufacture of religious objects, particularly cult statuettes which individuals could purchase to stand in their own household shrines, and objects for use in votive contexts, which might, for example, include false coins like the bronze *denarii* found at Maryport.[24]

As well as the cults of these functional national or tribal gods, the movement of people around the empire brought in an increasing number of so-called 'mystery' cults. In contrast to the very public rituals of the state cults, these were private matters in which normally small

52. Temple of Mithras, Carraw-burgh. The temple was originally recognised during drought conditions in 1949. Mithraism was one of a number of 'mystery cults' which enjoyed phases of popularity with members of the Roman army. Most Mithraea were cavernous in internal arrangement, with a raised dais on either side of a central nave for benches on which initiates reclined.

groups of individual initiates privately sought the support of their deity, and worshipped him/her for his/her beneficence, which often included the notion of suffering or dying for mankind; Christianity was but one of these, though ultimately victorious.

Shrines of such gods existed in the frontier zone and its hinterland: the temples of Mithras at Carrawburgh and Housesteads are well known,[25] and Mithraic sculpture is known from other sites. A temple was certainly built at York in the early third century to the Egyptian deities (*RIB* 658), though it would seem likely that this was a temporary expedient to please the entourage of Septimius Severus, who was devoted to these gods and used York as the base for his northern campaigns. Evidence of even more recondite cults, such as that of Jupiter of Doliche, has come from Corbridge (*RIB* 1131) and Ribchester (*RIB* 587); on the former of these, the god's consort, Juno Caelestis, is equated with Brigantia. Not only did these cults cater for relatively small numbers of devotees, as the size of surviving shrines makes clear, but they were active probably only for short periods at a time. Military personnel moved around, and, in any case, a devotee of senior status was usually required both to satisfy the nature of cult hierarchies and to defray expenses.

In view of the boost given to Christianity by its adoption by Constantine I, it is surprising that so little evidence of it has been found in the frontier zone and its hinterland.[26] There are no known churches in the area, and what evidence there is consists largely of cryptograms of various kinds, the significance of many of which is not beyond dispute. The earliest evidence – if, indeed, its significance is Christian – is provided by a fragment of a well-known word-square which was found in the *vicus* at Manchester in a context dating to the second half of the second century.[27] From Maryport, a fragmentary inscription (*RIB* 856) bears a Christogram, whilst from Brougham (*RIB* 787) and Carlisle (*RIB* 955), there are tombstones which convey the age of the deceased with an allegedly Christian formula. Most recently, a salt pan was found near Crewe, which suggests the possibility of the involvement of the early church in the salt industry.[28]

At the edges of the *vici*, lining the roads leading out, were the cemeteries; few fort and *vicus* cemeteries have been studied in detail in the north, though tombstone inscriptions, of course, inform us of some of those buried – albeit those who were sufficiently wealthy to be able to afford a tombstone. Many of these belong to soldiers, but some to civilians, either individually or in families. A few belong to people who were evidently of British origin, such as Rianorix and perhaps Spurcio

53. The Cemetery, Low Borrow Bridge. By law cemeteries were located outside settlement areas; this one, situated about a mile to the south of the fort, consisted of sub-rectangular and sub-circular burial plots (visible here as differences in soil colour) containing cremation urns and a few inhumations in the 'crouch' position.

of Maryport (*RIB* 862 and 863); from the same site is a tombstone to a man (*RIB* 864) who was born in Galatia, and who died there but strongly desired to be returned to Maryport for burial. Most recently, some excavation has taken place on the cemetery at Low Borrow Bridge;[29] this showed that the majority of burials were cremations, though a few were in the pre-Roman 'crouch' position. Clearly evident were sub-rectangular and sub-circular enclosures which formed burial plots, perhaps purchased by military burial clubs.

Whilst some of the *vici* – particularly those which were of greater significance – may have formally terminated with an enclosing wall or rampart, many display thinning settlement merging into the countryside. In some cases, farms approached very close to the forts themselves, as at Maiden Castle-on-Stainmore, or the large complex at Low Carlingill, just to the south of Low Borrow Bridge.

The domestic structures of the countryside of the frontier zone owed little to Romanised prototypes further south, unless an apparent move from sub-circular to sub-rectangular is significant in this respect. There are, however, very few examples of the type of structure known in the lowland zone as *villas*: Northumberland and Cumbria have none, northern Cheshire has one, whilst there are a few in Durham and Yorkshire. If it is right that these belonged to aristocratic families who wished to take advantage of the military market for their produce, then the somewhat higher incidence east of the Pennines reflects both the greater development of the rural economy in pre-Roman times, and

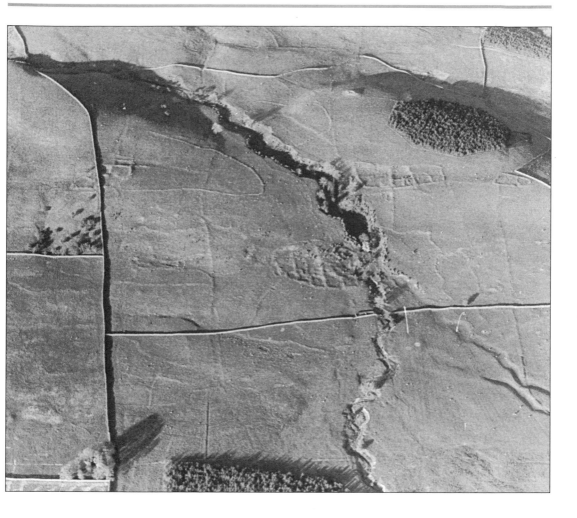

54. Romano-British landscape, Eller Beck. This landscape on the eastern slopes of the Lune valley consists of small nuclei (representing farmsteads) and larger enclosures.

the relatively early establishment of the *civitas* of the Brigantes, around Aldborough.

In the region as a whole, forestry clearance at the outset of the Roman occupation presented a patchy picture, though broadly was less advanced in the north and west of the region than in the south and east. Indeed, some forestation remained largely in tact until relatively late in the occupation. The limited clearance that had taken place before the occupation was presumably in pursuit of land largely for grazing purposes, but also for arable farming. After the onset of occupation, then a pressing reason for clearance – and in some areas it was very thorough – was the need for timber for building and burning.[30] This larger-scale clearance obviously carried serious implications: the higher ground was probably already clear of forest, but the areas of clearance extended down the fellsides. Whilst immediately

137

this provided land – largely for grazing – in the longer term it speeded the process of soil erosion, so that upland environments will have tended to become less useful, except for rough pasture, whilst the soils of the valley floors will have become richer. Not surprisingly, such land came to be viewed as increasingly important for arable purposes, and thus regarded as 'premium land', some of which was consequently ear-marked for veteran settlement. Further consequences of timber clearances were the destruction of habitats of wild animals which were important as a means of subsistence for some, and that inevitably timber became a scarcer commodity for building. Thus, some rural buildings may have come to make more use of construction wholly or partly in stone.[31]

Fieldwork has made patchy progress in determining the workings of the agricultural economy, and in many areas subsequent centuries of agricultural activity have come close to destroying the evidence. Further, since few such sites have been excavated, and since those which have have produced little artefactual evidence, the dating of them between the late prehistoric and early medieval periods can prove to be a hazardous undertaking.[32]

55. Romano-British farmstead at Castle Hill, Leck. This site is typical of circular farmsteads found in the north of Britain; many of these enjoyed a long life from the prehistoric period into the post-Roman 'Dark Ages'. The internal structures are demonstrated by the plan in Figure 15.

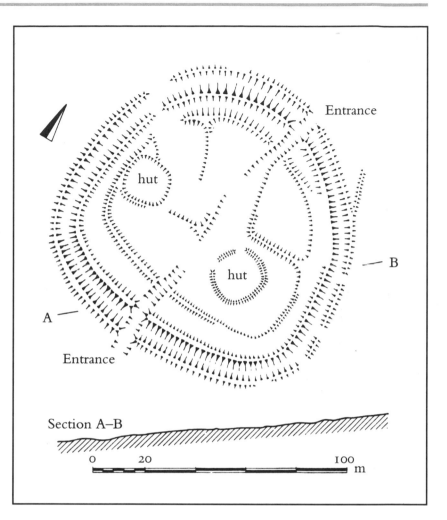

Figure 15. Castle Hill, Leck: Romano-British farmstead.

In the west, in particular, the land between farms appears to have been organised in two ways: some appears to be divided into small sub-rectangular fields – for example, the Eller Beck system in Lunesdale[33] – which is probably best seen as arable land. In other cases, the dikes (or turf walls) found at higher altitudes in eastern Cumbria are best explained in relation to stock management. The distinction of land characterised by these enclosure systems is not static in the short or long term. Presumably adjustments were made to land usage from year to year, depending upon grazing or arable land required, whilst in the longer term soil erosion may have reduced the land that remained suitable for arable cultivation. In any case, climatic changes may have had a part to play in this, as well as 'market response'. For example, the authorities may have been flexible, as they clearly were in Germany, over the form in which taxes were paid; it might have been normal

56. Romano-British farmstead: Colt Park, Ribblesdale. The sites of Romano-British farmsteads are rarely well preserved in the valley floors. On higher ground, however, where the land is not subject to ploughing damage, the outlines of buildings and fields often survive clearly.

to pay in grain, but oxhides or even fleeces were equally serviceable. Further, farmers might realise a better return in tanning and textiles than in grain.[34]

For the late first and early second centuries, the Vindolanda tablets provide our clearest evidence for the commodities and raw materials that were passing between native and Roman. It is clear that grain played an important part in this relationship — for use as food or for making beer; it is suggested that some areas in the frontier hinterland — for example, the Eden valley and Durham[35] — may have been producing sufficient to supply adjacent forts, although much was probably moved in by road or sea. It is likely on the evidence of the watermill at Haltwistle Burn that the army itself took on responsibility for processing the raw material.[36]

Many different animal bones are represented in archaeological deposits, and meats mentioned in the tablets; some, however, probably represented just occasional acquisitions to suit perhaps a particular taste or a special time; the bulk of evidence relates to cattle and sheep. These staple meats were sold from animals evidently slaughtered at an optimum age[37] — a clear sign that here at any rate local producers responded to the market. Many farms may have taken on a role as centres of cottage industries; with the popularity of the cloak, known as *birrus Britannicus*, farmers may have turned to weaving. Similarly, many may have seen a future in exploiting the north's natural resources, though in many cases the military units may have done this for themselves; there seems a strong case that the exceptionally well-defended site at Whitley Castle

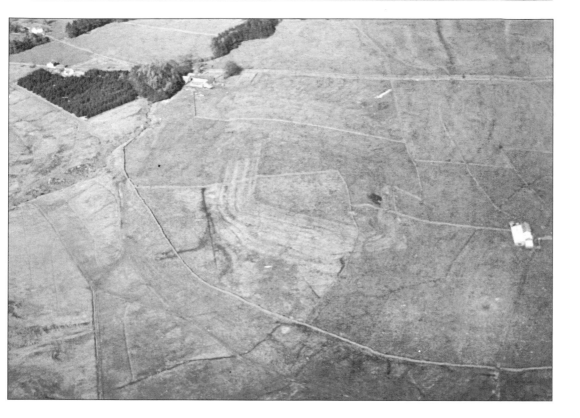

57. Whitley Castle fort. This well-defended fort in the north Pennines enjoyed a direct road link to Carvoran on Hadrian's Wall. The purpose of the fort may have been security interests surrounding the operation of the lead and silver industries.

was involved in the lead and silver industries. But iron working has been identified not just in the *vici*, but also on rural sites, too.[38]

In all, we see the farmer of the frontier zone responding to the demands and opportunities presented by a garrison of the Roman army and its camp followers. Rarely, however, could those working within the near vicinity of a fort supply it totally; in those circumstances we might expect a civilian community to be able to stand on its own without the necessary presence of a garrison. In most cases, however, when a garrison moved on, so too did the contracts to supply it, leaving a civilian community with no means to survive by the business which it could do with local farmers. It had, therefore, no alternative but to pass on also. However, even if the local farmer did not progress to the role of sole supplier, he did make significant strides. To dismiss him as a rebellious or potentially rebellious native is clearly inappropriate; he was sufficiently alert and worldly-wise to know that the frontier and its hinterland had more to offer him than 'blood, sweat and tears'.

Within the frontiers devised and guarded by Rome, the British slowly but surely adapted; by the late fourth century, their old ways were but a memory; for many, Romano-British had become a truer description of themselves; they would have seen little reason to agree with Tacitus' eloquent Caledonian chieftain, Calgacus, when he said: 'They create a desolation and call it peace'. The truth for Britain, as for Germany, was that the native population became 'different without knowing it'. This ultimately was the proof of success of the Roman frontiers in Britain.

Epilogue

THE frontiers of Roman Britain have excited the interest of a succession of generations of people who have been involved in both 'professional' and 'amateur' capacities. It is one of the great successes of Britain's attitude to its heritage that both have happily co-operated and interacted in the developing understanding of the frontiers of Roman Britain; for just as frontier studies have involved what can only be described as a 'roll call' of the great amongst the professional practitioners, so it is no accident that an amateur, Joseph Robinson of Maryport, is widely acknowledged as the founding father of studies of the Cumberland coast.

The landmarks in our developing knowledge are by no means limited to the late twentieth century; over the years, fieldwork, excavations of all types and sizes, studies of artefactual evidence, ingenious interpretations of classical sources have made major contributions. Aerial reconnaissance and science-based disciplines continue to do so. People have never been afraid to offer their view on this or that aspect of the frontiers, whether it be an aspect of major and far-reaching significance or one of detail. Such views have been contested, often vigorously, but all make a contribution – whether it be on the purpose of Hadrian's Wall, or whether the Wall was painted.

Often, archaeological evidence is not capable of absolute interpretation; a view based upon one type of evidence may cause experts in other areas of study to reconstruct their views completely. In this way, there is always something new to engage the interest. Admittedly, some of an interpretative problems are caused by the paucity of relevant written sources; the incessant debate about aspects of the northern frontier in the second century A.D. is kept alive partly because of this paucity, but partly, too, because what does survive often lacks the precision to permit categorical statements to be made. In the last few decades, the discovery in considerable quantity of writing tablets at sites such as Vindolanda and Carlisle not only opens up a completely new insight into social, political and economic aspects of our study, but also carries the promise that what has been found relating to a relatively narrow band of time may be extended by new discoveries to other periods; further, small-scale discoveries at other sites suggest that there may well be a wider geographical potential of such evidence. To be made aware of soldiers' attitudes to the British or of the fact that mundane events such as birthday parties were organised on the frontier opens the door on previously unrealised aspects of frontier studies.

Although over the years much excavation has been carried out on frontier sites, with only a few exceptions these have concerned what amounts to a tiny proportion of the ground area that is potentially relevant. In such circumstances, we have to ask whether we can yet have confidence in 'models of occupation' of whole frontier systems that are based upon what a statistician would regard as an unacceptably small sample of the material potentially available. Indeed, some recent excavations and studies have suggested that we may need to unravel earlier models and start again – as indeed has already happened in some areas of frontier studies. The mere fact that major sites whose presence was never suspected can still be discovered should indicate that we have a lot still to learn, and that what we now accept as indisputable truth may in fact be very fragile. In any case, whilst our study of military aspects of frontier life may be comparatively well advanced, much remains to be understood in detail as to how the local people reacted to the new presence.

By a gradual process, we shall of course shed untenable ideas and substitute new theories, many of which will probably in their turn prove to be equally vulnerable. However, the application of more science-based techniques will undoubtedly elevate the potential for absolute answers – at least in matters of detail. Many of today's questions will be answered and theories altered or abandoned, and in the process new questions will be posed; the study of the frontiers is an on-going process. At the end of the day, some questions may prove to be incapable of resolution. It is, however, a tribute to the enthusiasm of those engaged in the study of the past that this will not lead to frustration, so much as to spur the researcher, professional and amateur, to greater endeavour. As has recently been noted, the fact that the site of Agricola's victory at *Mons Graupius* remains elusive prompts intensified study and ever greater ingenuity.

In this way, our heritage as exemplified by Roman frontier sites will continue to engage the attention of scholars. At the same time, we may be sure that these sites will also continue to attract the interest of and give pleasure to countless others for whom the academic questions are dwarfed by the images which those sites evoke.

APPENDIX I

The Classical Sources

A GREAT MANY MEN wrote historical works under the Roman emperors; some of them comprised chronological accounts of particular periods, such as Tacitus' *Histories* (A.D. 69–96) and his *Annals* (A.D. 14–68). Others, such as Suetonius, wrote *Lives* or biographies, which generally did not accept a chronological framework, but treated their subjects by themes. Most of what was written in antiquity has, of course, perished without trace, though it was undoubtedly used by those writers whose works have survived. We are left, however, with a problem of source evaluation, for Roman writers seldom do more than to allude to their sources, usually without naming them.

We have to appreciate that the Romans had no knowledge of what today we should regard as historiography. In the first place, most 'writing' was done initially for a listening audience who would be expecting to a large degree to be entertained by what they heard. It is clear that some at least of what was produced was dismissed as 'boring', and that may have been because authors were straining too hard to impress with 'verbal fireworks', and were rather short on substance. Secondly, there was a tendency to see most motivation as inspired by character, and a tendency to view character as essentially immutable, and only *revealed* by events.

The political atmosphere was also seen as a drawback; some emperors were both suspicious and repressive; they tended to lead to contemporary writers being unduly sycophantic during emperors' lifetimes and boldly and excessively critical after their deaths. There was also a problem with the flow of information; many decisions were taken by emperors within their own small circles of advisers whose deliberations might be the subjects of rumour, but rarely of fact. Further, many, though not all, writers were themselves active or retired politicians and administrators who might entertain a very subjective view of events, or even be trying to salve a bad conscience.

A final point to bear in mind is that Britain was a long way from the centre of the empire, and not a subject of vast concern to many Romans who might not be particularly interested in disentangling fact from fiction, and who would have little concern about the *minutiae* of places where frontiers and forts were established, or of details of landscapes against which battles were fought. To a Roman audience, a far-off province, such as Britain, assumed an importance if its governor or armies were main players on the imperial scene. Questions of morale, of bravery or cowardice, of leadership and heroism – these would be the chief points of identification between audience and subject matter. Most battle scenes cannot now be placed securely, and campaign routes can only occasionally be elucidated; the oral nature of 'publication' gave no scope for explanatory maps, diagrams and footnotes. The kind of material requiring such elucidation was, therefore, omitted.

Thus, rather than the archaeologist turning for help to Roman writers, more often than not students of Roman historiography turn to the work of archaeology to help them understand the accounts of Roman Britain left by Roman writers.

The chief surviving writers

Publius Cornelius TACITUS (c. A.D. 55–120). Tacitus originated probably from Belgic Gaul, and represented the first generation of his family to enter the senate; the fact that he was chosen as the son-in-law of Gnaeus Julius Agricola (governor of Britain, A.D. 77–83) is indicative of his promise; he reached the consulship in A.D. 97 after moving through the senatorial career under all the Flavian emperors. He became proconsul of Asia in c.A.D. 112. Most of his writing came after his consulship; his biography of his father-in-law, Agricola, and a treatise on the tribes of Germany were published in A.D. 98; his *Histories*, covering the period, A.D. 69–96 (though now largely lost), was published in c.A.D. 106, and some ten years or so later came the *Annals*. This covered the period A.D. 14–68, though portions of it, including the account of Claudius' invasion of Britain in A.D. 43, are lost.

Gaius SUETONIUS Tranquillus (c. A.D. 70–140). Suetonius was a school-master by profession and a member of Rome's second social order, the equestrians; he rose to senior administrative office in the service of emperors under Trajan and Hadrian, reaching the imperial secretariat, which gave him access to a wealth of imperial letters and papers. He was sacked in c.A.D. 122 apparently after some indiscretion, and never regained office. By nature a compiler of information and curiosities, he wrote a large amount, of which the most complete is now his *Lives of the Caesars*, biographies of the first twelve emperors from Julius Caesar to Domitian. These contain some information about Britain, in so far as his subjects were involved in the conquest and occupation of the province.

Cassius DIO Cocceianus (*c.* A.D. 163–230). Dio was a Greek from Nicaea in the province of Bithynia; his father reached the consulship and went on to hold a number of provincial governorships. Dio followed his father into the senate, achieving the rare distinction of holding two consulships – in *c.* A.D. 205 and in 229, with the emperor, Severus Alexander, as his colleague. Although favoured by the Severans, Dio appears not to have entertained a high opinion of them. He remained active in administration between 200 and 230, and appears to have done the bulk of his writing between *c.* A.D. 211 and 229. He set out to write (in Greek) a history of Rome from the foundation of the city down to his own times; most of his account of the period from 68 B.C. to A.D. 46 survives intact, whilst much of the remainder is covered by the Byzantine eiptomators.

When he can be directly compared with other writers, Dio is not outstandingly accurate, and has a penchant for good stories, particularly those that have a moral to point. He also tends to assume that constitutional and political practices of his own day were relevant to earlier periods. His greatest value lies in his account of events contemporary to himself.

HERODIAN (*c.* A.D. 170–250). Little is known about Herodian's life, though it seems safest to assume that, whatever his origins, he rose to equestrian status and saw service in the imperial administration. Various cities of origin have been canvassed, and of them Antioch (in Syria) seems the most likely. His account covers the period from A.D. 180 (the accession of Commodus) to 238 (the accession of Gordian III); his work is generally regarded as less reliable than Dio's, but superior to those of the writers of the Augustan History – perhaps an effort to be accurate vitiated by a degree of ignorance and an inability to resist rhetorical embellishment. Like Suetonius, however, his job appears to have given him access to imperial documents, and if, as some suppose, his patron in Rome was a senator, then that may have opened further sources to him.

Writers of the AUGUSTAN HISTORY. Despite the title, the Augustan History is, in fact, a collection of imperial biographies compiled ostensibly by six different authors in the period of Diocletian and Constantine – Aelius Spartianus, Julius Capitolinus, Aelius Lampridius, Flavius

Vopiscus, Vulcacius Gallicanus and Trebellius Pollio. However, the broad agreement amongst scholars is now that in fact this 'scenario' is an elaborate piece of deceit, perpetrated for unknown reasons, and that the Augustan History was the work of one author writing in the late fourth century. The work starts with the *Life of Hadrian* and continues down to the late third century; because there is no formal introduction, it is widely believed that a portion is missing from the beginning which contained *Lives* of Nerva and Trajan, and thus maintained a continuation from Suetonius. The *Lives* are of very variable quality, the later ones in particular being regarded as largely fictional or gathered together through extracts taken uncritically from other authors; it can be shown that in many cases, documents which purport to be quoted verbatim are totally fictional. However, in general the earlier *Lives* (down to the Severi) are regarded as achieving a higher standard than the later ones.

AMMIANUS Marcellinus (*c.* A.D. 330–395). Like Herodian, Ammianus was a Greek from Antioch in Syria; but, unlike Herodian, Ammianus (for whatever reason) preferred Rome, and wrote in Latin. His *History of Rome* started with the accession of Nerva in A.D. 96, perhaps indicating that Ammianus saw himself as the 'literary heir' of Tacitus. Certainly, one of his complaints about the Roman aristocracy of his own day was the fact that they preferred superficial imperial biographies to serious works of history. A little over half of Ammianus' *History* survives (Books 14–31), covering the period, A.D. 354–378; this shows the relatively short space that was devoted to the first two-and-a-half centuries of the historian's brief. Most of the research work was done in the late 380s and early 390s, and the *History* was published *c.*A.D. 392. Ammianus evidently saw Julian's reign as the climax of his work; Julian was for him the embodiment of all the greatest qualities of earlier emperors, and a man who held out a promise that Rome could return to a golden age of virtue, justice and territorial integrity. Julian's successors failed to deliver on the promise. Although some threads of his work are biographical, even autobiographical, Ammianus stands as a historian because, as for his historical predecessors, so for him the public affairs of Rome were more important than the acts and fates of individual emperors.

ZOSIMUS (*c.*A.D. 450–500): Zosimus was a Greek historian, of whom little is known; he wrote his *New History* to cover the period from Augustus to *c.*A.D. 410, devoting over half of the work to events of the fourth century. A pagan himself, he attributed the decline of Rome to the decline of paganism, criticising the prominent Christian emperors, such as Constantine I and Theodosius, and, like Ammianus, taking Julian as his chief hero. Zosimus enjoyed administrative posts, and thus had first-hand knowledge of the mechanics of government. He is regarded as chiefly important for his account of events in Britain at the turn of the fourth and fifth centuries, for which his main source appears to have been the histories (or memoirs) of Olympiodorus of Thebes (Egypt), whose work (now largely lost) covered the period from A.D. 407 to 425 in twenty-two books. Other Greek sources of Zosimus' accounts of earlier events are Dexippus of Athens (of the third century) and the fourth-century sophist, Eunapius of Sardis.

Such is the shortage of surviving ancient literature which covers the affairs of Roman Britain that various other individual references have to be pressed into service. The reliability of many of these cannot be tested, though since many of them are from the works of poets, we have to expect a certain degree of licence. Examples of such works are:

The *Silvae* of Papinius Statius (writing in the late first century A.D.), which contain references to Britain in the period of civil war (A.D. 69–70).

The *Satires* of Juvenal (writing in the early second century A.D.), which refer to the Brigantes and a chieftain of theirs, named Arviragus (*c*.A.D. 100).

The *Latin Panegyrics* of fourth-century emperors, which in a number of references suggest Britain as a kind of paradise at that time.

The *Consulship of Stilicho* of the court poet, Claudian (writing in the early fifth century A.D.), who provides almost the only evidence of Stilicho's activities in Britain in the latest years of the fourth century.

Chief References

Caesar's incursions in 55 and 54 B.C.:

Caesar, *Gallic War* IV. 20–28; V. 8–23
Dio Cassius, *Roman History* 39.51–53; 40. 1–3

Caligula's 'abortive invasion' (A.D. 40):

Suetonius, *Life of Caligula* 44–46
Dio Cassius, *Roman History* 59.21

Claudius' Invasion (A.D. 43):

Dio Cassius, *Roman History* 60.19–23
Suetonius, *Life of Claudius* 17
Life of Vespasian 4

The mid-first century A.D.:

Tacitus, *Annals* XII. 31–40; XIV. 29–39
Dio Cassius, *Roman History* 62. 1–12

The Flavian Period:

Tacitus, *Life of Agricola*
Dio Cassius, *Roman History* 66.20

Hadrianic Events:

SHA, *Hadrian* 5, 2; 11, 2; 12, 6

The Antonine Period:

SHA, *Antoninus* 5, 4
Marcus 8, 7–8; 22, 1
Commodus 6, 2; 8, 4; 13, 5
Pertinax 3, 5–10
Dio Cassius, *Roman History* 73. 8–9

The Severan Period:

SHA *Clodius Albinus* 13, 4
Septimius Severus 18–19; 23, 3
Dio Cassius *Roman History* 75. 5; 76. 11–16; 77. 1
Herodian, *Roman History* II.15; III. 6–7; III. 14–15

The fourth century and beyond:

Ammianus Marcellinus, *Roman History* XX.1; XXVI.4; XXVII.8;
XXVIII.3
Zosimus, *Roman History* VI. 2–5

The Coin Evidence
for Roman Britain

ROMAN COINS of the imperial period were frequently used to communicate the emperors' views of contemporary events and to bring major successes to public attention. Since a number of policy initiatives in Britain enjoyed high-profile status, it is not surprising that they found expression on the coinage.

1. Claudius' invasion of Britain in A.D. 43 was depicted on *aurei* and *denarii* between A.D. 46 and 50 (*RIC* I² (Claudius), 30, 33, 34, 44, 45). The coins show a triumphal arch, as set up in both Rome and Colchester, and bearing on the architrave the legend DE BRITAN. The invasion was also commemorated on a silver didrachm from Caesarea (in Cappadocia); this coin showed Claudius riding in a quadriga over the legend DE BRITANNIS (*RIC* I² (Claudius), 122).

2. It has been argued that Agricola's victory over the Caledonians at Mons Graupius was celebrated on Domitian's coinage. A *sestertius* of A.D. 84 shows a cavalryman riding down a barbarian enemy, and the legend connects the event with Domitian's seventh imperial acclamation (Buttrey, *Documentary Evidence*, 1980), which occurred around September, A.D. 84. The problem is that if the battle was in A.D. 83, then the salutation is too late; if, on the other hand, it was in A.D. 84, then the salutation would be too early (Hanson, *Agricola and the Conquest of the North*, 42; Kraay, 'Two new *sestertii* of Domitian'). It is safest *not* to take the coin as referring to Agricola's victory.

3. Hadrian's accession in A.D. 117 came at a time of disturbance in Britain, which had to be dealt with as a matter of urgency. *Asses* of A.D. 119 and 120 (Hill, *Dating and Arrangement of Coins*, 1970, nos 141 and 177) show Britannia seated facing front and in the 'dejected' pose; her foot rests on a pile of stones which some have taken as representative of Hadrian's Wall; the coins, however, are too early for that, but presumably commemorate a victory won by Q. Pompeius Falco (Toynbee, '"Britannia" on Roman Coins').

4. Hadrian visited Britain in *c*.A.D. 121–122; it is thought by some that an *aureus* of A.D. 120 showing a reclining river goddess may herald that visit by referring to the river Tyne (*Tina*; Hill, *Dating and Arrangement of Coins*, no. 165; Toynbee, *The Hadrianic School*, 1934). It is also thought that *sestertii* and *asses* of A.D. 136 (Hill, *Dating and Arrangement of Coins*, nos 615, 617, 620A (misspelt), 621) which have the legend BRITANNIA, and show the personification much as in the earlier 'victory' types, may commemorate the visit. Particularly referring to the visit is a *sestertius* of A.D. 136 commemorating Hadrian's arrival (ADVENTVI AVG BRITANNIAE: Hill, *Dating and Arrangement of Coins*, no. 701); perhaps significantly there was no issue in Britain's case of a coin commemorating Hadrian as 'Restorer' (RESTITVTOR) of the visited province. The design on the reverse of the ADVENTVS coin is of Hadrian sacrificing over an altar, and faced by Britannia. Finally, in these coins commemorating the visits, a series of A.D. 137 refers especially to Hadrian's connection with the provincial armies; the coins show Hadrian addressing troops (*adlocutio*) with variants of a legend, EXERCITVS BRITANNICVS (Hill, *Dating and Arrangement of Coins*, nos 872, 873, 881).

5. A number of coins of Antoninus Pius' reign refer to Britain; a sign of the importance to Antoninus of the advance into Scotland is the fact that whole issues of A.D. 143 (Hill, *Dating and Arrangement of*

58. *Solidi* of Theo-
dosius (*left*: from Mun-
caster Castle) and
Valenturian II (*right*:
from Carlisle).
These gold coins are
amongst the latest
found in the frontier
zone; the coin of
Theodosius was found
in *c.* 1800 beneath the
foundations of a Pele
tower, and *may* indi-
cate the presence of a
Roman coastal watch-
tower above the fort
at Ravenglass. The
significance of the
coin from Carlisle lies
in the fact that it was
found during excav-
ation in 1988 in a
building that conti-
nued in a Romanised
form for some consid-
erable period after the
level in which the
coin was found. Since
the coin itself was is-
sued as late as A.D.
392, it suggests that
Carlisle remained
'Romanised' well into
the fifth century.

Coins, nos 526–530, 544–558) were devoted to Britannia, to Victory, to Jupiter, Mars and Hercules and to Antoninus' relations with
his troops. Legends on coins of all denominations include IOVI
VICTORI, BRITANNIA and DISCIPLINA AVG; prominent too, is
Antoninus' imperial salutation (IMPERATOR II) and personifications
of Victoria, in one case holding a shield inscribed with the letters,
BRITAN. In all cases, Britain looks alert and prosperous.

6. In contrast is an *as* of A.D. 154–5, depicting a 'dejected' Britannia,
with the legend BRITANNIA COS IIII S C. It is assumed that this
represents an indication of trouble in the northern frontier area in
Antoninus' later years, which may have led to a temporary evacuation of the Antonine Wall.

7. Although Marcus Aurelius did not overtly refer to events in Britain
on his coinage, some have assumed that the re-issue by Marcus
Aurelius and Lucius Verus of the LEG VI type of Marcus Antonius'
legionary series of 32–1 B.C. (Crawford, *Roman Republican Coinage*,
1974, no. 544) was significant (*RIC* (Marcus) 443). Two legions
bore the number, six – VICTRIX in Britain and FERRATA in the east.

8. Commodus took the title BRITANNICVS for the victories of Ulpius
Marcellus in A.D. 181–4; coins were issued in A.D. 184–5 to
commemorate the event; they show Britannia and Victoria on the
reverse with the legends including BRITT, VICT BRIT and VIC BRIT;
Commodus included BRIT in the imperial titulary on the obverse
(*RIC* (Commodus), 437, 440, 451, 452). Commemorative medal-
lions were also struck at the beginning of A.D. 185 to publicise the
event.

9. The presence in Britain between A.D. 209 and 211 of Septimius
Severus and his family and entourage received large-scale publicity
on the coinage issued in the names of Severus himself and of his
sons, Caracalla and Geta. As was the case with Antoninus Pius,
whole issues were devoted to themes of warfare, Britain and victory
between A.D. 208 (the departure from Rome) and 211 (Severus'
death in Britain). Gods are commemorated (particularly Jupiter and
Mars), as is Victory (named VICTORIA BRITANNICA). Severus and
his sons are also shown in various triumphant situations (see Hill,
The Coinage of Septimius Severus, nos 952–1242), and all three added
BRIT to the imperial titulary on the obverse of the coins. It is also
striking that the victories were considered to be of sufficient significance to be commemorated on Greek coins struck in Alexandria
(Milne, *A Catalogue of Alexandrian Coins*, no. 2726). Of particular

interest in the interpretation of the events of these campaigns are the 'bridge' coins of Caracalla, with the legend, TRAIECTVS (*RIC* (Caracalla), 441; Hill, *The Coinage of Septimius Severus*, no. 953; Robertson, *The Bridges on Severan Coins*).

10. Although, subsequently, Britain produced coins from the London mint (A.D. 287–324), and at various times in the later third and fourth centuries was flooded with locally made irregular issues and 'enjoyed' emperors, such as Carausius and Allectus, who were based in Britain, there are few other specific references on the coinage to events in Britain. It is, of course, possible, that some of the imperial 'virtues' which are commemorated refer to Britain (for example, PAX). There is a possible reference on two *aurei* of Victorinus (the rebel emperor of the *Imperium Galliarum*, A.D. 269–71), in the form of commemorations of Legion XX *Valeria Victrix* (*RIC* (Victorinus), 21–2).

Two coins of Carausius have unusual references – EXPECTATE VENI, showing Britannia welcoming Carausius (*RIC* (Carausius), 216–19), and GENIO BRITANNI (*RIC* (Carausius), 240). The rebellion of Carausius and Allectus was brought to an end in A.D. 296 by Constantius I, who commemorated the event on the famous 'Arras' medallion, which shows a mounted Constantius disembarking from a barge, being welcomed by a figure kneeling in suppliant fashion in front of the gates of London. The legend is REDDITOR LVCIS AERTERNAE ('Restoror of Eternal Light'), which had both political and religious connotations.

The Dispositions of Legions in the First and Second Centuries A.D.

A) AT THE TIME OF AUGUSTUS' DEATH (A.D. 14)   25 legions

Nearer Spain	IV Macedonica, VI Victrix, X Gemina	3
Upper Germany	II Augusta, XIII Gemina, XIV Gemina Martia Victrix, XVI Gallica	4
Lower Germany	I Germanica, V Alaudae, XX Valeria Victrix, XXI Rapax	4
Upper Illyria	VII Macedonica, XI ('Actiaca')	2
Lower Illyria	VIII Augusta, IX Hispana, XV Apollinaris	3
Macedonia/Moesia	IV Scythica, V Macedonica	2
Syria	III Gallica, VI Ferrata, X Fretensis, XII Fulminata	4
Egypt	III Cyrenaica, XXII Deiotariana	2
Africa	III Augusta	1

B) THE REIGN OF CLAUDIUS (c. A.D. 46)   27 legions

Nearer Spain	VI Victrix, X Gemina	2
Britain	II Augusta, IX Hispana, XIV Gemina Martia Victrix, XX Valeria Victrix	4
Upper Germany	IV Macedonica, XXI Rapax, XXII Primigenia, XVI Gallica	4
Lower Germany	I Germanica, V Alaudae, XV Primigenia, XVI Gallica	4
Dalmatia	VII Claudia Pia Fidelis, XI Claudia Pia Fidelis	2
Pannonia	XIII Gemina, XV Apollinaris	2
Moesia	IV Scythica, V Macedonica, VIII Augusta	3
Syria	III Gallica, VI Ferrata, X Fretensis, XII Fulminata	4
Egypt	III Cyrenaica, XXII Deiotariana	2
Africa	III Augusta	1

(*Note*: VII Macedonica and XI ('Actiaca') were both renamed Claudia Pia Fidelis following their loyalty to Claudius during an attempted rebellion in Dalmatia in A.D. 42).

C) THE REIGN OF NERO (*c*.A.D. 63)   27 legions

Nearer Spain	VI Victrix	I
Britain	II Augusta, IX Hispana, XIV Gemina	
	Martia Victrix, XX Valeria Victrix	4
Upper Germany	IV Macedonica, XXI Rapax,	
	XXII Primigenia	3
Lower Germany	I Germanica, V Alaudae, XV Primigenia,	
	XVI Gallica	4
Dalmatia	XI Claudia Pia Fidelis	I
Pannonia	X Gemina, XIII Gemina	2
Moesia	VII Claudia Pia Fidelis, VIII Augusta	2
Syria/Armenia	IV Scythica, X Fretensis, XII Fulminata,	
	V Macedonica, VI Ferrata, XV Apollinaris,	
	III Gallica	7
Egypt	III Cyrenaica, XXII Deiotariana	2
Africa	III Augusta	I

D) THE CIVIL WAR (late in A.D. 68)   30 legions

Nearer Spain	VI Victrix, X Gemina	2
Britain	II Augusta, IX Hispana,	
	XX Valeria Victrix	3
Upper Germany	IV Macedonica, XXI Rapax,	
	XXII Primigenia	3
Lower Germany	I Germanica, V Alaudae, XV Primigenia,	
	XVI Gallica	4
Gaul (Lugdunensis)	I Italica	I
Rome	I Adiutrix	I
Dalmatia	XI Claudia Pia Fidelis, XIV Gemina	
	Martia Victrix	2
Pannonia	VII Galbiana, XIII Gemina	2
Moesia	III Gallica, VII Claudia Pia Fidelis,	
	VIII Augusta	3
Syria	IV Scythica, VI Ferrata, XII Fulminata	3
Judaea	V Macedonica, X Fretensis,	
	XV Apollinaris	3
Egypt	III Cyrenaica, XXII Deiotariana	2
Africa	III Augusta	I

(*Note*: I Adiutrix was formed from the fleet in Nero's last months; VII Galbiana was raised by Galba in Spain in April, A.D. 68).

E) VESPASIAN'S REORGANISATION (*c.* A.D. 71)   29 legions

Spain	VII Gemina (= ex-Galbiana)	1
Britain	II Augusta, IX Hispana,	
	XX Valeria Victrix	3
Upper Germany	I Adiutrix, VIII Augusta, XI Claudia	
	Pia Fidelis, XIV Gemina Martia Victrix	4
Lower Germany	II Adiutrix, VI Victrix, X Gemina,	
	XXI Rapax	4
Pannonia	XIII Gemina, XV Apollinaris,	
	XXII Primigenia	3
Moesia	I Italica, IV Flavia, V Alaudae,	
	V Macedonica, VII Claudia Pia Fidelis	5
Syria	III Gallica, IV Scythica, VI Ferrata	3
Cappadocia	XII Fulminata, XVI Flavia	2
Judaea	X Fretensis	1
Egypt	III Cyrenaica, XXII Deiotariana	2
Africa	III Augusta	1

(*Note*: I Germanica, IV Macedonica, XV Primigenia, and XVI Gallica were disbanded by Vespasian after disgrace in the Batavian war; they were replaced by IV and XVI Flavia. II Adiutrix was recruited probably by Otho in A.D. 69, though some believe that it was formed from the Ravenna fleet after its defection to Vespasian in A.D. 69 – Tacitus *Histories* III.12).

F) THE REIGN OF VESPASIAN (*c.* A.D. 75)   29 legions

Spain	VII Gemina	1
Britain	II Adiutrix, II Augusta, IX Hispana,	
	XX Valeria Victrix	4
Upper Germany	I Adiutrix, VIII Augusta, XI Claudia	
	Pia Fidelis, XIV Gemina Martia Victrix	4
Lower Germany	VI Victrix, X Gemina, XXI Rapax,	
	XXII Primigenia	4
Dalmatia	IV Flavia	1
Pannonia	XIII Gemina, XV Apollinaris	2
Moesia	I Italica, V Alaudae, V Macedonica,	
	VII Claudia Pia Fidelis	4
Cappadocia	XII Fulminata, XVI Flavia	2
Syria	III Gallica, IV Scythica, VI Ferrata	3

Judaea	X Fretensis	I
Egypt	III Cyrenaica, XXII Deiotariana	2
Africa	III Augusta	I

G) THE REIGN OF TRAJAN (c. A.D. 110)   30 legions

Spain	VII Gemina	I
Britain	II Augusta, IX Hispana, XX Valeria Victrix	3
Upper Germany	VIII Augusta, XXII Primigenia	2
Lower Germany	I Minervia, VI Victrix	2
Upper Pannonia	X Gemina, XIV Gemina Martia Victrix, XV Apollinaris	3
Lower Pannonia	II Adiutrix Pia Fidelis	I
Upper Moesia	IV Flavia, VII Claudia Pia Fidelis, XXX Ulpia Victrix, II Traiana	4
Lower Moesia	I Italica, V Macedonica, XI Claudia Pia Fidelis	3
Dacia	I Adiutrix Pia Fidelis, XIII Gemina	2
Cappadocia	XII Fulminata, XVI Flavia	2
Syria	III Gallica, IV Scythica, VI Ferrata	3
Judaea	X Fretensis	I
Egypt	III Cyrenaica, XXII Deiotariana	2
Africa	III Augusta	I

(*Note*: During the Flavian/Trajanic periods, V Alaudae and XXI Rapax were replaced by I Minervia, II Traiana, and XXX Ulpia Victrix).

H) THE DEATH OF HADRIAN (A.D. 138)   28 legions

Spain	VII Gemina	I
Britain	II Augusta, VI Victrix, XX Valeria Victrix	3
Upper Germany	VIII Augusta, XXII Primigenia	2
Lower Germany	I Minervia, XXX Ulpia Victrix	2
Upper Pannonia	I Adiutrix, X Gemina, XIV Gemina Martia Victrix	3
Lower Pannonia	II Adiutrix	I
Upper Moesia	IV Flavia, VII Claudia Pia Fidelis	2
Lower Moesia	I Italica	I
Dacia	V Macedonica, XI Claudia Pia Fidelis, XIII Gemina	3
Cappadocia	XII Fulminata, XV Apollinaris	2
Syria	IV Scythica, XVI Flavia	2

Judaea	VI Ferrata, X Fretensis	2
Arabia	III Cyrenaica	1
Phoenicia	III Gallica	1
Egypt	II Traiana	1
Africa	III Augusta	1

(*Note*: IX Hispana and XXII Deiotariana have disappeared from the list – both probably during the Jewish Rebellion of A.D. 132; IX Hispana was transferred from Britain in *c.*A.D. 122).

I) THE REIGN OF MARCUS AURELIUS (*c.* A.D. 170) 30 legions

Spain	VII Gemina	1
Britain	II Augusta, VI Victrix, XX Valeria Victrix	3
Upper Germany	VIII Augusta, XXII Primigenia	2
Lower Germany	I Minervia, XXX Ulpia Victrix	2
Upper Pannonia	I Adiutrix, X Gemina, XIV Gemina Martia Victrix	3
Lower Pannonia	II Adiutrix Pia Fidelis	1
Upper Moesia	IV Flavia, VII Claudia Pia Fidelis	2
Lower Moesia	I Italica, V Macedonica XI Claudia Pia Fidelis	3
Dacia	XIII Gemina	1
Noricum	II Italica	1
Raetia	III Italica	1
Cappadocia	XII Fulminata, XV Apollinaris	2
Syria	III Gallica, IV Scythica, XVI Flavia	3
Judaea	VI Ferrata, X Fretensis	2
Arabia	III Cyrenaica	1
Egypt	II Traiana	1
Numidia	III Augusta	1

(*Note*: II and III Italica were legions newly raised for Marcus Aurelius' German campaigns. Septimius Severus added three more legions – I, II and III Parthica –, bringing the total to 33 legions. I and III Parthica were stationed in Mesopotamia, and II Parthica in Italy).

Area Distribution

A.D.	14	46	63	68	71	75	110	138	170	200
Britain	—	4	4	3	3	4	3	3	3	3
Italy	—	—	—	1	—	—	—	—	—	1
Germany and the West	11	9	8	10	9	9	5	5	5	5
Central and eastern Europe	7	7	5	7	8	7	13	10	12	12
The east	4	4	7	6	6	6	6	7	8	10
North Africa	3	3	3	3	3	3	3	3	2	2
Total	25	27	27	30	29	29	30	28	30	33

Notes and References

NOTES TO CHAPTER 1

1. T. W. Potter, *Roman Britain* (London, 1983), p. 27.
2. E. Gjerstad, *Legends and Facts of Early Roman History* (Lund, 1962).
3. D. C. A. Shotter, *The Fall of the Roman Republic* (London, 1994).
4. D. C. A. Shotter, *Augustus Caesar* (London, 1991).
5. Tacitus, *Annals*, I.2.
6. Dio Cassius, *Roman History*, 56.18, 2.
7. Tacitus, *Annals*, I.11.
8. A. R. Birley, *Septimius Severus: the African Emperor* (London, 1971).
9. S. Williams, *Diocletian and the Roman Recovery* (London, 1985).

NOTES TO CHAPTER 2

1. L. J. F. Keppie, 'Legio VIII Augusta and the Claudian Invasion', *Britannia*, ii (1971), 149–55; P. Holder, *The Roman Army in Britain* (London, 1982).
2. H. R. Hurst, *Kingsholm* (Gloucester, 1985).
3. P. Bidwell, *Roman Exeter: Fortress and Town* (Exeter, 1980).
4. D. E. Eichholz, 'How long did Vespasian Serve in Britain?', *Britannia*, iii (1972), 149–63.
5. Suetonius, *Life of Vespasian*, 4.
6. P. Salway, *Roman Britain* (Oxford, 1981), p. 95ff.
7. Tacitus, *Annals*, XII.31.
8. S. S. Frere and J. K. St Joseph, 'The Roman Fortress at Longthorpe', *Britannia*, v (1974), 1–129 (esp. p. 6ff).
9. E. B. Birley, *Roman Britain and the Roman Army* (Kendal, 1953), p. 1ff.
10. M. R. Hull, *Roman Colchester* (Oxford, 1958).
11. Tacitus, *Annals*, XII.39.
12. V. E. Nash-Williams (revised M. G. Jarrett), *The Roman Frontier in Wales* (Cardiff, 1969), p. 6.
13. Tacitus, *Life of Agricola*, 14; *Annals*, XII.40 and XIV.29.

14. Suetonius, *Life of Nero*, 18.
15. Dio Cassius, *Roman History*, 62.2, 1.
16. E. B. Birley, *Roman Britain and the Roman Army*, p. 1ff.
17. G. Webster, *Boudica* (London, 1978).
18. N. J. Higham, *The Northern Counties to A.D. 1000* (London, 1986), p. 179.
19. D. Fishwick, 'Templum divo Claudio Constitutum', *Britannia*, iii (1972), 164–81.
20. M. Griffin, 'Nero's Recall of Suetonius Paullinus', *Scripta Classica Israelica*, iii (1976–7), 138–52.
21. Tacitus, *Annals*, XIV.38–39.
22. Tacitus, *Life of Agricola*, 16.

NOTES TO CHAPTER 3

1. Tacitus, *Life of Agricola*, 16, 3; *Annals*, XIV.39.
2. Tacitus, *Annals*, XII. 40, 2–3.
3. Tacitus, *Life of Agricola*, 17,1.
4. N. J. Higham, *The Northern Counties to A.D. 1000*, p. 146.
5. I. A. Richmond, 'Queen Cartimandua', *JRS*, xliv (1954), 43–52.
6. G. D. B. Jones, 'The Romans in the North-West', *Northern History*, iii (1968), 1–26.
7. Tacitus, *Annals*, XII.40 and *Histories*, III.45; W. S. Hanson and D. B. Campbell, 'The Brigantes: From Clientage to Conquest', *Britannia*, xvii (1986), 73–89.
8. D. C. A. Shotter, 'Rome and the Brigantes: Early Hostilities, *CW*^{2}, xciv (1994), 21–34.
9. G. B. Townend, 'Some Flavian Connections', *JRS*, li (1961), 54–62.
10. E. B. Birley, 'The Adherence of Britain to Vespasian', *Britannia*, ix (1978), 243–5
11. E. B. Birley, *Roman Britain and the Roman Army*, p. 13.
12. P. Salway, *Roman Britain*, p. 133.
13. G. B. Townend, 'Some Flavian Connections', *JRS*, li (1961), 54–62; A. R. Birley, 'Petillius Cerialis and the Conquest of Brigantia', *Britannia*, iv (1973), 179–190.

14. Tacitus, *Life of Agricola*, 8, 2–3.
15. R. S. O. Tomlin, 'The Twentieth Legion at Wroxeter and Carlisle in the first century: the Epigraphic Evidence', *Britannia*, xxiii (1992), 141–58.
16. G. Webster, 'The Military Situations in Britain between A.D. 43 and 71', *Britannia*, i (1970), 179–97; A. R. Birley, 'Petillius Cerialis and the Conquest of Brigantia', *Britannia*, iv (1973), 179–190.
17. R. E. M. Wheeler, *The Stanwick Fortifications* (Oxford, 1954).
18. E. B. Birley, *Roman Britain and the Roman Army*, p. 13; B. Dobson, 'Roman Durham', *Transactions of the Architectural and Archaeological Society of Durham and Northumberland*, iii (1970), 31–43.
19. I. A. Richmond and J. McIntyre, 'The Roman Camps at Rey Cross and Crackenthorpe', *CW²*, xxxviii (1938), 50–61.
20. M. R. McCarthy, *Carlisle: History and Guide*, (Gloucester, 1993), p. 3.
21. J. Evans and C. Scull, 'Fieldwork on the Roman Fort Site at Blennerhasset, Cumbria', *CW²*, xc (1990), 127–37.
22. N. J. Higham and G. D. B. Jones, *The Carvetii* (Gloucester, 1985), p. 68ff.
23. M. G. Jarrett, *Maryport, Cumbria: A Roman Fort and its Garrison* (Kendal, 1976).
24. N. J. Higham, *The Northern Counties to A.D. 1000*, p. 146.
25. W. S. Hanson, C. M. Daniels, J. N. Dore and J. P. Gillam, 'The Agricolan Supply Base at Red House, Corbridge', *Arch. Ael.⁵*, vii (1979), 1–98.
26. W. S. Hanson, 'The First Roman Occupation of Scotland', pp. 15–43, in W. S. Hanson and L. J. F. Keppie (eds), *Roman Frontier Studies* (Oxford, 1980), (*BAR*, Int. Series 71).
27. D. J. Breeze, *The Northern Frontiers of Roman Britain* (London, 1982), p. 42.
28. Tacitus, *Life of Agricola*, 23.
29. D. J. Breeze, *The Northern Frontiers of Roman Britain*, p. 46.
30. W. S. Hanson and G. S. Maxwell, 'An Agricolan Praesidium on the Forth–Clyde Isthmus (Mollins, Strathclyde)', *Britannia*, xi (1980), 43–9.
31. N. Reed, 'The Fifth Year of Agricola's Campaigns', *Britannia*, ii (1971), 143–8.
32. D. J. Breeze, *The Northern Frontiers of Roman Britain*, p. 53.
33. Ptolemy, *Geographia*, II.3,7.
34. Tacitus, *Life of Agricola*, 26.
35. D. J. Breeze, *The Northern Frontiers of Roman Britain*, p. 31.
36. D. J. Breeze, *The Northern Frontiers of Roman Britain*, p. 62.
37. Tacitus, *Life of Agricola*, 25.
38. G. S. Maxwell, *The Romans in Scotland* (Edinburgh, 1989); G. S. Maxwell, *A Battle Lost: Romans and Caledonians at Mons Graupius* (Edinburgh, 1990).
39. W. S. Hanson, *Agricola and the Conquest of the North* (London, 1987).
40. B. W. Jones, *The Emperor Domitian* (London, 1992), p. 128ff.
41. Frontinus, *Strategemata*, I.1,8.
42. A. R. Birley, 'Petillius Cerialis and the Conquest of Brigantia', *Britannia*, iv (1973), 179–90.
43. A. S. Hobley, 'The Numismatic Evidence for the post-Agricolan abandonment of the Roman frontier in northern Scotland, *Britannia*, xx (1989), 69–74.
44. D. J. Breeze, *The Northern Frontiers of Roman Britain*, p. 61.
45. G. D. B. Jones, 'The Emergence of the Tyne–Solway Frontier', pp. 98–107, in V. A. Maxfield and M. J. Dobson (eds), *Roman Frontier Studies* (Exeter, 1989).
46. A. S. Hobley, 'The Numismatic Evidence for the post-Agricolan abandonment of the Roman frontier in northern Scotland', *Britannia*, xx (1989), 69–74.
47. D. J. Breeze, 'The Roman Army in Cumbria', *CW²*, lxxxviii (1988), 9–22.

NOTES TO CHAPTER 4

1. B. Dobson, 'Agricola's Life and Career', *Scot. Arch. Forum*, xii (1981), 1–13.
2. D. J. Breeze and B. Dobson, 'Roman Military Deployment in North England', *Britannia*, xvi (1985), 1–19.
3. D. C. A. Shotter, *Romans and Britons in North-West England* (Lancaster, 1993), p. 32.
4. P. Graystone, *Walking Roman Roads in East Cumbria* (Lancaster, 1994).
5. M. R. McCarthy, *Carlisle: History and Guide*.
6. W. S. Hanson *et al.*, 'The Agricolan Supply Base at Red House, Corbridge', *Arch. Ael.⁵*, vii.
7. E. B. Birley, R. Birley and A. R. Birley, *Vindolanda II: The Early Wooden Forts* (Hexham, 1993).
8. Tacitus, *Histories*, I.2, 1.
9. Juvenal, *Sat.* IV. 127; XIV. 196.
10. Spartianus, *Life of Hadrian*, 5.2.
11. P. V. Hill, *The Dating and Arrangement of the*

Undated Coins of Rome, A.D. 98–148 (London, 1970), p. 155.

12. Suetonius, *Life of Domitian*, 10.

13. A. R. Birley, *The People of Roman Britain* (London, 1979), p. 39.

14. E. B. Birley, R. Birley and A. R. Birley, *Vindolanda II The Early Wooden Forts*, p. 23.

15. E. B. Birley, R. Birley and A. R. Birley, *Vindolanda II The Early Wooden Forts*, p. 37.

16. A. S. Hobley, 'The Numismatic Evidence for the post-Agricolan abandonment of the Roman frontier in northern Scotland', *Britannia*, xx (1989), 69–74.

17. G. D. B. Jones, 'The Emergence of the Tyne–Solway Frontier', pp. 98–107, in Maxfield and Dobson, *Roman Frontier Studies* (1990).

18. G. D. B. Jones, 'The Emergence of the Tyne–Solway Frontier', pp. 98–107, *Roman Frontier Studies*; G. D. B. Jones, *Hadrian's Wall from the Air* (Preston, 1996).

19. N. J. Higham and G. D. B. Jones, *The Carvetii*, p. 26ff.

20. I am grateful to Professor Barri Jones of Manchester University for allowing me to make use of this material prior to its full publication (*Britannia*, xxvi (1995), p. 343).

21. A. K. Bowman and J. D. Thomas, *Vindolanda: The Latin Writing-Tablets* (London, 1983), pp. 105–11.

22. E. B. Birley, *Research on Hadrian's Wall* (Kendal, 1961), p. 132ff.

23. E. B. Birley, *Research on Hadrian's Wall*, p. 147ff.

24. D. J. Breeze, 'The Roman Army in Cumbria', *CW*^{2}, lxxxviii.

25. G. D. B. Jones, 'The Emergence of the Tyne–Solway Frontier', *Roman Frontier Studies* (1990), p. 105.

26. D. C. A. Shotter and A. J. White, *The Roman Fort and Town of Lancaster* (Lancaster, 1990); G. D. B. Jones and D. C. A. Shotter, *Roman Lancaster* (Manchester, 1988).

27. J. Walker (ed.), *Castleshaw: The Archaeology of a Roman Fortlet* (Manchester, 1989).

28. G. D. B. Jones and D. C. A. Shotter, *Roman Lancaster*.

29. R. Hogg, 'Excavation of the Roman auxiliary tilery, Brampton', *CW*^{2}, lxv (1965), 133–68.

30. J. Hinchliffe and J. H. Williams, *Roman Warrington* (Manchester, 1992).

31. D. C. A. Shotter, 'The Romans in South Cumbria, *CW*^{2}, xcv (1995), p. 73.

32. H. Schönberger, 'The Roman Frontier in Germany: An Archaeological Survey', *JRS*, lix (1969), 144–97.

33. Spartianus, *Life of Hadrian*, 5.2.

34. D. C. A. Shotter, 'Three Early Imperial Coinhoards from Lancashire', *Coin Hoards*, iv (1978), pp. 45–5.

35. P. V. Hill, *The Dating and Arrangement of the Undated Coins of Rome, A.D. 98–148*, nos 141 and 145.

36. P. V. Hill, *The Dating and Arrangement of the Undated Coins of Rome, A.D. 98–148*, p. 54, nos 160 and 165.

37. J. M. C. Toynbee, '"Britannia" on Roman Coins of the second century A.D.', *JRS*, xiv (1924), 142–57; J. M. C. Toynbee, *The Hadrianic School* (Cambridge, 1934).

NOTES TO CHAPTER 5

1. M. G. Jarrett, 'An Unnecessary War', *Britannia*, vii (1976), 145–51.

2. D. C. A. Shotter, 'Three Early Imperial Coinhoards from Lancashire', *Coin-hoards*, iv, p. 44ff; D. C. A. Shotter, *Roman Coins from North-West England* (Lancaster, 1990), p. 212ff.

3. Spartanus, *Life of Hadrian*, 5–7; Dio Cassius, *Roman History* 68.1–5.

4. M. G. Jarrett, 'An Unnecessary War', *Britannia*, vii (1976), p. 150.

5. J. M. C. Toynbee, *The Hadrianic School*, p. 139; P. V. Hill, *The Dating and Arrangement of the Undated Coins of Rome, A.D. 98–148*, no. 165.

6. T. W. Potter, *Roman Britain*, p. 28.

7. D. J. Breeze and B. Dobson, *Hadrian's Wall* (London, 1976), p. 55ff.

8. P. S. Austen, 'Recent Excavations on Hadrian's Wall at Burgh-by-Sands', *CW*^{2}, xciv (1994), 35–54.

9. A. W. Lintott, *Imperium Romanum* (London, 1993), p. 122ff.

10. Tacitus, *Life of Agricola*, 19.

11. B. Haywood, 'The *Vallum* – its Problems Restated', pp. 85–94, in M. G. Jarrett and B Dobson (eds), *Britain and Rome* (Kendal, 1966).

12. P. S. Austen, 'Recent Excavations on Hadrian's Wall at Burgh-by-Sands', *CW*^{2}, xciv.

13. M. W. C. Hassall, 'The Date of the Rebuilding of Hadrian's Turf Wall in stone', *Britannia*, xv (1984), pp. 242–4.

14. J. D. Cowan and I. A. Richmond, 'The Rudge Cup', *Arch. Ael.*^{4}, xii (1935), 310–42.

NOTES TO CHAPTER 6

1. R. L. Bellhouse, *Joseph Robinson of Maryport: Archaeologist Extraordinary* (Ilkley, 1992); E. B. Birley, *Research on Hadrian's Wall*, pp. 214–26.

2. R. L. Bellhouse, 'The Roman Fort at Burrow Walls, near Workington', *CW²*, lv (1955), 30–45.

3. M. G. Jarrett, *Maryport, Cumbria: A Roman Fort and its Garrison*; M. G. Jarrett, 'An Unnecessary War', *Britannia*, vii (1976).

4. R. L. Bellhouse, *Roman Sites on the Cumberland Coast* (Kendal, 1989), pp. 1–3.

5. D. J. Wooliscroft, 'Signalling and the Design of the Cumberland Coast System', *CW²*, xciv (1994), 55–64.

6. R. L. Bellhouse, *Joseph Robinson of Maryport: Archaeologist Extraordinary*.

7. F. G. Simpson and K. S. Hodgson, 'The Coastal Milefortlet at Cardurnock', *CW²*, xlvii (1947), 78–127.

8. N. J. Higham and G. D. B. Jones, 'Frontier, Fort and Farmers: Cumbria Aerial Survey, 1974–5', *Arch. J.*, cxxxii (1975), 16–53; G. D. B. Jones, 'The Western Extension of Hadrian's Wall', *Britannia*, vii (1976), 236–43; G. D. B. Jones, 'The Solway Frontier: Interim Report 1976–81', *Britannia*, xiii (1982), 283–97; G. D. B. Jones, 'The Emergence of the Tyne–Solway Frontier', *Roman Frontier Studies*; T. W. Potter, 'The Biglands Milefortlet and the Cumberland Coast Defences', *Britannia*, viii (1977), 149–83; T. W. Potter, *The Romans in North-West England* (Kendal, 1979).

9. R. L. Bellhouse and G. G. S. Richardson, 'The Trajanic Fort at Kirkbride: the terminus of the Stanegate Frontier', *CW²*, lxxxii (1982), 35–50.

10. T. W. Potter, 'The Biglands Milefortlet and the Cumberland Coast Defences, *Britannia*, viii (1977), p. 152.

11. *Britannia*, xxiii (1992), 270–1.

12. G. D. B. Jones, 'Excavations on a Coastal tower, Hadrian's Wall; Campfield Tower 2B, Bowness-on-Solway', *MAB*, viii (1993), 31–9.

13. G. D. B. Jones, 'The Solway Frontier: Interim Report', *Britannia*, xiii (1982), p. 286.

14. Spartianus, *Life of Hadrian*, 12.6.

15. T. W. Potter, *The Romans in North-West England*, p. 50.

16. R. L. Bellhouse, *Roman Sites on the Cumberland Coast*, p. 57f.

17. D. C. A. Shotter, 'Roman Coin-finds in Cumbria', *CW²*, lxxxix (1989), 41–50.

18. T. W. Potter, *The Romans in North-West England*, p. 48.

19. R. L. Bellhouse, *Roman Sites on the Cumberland Coast*, p. 31.

20. T. W. Potter, 'Excavations at Bowness-on-Solway, 1973', *CW²*, lxxv (1975), 29–57.

21. T. W. Potter, *The Romans in North-West England*, pp. 49 and 330.

22. M. G. Jarrett, *Maryport, Cumbria: A Roman Fort and its Garrison*, p. 46.

23. F. G. Simpson and K. S. Hodgson, 'The Coastal Milefortlet at Cardurnock', *CW²*, xlvii.

24. T. W. Potter, 'The Biglands Milefortlet and the Cumberland Coast Defences', *Britannia*, viii (1977), p. 183.

25. G. D. Keevil, M. R. McCarthy and D. C. A. Shotter, 'A *Solidus* of Valentinian II from Scotch Street, Carlisle, *Britannia*, xx (1989), pp. 254–5.

26. R. L. Bellhouse, *Roman Sites on the Cumberland Coast*, p. 59.

27. G. D. B. Jones, 'The Solway Frontier: Interim Report 1976–81,' *Britannia*, xiii (1982), p. 288ff.

28. T. W. Potter, 'The Biglands Milefortlet and the Cumberland Coast Defences', *Britannia*, viii (1977).

29. M. G. Jarrett, 'The Garrison of Maryport and the Roman Army in Britain', pp. 27–40, in M. G. Jarrett and B. Dobson (eds), *Britain and Rome* (Kendal, 1966).

NOTES TO CHAPTER 7

1. Pausanias, *Description of Greece*, VIII.43.

2. J. G. F. Hind, 'The "Genounian" Part of Britain', *Britannia*, viii (1977), 229–48.

3. D. J. Breeze, 'A Roman Fortlet at Barburgh Mill, Dumfriesshire', *Britannia*, v (1974), 130–62.

4. D. J. Breeze, *The Northern Frontiers of Roman Britain*, p. 110.

5. A. S. Robertson, M. Scott and L. J. F. Keppie, *Bar Hill: A Roman Fort and its Finds* (Oxford, 1975)., (*BAR* 16).

6. I. A. Richmond, 'Excavations at the Roman Fort of Newstead', *PSAS*, lxxxiv (1950), 1–37.

7. D. J. Breeze, *Roman Scotland: some recent excavations* (Edinburgh, 1979).

8. B. R. Hartley, 'The Roman Occupation of Scotland: The Evidence of Samian Ware', *Britannia*, iii (1972), 1–55.

9. T. W. Potter, 'The Biglands Milefortlet and the Cumberland Coast Defences', *Britannia*, viii (1977).

10. G. D. B. Jones, 'Excavations on a Coastal tower, Hadrian's Wall; Campfield Tower 2B, Bowness-on-Solway', *MAB*, viii.

11. G. D. B. Jones, 'The Solway Frontier: Interim Report 1976–81', *Britannia*, xiii (1982).

12. M. G. Jarrett, *Maryport, Cumbria: A Roman Fort and its Garrison*.

13. J. M. C. Toynbee, '"Britannia" on Roman Coins of the second century A.D.', *JRS*, xiv.

14. M. P. Speidel, 'The Chattan War, the Brigantian Revolt, and the loss of the Antonine Wall', *Britannia*, xviii (1987), 233–7.

15. A. S. Robertson, 'Romano-British Coin Hoards', pp. 12–36, in P. J. Casey and R. Reece (eds), *Coins and the Archaeologist* (Oxford, 1974), (*BAR*, 4).

16. M. P. Speidel, 'The Chattan War, the Brigantian Revolt, and the loss of the Antonine Wall', *Britannia*, xviii (1987), 233–7.

17. D. J. Breeze, 'The Abandonment of the Antonine Wall: its date and implications', *Scot. Arch. Forum*, vii (1975), 67–80.

18. A. S. Robertson, 'A Hoard of Roman Silver Coins from Briglands, Rumbling Bridge, Kinross-shire', *PSAS*, xc (1957), 241–6.

19. R. Reece, 'Coins and Frontiers: The Falkirk Hoard reconsidered', pp. 119–29, in W. S. Hanson and L. J. F. Keppie (eds), *Roman Frontier Studies, 1979* (Oxford, 1980), (*BAR*, Int. Series 71).

20. B. R. Hartley, 'The Roman Occupation of Scotland: The Evidence of Samian Ware', *Britannia*, iii (1972), 1–55.

21. D. C. A. Shotter, 'Coin Evidence and the Northern Frontier in the Second Century A.D.', *PSAS*, cvii (1976), 81–91.

22. T. W. Potter, *The Romans in North-West England*, p. 362.

23. Dio Cassius, *Roman History*, 72.16, 2.

NOTES TO CHAPTER 8

1. *Life of Marcus*, 8.2–8 and 22.1.

2. *Life of Commodus*, 8.4.

3. Dio Cassius, *Roman History*, 73.8.

4. R. W. Davies, '"Singulares" and Roman Britain', *Britannia*, vii (1976), 134–44.

5. *JRS*, liii (1963), 160.

6. T. W. Potter, *The Romans in North-West England*, p. 362.

7. Dio Cassius, *Roman History*, 75.5.

8. D. J. Breeze, *The Northern Frontiers of Roman Britain*, p. 129.

9. A. Ferrill, *Roman Imperial Grand Strategy* (Lanham, 1991); D. J. Breeze, *The Northern Frontiers of Roman Britain*, p. 130f.

10. T. W. Potter, *The Romans in North-West England*, p. 361ff.

11. Dio Cassius, *Roman History*, 77.11ff; Herodian III, 14–15; A. R. Birley, *Septimius Severus*, 244ff.

12. N. Reed, 'The Scottish Campaigns of Septimius Severus', *PSAS*, cvii (1976), 92–102.

13. G. R. Stephens, 'A Severan Vexillation at Ribchester', *Britannia*, xviii (1987), 239–42.

14. P. V. Hill, *The Coinage of Septimius Serverus and his family of the mint of Rome, A.D. 193–217* (London, 1977), pp. 27–8; A. S. Robertson, 'The Bridges on Severan coins of A.D. 208 and 209', pp. 131–9, in W. S. Hanson and L. J. F. Keppie (eds), *Roman Frontier Studies, 1979* (Oxford, 1980), (*BAR*, Int. Series, 71).

15. J. Dore and J. P. Gillam, *The Roman Fort at South Shields* (Newcastle-upon-Tyne, 1979).

NOTES TO CHAPTER 9

1. D. J. Breeze, *The Northern Frontiers of Roman Britain*, p. 137.

2. J. P. Gillam, 'Also, Along the Line of the Wall', *CW²*, xlix (1949), 38–58; R. Goodburn and P. Bartholomew (eds), *Aspects of the Notitia Dignitatum* (Oxford, 1976), (*BAR* Supplement 15).

3. D. J. Breeze, *The Northern Frontiers of Roman Britain*, p. 144f.

4. C. M. Daniels, 'Excavations at Wallsend and the fourth-century barracks on Hadrian's Wall', pp. 173–93, in W. S. Hanson and L. J. F. Keppie (eds), *Roman Frontier Studies, 1979* (Oxford, 1980), (*BAR*, Int. Series 71).

5. *JRS*, lv (1965), 224, from Brougham; N. J. Higham and G. D. B. Jones, *The Carvetii* (Gloucester, 1985).

6. M. R. McCarthy, *Carlisle: History and Guide*.

7. R. Birley, *Vindolanda* (London, 1977).

8. I. A. Richmond and K. A. Steer, 'Castellum Veluniate and Civilians on a Roman frontier', *PSAS*, xc (1957), 1–6.

9. D. J. Breeze, *The Northern Frontier of Roman Britain*, p. 152.

10. N. J. Higham, *The Northern Counties to A.D. 1000*, p 182ff.

11. P. A. G. Clack, 'The Northern Frontiers: Farmers in the Military Zone', pp. 377–402, in D. Miles (ed), *The Romano-British Countryside* (Oxford, 1982), (*BAR*, 103i).

12. K. Branigan (ed), *Rome and the Brigantes* (Sheffield, 1980).

13. G. D. B. Jones, *Hadrian's Wall from the Air* (Preston, 1996); N. J. Higham and G. D. B. Jones, 'Frontier, Forts and Farmers: Cumbria Aerial Survey, 1974–5', *Arch. J.* cxxxii; R. A. C. Lowndes, 'Celtic' fields, farms and burial mounds in the Lune Valley', *CW²*, lxiii (1963), 77–95; R. A. C. Lowndes, 'Excavations of a Romano-British farmstead at Eller Beck, *CW²*, lxiv (1964), 6–13; D. C. A. Shotter and A. J. White, *The Romans in Lunesdale* (Lancaster, 1995).

14. N. Shiel, *The Episode of Carausius and Allectus* (Oxford, 1977), (*BAR*, 40).

15. I. A. Richmond, K. S. Hodgson and J. K. St Joseph, 'The Roman Fort at Bewcastle', *CW²*, xxxviii (1938), 195–239; P. S. Austen, *Bewcastle and Old Penrith: A Roman Outpost Fort and a Frontier vicus* (Kendal, 1991), p. 50.

16. D. C. A. Shotter, *Roman Coins from North-West England*.

17. *Pan. Lat. Vet.* VIII.11, 4.

18. Ammianus Marcellinus, *Roman History* XXVII.8, 5.

19. J. J. Wilkes, 'Early Fourth-Century Rebuilding in Hadrian's Wall Forts', pp. 114–38, in M. G. Jarrett and B. Dobson (eds), *Britain and Rome* (Kendal, 1966).

20. E. B. Birley, 'The Roman Fort at Low Borrow Bridge', *CW²*, xlvii (1947), 1–19.

21. R. L. Bellhouse, 'The Roman Fort at Burrow Walls, near Workington', *CW²*, lv (1955), 30–45.

22. N. J. Higham, *The Northern Counties to A.D. 1000*, p. 235f; J. G. F. Hind, 'Who betrayed Britain to the Barbarians in A.D. 367?', *Northern History*, xix (1983), 1–7.

23. Ammianus Marcellinus, *Roman History*, XXI.1.

24. D. C. A. Shotter, '*Numeri Barcariorum*: a note on *RIB* 601', *Britannia*, iv (1973), 206–9.

25. A. S. Johnson, *Later Roman Britain* (London, 1980), p. 64.

26. T. W. Potter, *The Romans in North-West England*, p. 12f.

27. D. C. A. Shotter, *Romans and Britons in North-West England*, p. 93f.

28. A. S. Johnson, *The Roman Forts of the Saxon Shore* (London, 1976).

29. Ammianus Marcellinus, *Roman History*, XX. 1, 1.

30. Ammianus Marcellinus, *Roman History*, XX. 1.

31. Ammianus Marcellinus, *Roman History*, XXVII. 8.

32. D. J. Breeze and B. Dobson, *Hadrian's Wall*, p. 221.

33. T. W. Potter, *The Romans in North-West England*.

34. A. Dornier, 'The Province of Valentia', *Britannia*, xiii (1982), p. 253.

35. A. S. Johnson, *Later Roman Britain*, p. 98.

36. B. Dobson, 'Roman Durham', *Trans. Archit. and Archaeol. Soc. of Durham and Northumberland*, iii (1970), 31–43.

37. P. S. Austen, *Bewcastle and Old Penrith: A Roman Outpost Fort and a Frontier vicus* (Kendal, 1991), p. 50.

38. Ammianus Marcellinus, *Roman History*, XXVII. 3.

39. P. J. Casey, 'Magnus Maximus in Britain', pp. 66–79, in P. J. Casey (ed), *The End of Roman Britain* (Oxford, 1979), (*BAR*, 71).

40. M. Miller, 'Stilicho's Pictish War', *Britannia*, vi (1975), 141–50.

41. Claudian, *De Consulatu Stilichonis*, II. 250–5.

NOTES TO CHAPTER 10

1. M. Millet, *The Romanisation of Britain* (Cambridge, 1990).

2. D. J. Breeze, *The Northern Frontiers of Roman Britain*, p. 151.

3. D. J. Breeze, *The Northern Frontiers of Roman Britain*, p. 152–3; M. F. Sekulla, 'The Roman Coins from Traprain Law', *PSAS*, cxii (1982), 285–94.

4. M. R. McCarthy, 'Woodland and Roman Forts', *Britannia*, xvii (1986), 339–43.

5. M. R. McCarthy, *Carlisle: History and Guide*, p. 2.

6. H. E. Kilbride-Jones, 'Excavation of a Native Settlement at Milking Gap, High Shield, Northumberland', *Arch. Ael.⁴*, xv (1938), 303–350; J. P. Gillam, 'Roman and Native, 122–197', pp. 60–90, in I. A. Richmond (ed), *Roman and Native in North Britain* (Edinburgh, 1958).

7. N. J. Higham, *The Northern Counties to A.D. 1000*, p. 178.

8. N. J. Higham, *The Northern Counties to A.D. 1000*, p. 179.

9. E. B. Birley, 'Old Penrith and its Problems', *CW²*, xlvi (1946), 27–38; P. S. Austen, *Bewcastle and Old Penrith: A Roman Outpost Fort and a Frontier vicus*.

10. R. H. Leech, 'The Roman Fort and *Vicus* at Ambleside: Archaeological Research in 1982', *CW²*, xciii (1993), 51–4.

11. Arrian, *Periplus*, 7.4–8.1.

12. W. F. Grimes, 'Holt, Denbighshire: The works-depot of the Twentieth Legion at Castle Lyons', *Y Cymmrodor*, xli, 1930.

13. R. Hogg, 'Excavation of the Roman auxiliary tilery, Brampton', *CW²*, lxv (1965), 133–68.

14. R. L. Bellhouse, 'Excavations in Eskdale: the Muncaster Roman Kilns', *CW*, lxi (1961), 47–56.

15. G. D. B. Jones and D. C. A. Shotter, *Roman Lancaster*, p. 85ff.

16. J. Hinchliffe and J. H. Williams, *Roman Warrington*.

17. For example, D. J. Smith, 'A Palmyrene Sculptor from South Shields', *Arch. Ael.*[4], xxxviii (1959), 203–10.

18. D. C. A. Shotter and A. J. White, *Romans in Lunesdale*.

19. T. W. Potter, *The Romans in North-West England*.

20. B. J. N. Edwards and P. V. Webster (eds), *Ribchester Excavations, Part II* (Cardiff, 1987), p. 55ff.

21. G. D. B. Jones, *Roman Manchester* (Altrincham, 1974).

22. *JRS* LIX (1969), 235; V. Nutten, 'A Greek Doctor at Chester', *Journal of the Chester Archaeological Society*, lv (1968), 7–13.

23. M. Henig, *Religion in Roman Britain* (London, 1984); M. Green, *The Religions of Civilian Roman Britain* (Oxford, 1976), (*BAR*, 24).

24. M. G. Jarrett, *Maryport, Cumbria: A Roman Fort and its Garrison* (Kendal, 1976).

25. I. A. Richmond and J. P. Gillam, 'The Temple of Mithras at Carrawburgh', *Arch. Ael.*[4], xxii (1951), 1–92.

26. D. Watts, *Christians and Pagans in Roman Britain* (London, 1990).

27. *Britannia*, x (1979), 353.

28. S. H. Penney and D. C. A. Shotter, 'A Salt-pan from Shavington, near Crewe', *Britannia*, xxvii (1996), forthcoming.

29. J. Lambert, N. Hair, C. L. E. Howard-Davis, R. M. Newman and T. M. Oliver, *Transect Through Time* (Oxford, 1996).

30. M. R. McCarthy, 'Woodland and Roman Forts', *Britannia*, xvii (1986).

31. N. J. Higham, *The Northern Counties to A.D. 1000*, p. 192f.

32. N. J. Higham and G. D. B. Jones, 'Excavation of two Romano-British Farm Sites in North Cumbria', *Britannia*, xiv (1983), 45–72.

33. R. A. C. Lowndes, 'Celtic' fields, farms and burial mounds in the Lune Valley', *CW*[2], lxiii (1963), 77–95; R. A. C. Lowndes, 'Excavations of a Romano-British farmstead at Eller Beck, *CW*[2], lxiv (1964), 6–13; N. J. Higham, *The Northern Counties to A.D. 1000*, p. 204.

34. D. Charlesworth and J. H. Thornton, 'Leather found in *Mediobogdum*, the Roman fort at Hardknott, *Britannia*, iv (1973), 141–51.

35. N. J. Higham, *The Northern Counties to A.D. 1000*, p. 222.

36. G. Simpson, 'Haltwhistle Burn, Corstopitum and the Antonine Wall', *Britannia*, v (1976), 317–39.

37. G. D. B. Jones, 'The North-Western Interface', pp. 93–106 in P. J. Fowler (ed), *Recent Work in Rural Archaeology* (Bradford-upon-Avon, 1975).

38. S. H. Penney, 'Romano-British Iron Extraction in north Lancashire', *CW*[2], lxxxiii (1983), 59–62.

Bibliography

P. S. Austen, *Bewcastle and Old Penrith: A Roman Outpost Fort and a Frontier vicus* (Kendal, 1991)

——, 'Recent Excavations on Hadrian's Wall at Burgh-by-Sands', *CW²*, xciv (1994), 35–54

R. L. Bellhouse, 'A Roman Post at Wreay Hall near Carlisle', *CW²* liii (1953), 49–51

——, 'The Roman Fort at Burrow Walls, near Workington', *CW²*, lv (1953), 30–45

——, 'Excavations in Eskdale: the Muncaster Roman Kilns', *CW²*, lxi (1961), 47–56

——, 'Hadrian's Wall: The Limiting Ditches in the Cardurnock Peninsula', *Britannia*, xii (1981), 135–42

——, 'Roman Sites on the Cumberland Coast: Milefortlet 17, Dubmill Point', *CW²*, lxxxvi (1986), 41–7

——, 'Roman Sites on the Cumberland Coast: Hadrian's Wall. The Fort at Bowness-on-Solway, a reappraisal', *CW²*, lxxxviii (1988), 33–53

——, *Roman Sites on the Cumberland Coast* (Kendal, 1989)

——, *Joseph Robinson of Maryport: Archaeologist Extraordinary* (Ilkley, 1992)

—— and G. G. S. Richardson, 'The Trajanic Fort at Kirkbride: the terminus of the Stanegate Frontier', *CW²*, lxxxii (1982), 35–50

P. Bidwell, *Roman Exeter: Fortress and Town* (Exeter, 1980)

A. R. Birley, *Septimius Severus: the African Emperor* (London, 1971)

——, 'Petillius Cerialis and the Conquest of Brigantia', *Britannia*, iv (1973), 179–90

——, *The People of Roman Britain* (London, 1979)

E. B. Birley, 'Old Penrith and its Problems', *CW²*, xlvi (1946), 27–38

——, 'The Roman Fort at Low Borrow Bridge', *CW²*, xlvii (1947), 1–19

——, *Roman Britain and The Roman Army* (Kendal, 1953)

——, *Research on Hadrian's Wall* (Kendal, 1961)

——, The Adherence of Britain to Vespasian, *Britannia*, ix (1978), 243–245

R. Birley, *Vindolanda* (London, 1977)

E. B. Birley, R. Birley and A. R. Birley, *Vindolanda II: The Early Wooden Forts* (Hexham, 1993)

M. C. Bishop and J. N. Dore, *Corbridge: Excavations of the Roman Fort and Town 1947–80* (London, 1989)

A. K. Bowman and J. D. Thomas, *Vindolanda: The Latin Writing-Tablets* (London, 1983)

K. Branigan (ed.), *Rome and the Brigantes* (Sheffield, 1980)

D. J. Breeze, 'A Roman Fortlet at Barburgh Mill, Dumfriesshire', *Britannia*, v (1974), 130–62

——, 'The abandonment of the Antonine Wall: its date and implications', *Scot. Arch. Forum*, vii (1975), 67–80

——, *Roman Scotland: some recent excavations* (Edinburgh, 1979)

——, *The Northern Frontiers of Roman Britain* (London, 1982)

——, 'The Roman Army in Cumbria', *CW²*, lxxxviii (1988), 9–22

—— and B. Dobson, *Hadrian's Wall* (London, 1976)

—— and B. Dobson, 'Roman Military Deployment in North England', *Britannia*, xvi (1985), 1–19

T. V. Buttrey, *Documentary Evidence for the Chronology of the Flavian Titulature* (Meisenheim, 1980)

P. J. Casey, 'Magnus Maximus in Britain', pp. 66–79 in P. J. Casey (ed.), *The End of Roman Britain* (BAR 71, Oxford, 1979)

——, *Carausius and Allectus: The British Usurpers* (London, 1994)

—— and R. Reece (eds), *Coins and the Archaeologist* (BAR 41, Oxford, 1974)

D. Charlesworth amd J. H. Thornton, 'Leather found in *Mediobogdum*, the Roman fort at Hardknott', *Britannia*, iv (1973), 141–52

P. A. G. Clack, 'The Northern Frontiers: Farmers in the Military Zone', pp. 377–402 in D. Miles (ed.), *The Romano-British Countryside* (BAR 103i, Oxford 1982)

A. S. E. Cleary, *The Ending of Roman Britain* (London, 1989)

R. G. Collingwood, 'Roman Signal-stations on the Cumberland Coast', *CW²*, xxix (1929), 138–65

J. D. Cowan and I. A. Richmond, 'The Rudge Cup', *Arch. Ael.*⁴, xii (1935), 310–42

M. H. Crawford, *Roman Republican Coinage* (Cambridge, 1974)

J. Crow, *Housesteads* (London, 1995)

C. M. Daniels, 'Excavations at Wallsend and the fourth-century barracks on Hadrian's Wall', pp. 173–93 in W. S. Hanson and L. J. F. Keppie (eds), *Roman Frontier Studies, 1979* (*BAR*, Int. Series 71, Oxford, 1980)

R. W. Davies, '*Singulares* and Roman Britain', *Britannia*, vii (1976), 134–44

D. Divine, *The North-West Frontier of Rome* (London, 1969)

B. Dobson, 'Roman Durham', *Trans. Archit. and Archaeol. Soc. of Durham and Northumberland*, iii (1970), 31–43

——, 'Agricola's Life and Career', *Scot. Arch. Forum*, xii (1981), 1–13

——, 'The Function of Hadrian's Wall', *Arch. Ael.*[5], xiv (1986), 1–30

J. Dore and J. P. Gillam, *The Roman Fort at South Shields* (Newcastle-upon-Tyne, 1979)

A. Dornier, 'The Province of Valentia', *Britannia*, xiii (1982), 253

B. J. N. Edwards and P. V. Webster (eds), *Ribchester Excavations, Part II* (Cardiff, 1987)

D. E. Eichholz, 'How long did Vespasian Serve in Britain?', *Britannia*, iii (1972), 149–63

J. Evans and C. Scull, 'Fieldwork on the Roman Fort Site at Blennerhasset, Cumbria', *CW*[2], xc (1990), 127–37

A. Ferrill, *Roman Imperial Grand Strategy* (Lanham, 1991)

D. Fishwick, 'Templum divo Claudio Constitutum', *Britannia*, iii (1972), 164–81

S. S. Frere and J. K. St Joseph, 'The Roman Fortress at Longthorpe', *Britannia*, v (1974), 1–129

J. P. Gillam, 'Also, Along the Line of the Wall', *CW*[2], xlix (1949), 38–58

——, 'Roman and Native, 122–197', pp. 60–90 in I. A. Richmond (ed.), *Roman and Native in North Britain* (Edinburgh, 1958)

—— and J. C. Mann, 'The Northern British Frontier from Antoninus Pius to Caracalla', *Arch. Ael.*[4], xlviii (1970), 1–44

E. Gjerstad, *Legends and Facts of Early Roman History* (Lund, 1962)

R. Goodburn and P. Bartholomew (eds), *Aspects of the Notitia Dignitatum* (*BAR*, Suppl. 15, Oxford, 1976)

P. Graystone, *Walking Roman Roads in East Cumbria* (Lancaster, 1994)

M. Green, *The Religions of Civilian Roman Britain* (*BAR* 24, Oxford, 1976)

M. Griffin, 'Nero's Recall of Suetonius Paullinus', *Scripta Classica Israelica*, iii (1976–77), 138–52

W. F. Grimes, 'Holt, Denbighshire: The works-depot of the Twentieth Legion at Castle Lyons', *Y Cymmrodor*, xli (1930)

W. S. Hanson, 'Roman Campaigns north of the Forth–Clyde Isthmus: The Evidence of Temporary Camps', *PSAS*, cix (1980), 140–50

——, 'The First Roman Occupation of Scotland, pp. 15–43 in W. S. Hanson and L. J. F. Keppie (eds), *Roman Frontier Studies 1979* (*BAR*, Int. Series 71, 1980)

——, *Agricola and the Conquest of the North* (London, 1987)

—— and D. B. Campbell, 'The Brigantes: From Clientage to Conquest', *Britannia*, xvii (1986), 73–89

—— and G. S. Maxwell, 'An Agricolan Praesidium on the Forth–Clyde Isthmus (Mollins, Strathclyde)', *Britannia*, xi (1980), 43–9

—— and G. S. Maxwell, *Rome's North-West Frontier* (Edinburgh, 1983)

——, C. M. Daniels, J. N. Dore and J. P. Gillam, 'The Agricolan Supply Base at Red House, Corbridge', *Arch. Ael.*[5], vii (1979), 1–98

B. R. Hartley, 'The Roman Occupation of Scotland: The Evidence of Samian Ware', *Britannia*, iii (1972), 1–55

—— and R. L. Fitts, *The Brigantes* (Gloucester, 1988)

M. W. C. Hassall, 'The Date of the Rebuilding of Hadrian's Turf Wall in Stone', *Britannia*, xv (1984), 242–4

M. Henig, *Religion in Roman Britain* (London, 1984)

B. Heywood, 'The *Vallum* – its Problems Restated', pp. 85–94 in M. G. Jarrett and B. Dobson (eds), *Britain and Rome* (Kendal, 1966)

N. J. Higham, *The Northern Counties to A.D. 1000* (London, 1986)

—— and G. D. B. Jones, 'Frontier, Forts and Farmers: Cumbria Aerial Survey, 1974–5', *Arch. J.*, cxxxii (1975), 16–53

—— and G. D. B. Jones, 'Excavation of two Romano-British Farm Sites in North Cumbria', *Britannia*, xiv (1983), 45–72

—— and G. D. B. Jones, *The Carvetii* (Gloucester, 1985)

P. V. Hill, *The Dating and Arrangement of the Undated Coins of Rome, A.D. 98–148* (London, 1970)

——, *The Coinage of Septimius Severus and his family of the mint of Rome, A.D. 193–217* (London, 1977)

J. Hinchliffe and J. H. Williams, *Roman Warrington* (Manchester, 1992)

J. G. F. Hind, 'The "Genounian" Part of Britain', *Britannia*, viii (1977), 229–38

——, 'Who betrayed Britain to the Barbarians in A.D. 367?', *Northern History*, xix (1983), 1–7

A. S. Hobley, 'The Numismatic Evidence for the post-Agricolan abandonment of the Roman frontier in northern Scotland', *Britannia*, xx (1989), 69–74

R. Hogg, 'Excavation of the Roman auxiliary tilery, Brampton, *CW*², lxv (1965), 133–68

P. Holder, *The Roman Army in Britain* (London, 1982)

M. R. Hull, *Roman Colchester* (Oxford, 1958)

H. R. Hurst, *Kingsholm* (Gloucester, 1985)

M. G. Jarrett, 'The Garrison of Maryport and the Roman Army in Britain', pp. 27–40 in M. G. Jarrett and B. Dobson (eds), *Britain and Rome* (Kendal, 1966)

——, *Maryport, Cumbria: A Roman Fort and its Garrison* (Kendal, 1976)

——, 'An Unnecessary War', *Britannia*, vii (1976), 145–51

A. S. Johnson, *The Roman Forts of the Saxon Shore* (London, 1976)

——, *Later Roman Britain* (London, 1980)

B. W. Jones, *The Emperor Domitian* (London, 1992)

G. D. B. Jones, 'The Romans in the North-West', *Northern History*, iii (1968), 1–26

——, *Roman Manchester* (Altrincham, 1974)

——, 'The North-Western Interface', pp. 93–106 in P. J. Fowler (ed.), *Recent Work in Rural Archaeology* (Bradford-upon-Avon, 1975)

——, 'The Western Extension of Hadrian's Wall', *Britannia*, vii (1976), 236–43

——, 'Archaeology and Coastal Change in the North-West', pp. 87–102 in F. H. Thompson (ed.), *Archaeology and Coastal Change* (London, 1979)

——, 'The Solway Frontier: Interim Report 1976–81', *Britannia*, xiii (1982), 283–97

——, 'The Emergence of the Tyne-Solway Frontier', pp. 98–107 in V. A. Maxfield and M. J. Dobson, (eds) *Roman Frontier Studies, 1989* (Exeter, 1990)

——, 'Excavations on a Coastal tower, Hadrian's Wall; Campfield Tower 2B, Bowness-on-Solway', *MAB*, viii (1993), 31–9

——, *Hadrian's Wall from the Air* (Preston, 1996)

—— and D. C. A. Shotter, *Roman Lancaster* (Manchester, 1988)

G. D. Keevil, M. R. McCarthy and D. C. A. Shotter, 'A *Solidus* of Valentinian II from Scotch Street, Carlisle', *Britannia*, xx (1989), 254–5

H. E. Kilbride-Jones, 'Excavation of a Native Settlement at Milking Gap, High Shield, Northumberland', *Arch.Ael.*⁴, xv (1938), 303–50

L. J. F. Keppie, 'Legio VIII Augusta and the Claudian Invasion', *Britannia*, ii (1971), 149–55

C. M. Kraay, Two new *sestertii* of Domitian, *American Num. Soc. Notes*, ix (1960), 109–16

J. Lambert, N. Hair, C. L. E. Howard-Davis, R. M. Newman and T. M. Oliver, *Transect Through Time* (Oxford, 1996)

R. H. Leech, 'The Roman Fort and Vicus at Amble-

side: Archaeological Research in 1982', *CW*², xciii (1993), 51–74

J. D. Leach and J. J. Wilkes, 'The military base at Carpow, Perthshire, Scotland; Summary of recent investigations (1964–70, 1975)', pp. 47–62 in J. Fitz (ed.), *Limes: Akten des XI Internationalen Limescongresses* (Budapest, 1978)

A. W. Lintott, *Imperium Romanum* (London, 1993)

R. A. C. Lowndes, '"Celtic" fields, farms and burial mounds in the Lune Valley', *CW*², lxiii (1963), 77–95

——, 'Excavations of a Romano-British farmstead at Eller Beck', *CW*², lxiv (1964), 6–13

J. C. Mann, 'The Northern Frontier after A.D. 369', *Glasgow Arch. J.*, iii (1974), 34–42

——, Hadrian's Wall: the last phases, pp. 144–51 in P. J. Casey (ed.), *The End of Roman Britain* (BAR, 71, Oxford, 1979)

V. A. Maxfield (ed.), *The Saxon Shore* (Exeter, 1989)

G. S. Maxwell, *The Romans in Scotland* (Edinburgh, 1989)

G. S. Maxwell, *A Battle Lost: Romans and Caledonians at Mons Graupius* (Edinburgh, 1990)

M. R. McCarthy, 'Woodland and Roman Forts', *Britannia*, xvii (1986), 339–43

——, *Carlisle: History and Guide* (Gloucester, 1993)

M. Miller, 'Stilicho's Pictish War', *Britannia*, vi (1975), 141–50

M. Millet, *The Romanisation of Britain* (Cambridge, 1990)

J. G. Milne, *A Catalogue of Alexandrian Coins* (London, 1971)

V. E. Nash-Williams (revised M. G. Jarrett), *The Roman Frontier in Wales* (Cardiff, 1969)

V. Nutten, 'A Greek Doctor at Chester', *Journ. Chester. Arch. Soc.*, lv (1968), 7–13

S. H. Penney, 'Romano-British Iron Extraction in north Lancashire', *CW*², lxxxiii (1983), 59–62

—— and D. C. A. Shotter, 'A Salt-Pan from Shavington, near Crewe', *Britannia*, xxvii (1996) (forthcoming)

T. W. Potter, 'Excavations at Bowness-on-Solway, 1973', *CW*², lxxv (1975), 29–57

——, 'The Biglands Milefortlet and the Cumberland Coast Defences', *Britannia*, viii (1977), 149–83

——, *The Romans in North-West England* (Kendal, 1979)

——, *Roman Britain* (London, 1983)

R. Reece, 'Coins and Frontiers: The Falkirk Hoard reconsidered', pp. 119–129 in W. S. Hanson and L. J. F. Keppie (eds), *Roman Frontier Studies, 1979* (BAR, Int. Series 71, Oxford, 1980)

N. Reed, 'The Fifth Year of Agricola's Campaigns', *Britannia*, ii (1971), 143–48

——, 'The Scottish Campaigns of Septimius Severus', *PSAS*, cvii (1976), 92–102

I. A. Richmond, 'Excavations at the Roman Fort of Newstead, 1947', *PSAS*, lxxxiv (1950), 1–37

——, Queen Cartimandua, *JRS*, xliv (1954), 43–52

——and J. P. Gillam, 'The Temple of Mithras at Carrawburgh', *Arch.Ael.*[4], xxii (1951), 1–92

——, K. S. Hodgson and J. K. St Joseph, 'The Roman Fort at Bewcastle', *CW*[2], xxxviii (1938), 195–239

—— and J. McIntyre, 'The Roman Camps at Rey Cross and Crackenthorpe', *CW*[2], xxxiv (1934), 50–61

—— and K. A. Steer, 'Castellum Veluniate and Civilians on a Roman frontier', *PSAS*, xc (1957), 1–6

A. S. Robertson, 'A Hoard of Roman Silver Coins from Briglands, Rumbling Bridge, Kinross-shire', *PSAS*, xc (1957), 241–6

——, Romano-British Coin Hoards', pp. 12–36 in P. J. Casey and R. Reece (eds), *Coins and the Archaeologist* (*BAR*, 4, Oxford, 1974)

——, *Birrens (Blatobulgium)* (Edinburgh, 1975)

——, *The Antonine Wall* (Glasgow, 1979)

——, The Bridges on Severan coins of A.D. 208 and 209', pp. 131–139 in W. S. Hanson and L. J. F. Keppie (eds), *Roman Frontier Studies, 1979* (*BAR*, Int. Series 71, Oxford, 1980)

——, M. Scott and L. J. F. Keppie, *Bar Hill: A Roman Fort and Its Finds* (*BAR* 16, Oxford, 1975)

P. Salway, *Roman Britain* (Oxford, 1981)

H. Schönberger, 'The Roman Frontier in Germany: An Archaeological Survey', *JRS*, lix (1969), 144–97

M. F. Sekulla, 'The Roman Coins from Traprain Law', *PSAS*, cxii (1982), 285–94

N. Shiel, *The Episode of Carausius and Allectus* (*BAR*, 40, Oxford, 1977)

D. C. A. Shotter, '*Numeri Barcariorum*: a note on *RIB* 601', *Britannia*, iv (1973), 206–9

——, 'Coin Evidence and the Northern Frontier in the Second Century A.D.', *PSAS*, cvii (1976), 81–91

——, 'Three Early Imperial Coin-hoards from Lancashire', *Coin Hoards*, iv (1978), 44–5

——, 'Roman Coin-finds in Cumbria', *CW*[2], lxxxix (1989), 41–50

——, *Roman Coins from North-West England* (Lancaster, 1990)

——, *Augustus Caesar* (London, 1991)

——, *Romans and Britons in North-West England* (Lancaster, 1993)

——, 'Rome and The Brigantes: Early Hostilities', *CW*[2], xciv (1994), 21–34

——, *The Fall of the Roman Republic* (London, 1994)

——, 'The Romans in South Cumbria', *CW*[2], xcv (1995)

—— and A. J. White, *The Roman Fort and Town of Lancaster* (Lancaster, 1990)

—— and A. J. White, *Romans in Lunesdale* (Lancaster, 1995)

F. G. Simpson and K. S. Hodgson, 'The Coastal Mile-fortlet at Cardurnock', *CW*[2], xlvii (1947), 78–127

G. Simpson, 'Haltwhistle Burn, Corstopitum and the Antonine Wall', *Britannia*, v (1976), 317–39

D. J. Smith, 'A Palmyrene Sculptor from South Shields', *Arch. Ael.*[4], xxxvii (1959), 203–10

M. P. Speidel, 'The Chattan War, the Brigantian Revolt, and the loss of the Antonine Wall', *Britannia*, xviii (1987), 233–7

G. R. Stephens, 'A Severan Vexillation at Ribchester', *Britannia*, xviii (1987), 239–42

R. S. O. Tomlin, 'The Date of the "Barbarian Conspiracy"', *Britannia*, v (1974), 303–9

——, 'The Twentieth Legion at Wroxeter and Carlisle in the first century: the Epigraphic Evidence', *Britannia*, xxiii (1992), 141–58

P. Topping, 'A "New" Signal Station in Cumbria', *Britannia*, xviii (1987), 298–300

G. B. Townend, 'Some Flavian Connections', *JRS*, li (1961), 54–62

J. M. C. Toynbee, '"Britannia" on Roman Coins of the second century A.D.', *JRS* xiv (1924), 142–57

——, *The Hadrianic School* (Cambridge, 1934)

J. Walker (ed.), *Castleshaw: The Archaeology of a Roman Fortlet* (Manchester, 1989)

D. Watts, *Christians and Pagans in Roman Britain* (London, 1990)

G. Webster, 'The Military Situations in Britain between A.D. 43 and 71', *Britannia*, i (1970), 179–97

——, *Boudica* (London, 1978)

R. E. M. Wheeler, *The Stanwick Fortifications* (Oxford, 1954)

C. R. Whittaker, *Frontiers of the Roman Empire* (London, 1994)

J. P. Wild, *The Textiles from Vindolanda, 1973–75* (Vindolanda Trust Report 3, 1977)

J. J. Wilkes, 'Early Fourth-Century Rebuilding in Hadrian's Wall Forts', pp. 114–38 in M. G. Jarrett and B. Dobson (eds), *Britain and Rome* (Kendal, 1966)

S. Williams, *Diocletian and the Roman Recovery* (London, 1985)

D. J. Woolliscroft, 'Signalling and the Design of the Cumberland Coast System', *CW*[2], xciv (1994), 55–64

R. P. Wright, 'Carpow and Caracalla', *Britannia*, v (1974), 289–92

Index

(Names of Roman Emperors are given in capital letters)

Abergavenny 19
Adminius 16
Aelius Caesar, Lucius 82
Africa 4, 11
Ager Publicus 4
Agricola, Gnaeus Julius 12, 20, 26, 27, 28, 29, 31, 32, 33, 34, 35, 37, 38, 39, 40, 41, 42, 43, 44, 53, 63, 84, 85, 86, 87, 102, 105, 132, 144, 151
agri decumates 12
Aire, river 30
Aldborough 24, 25, 60, 137
Alder, river 21
Alexandria 133, 153
ALLECTUS 112, 113, 114, 154
Alps 4, 83
Ambleside 50, 52, 99, 128, 131
Ammianus Marcellinus 114, 116, 120, 121, 122, 148, 149
Anglesey 19
Annandale 84, 85
Annia Lucilla 82
Annius Equester 48
Annius Verus, Marcus (S.V. AURELIUS, MARCUS)
Antigonus Papias, Flavius 133
Antioch 147
Antiochus 132
Antonine Itinerary 107
Antonine Wall 2, 35, 52, 64, 67, 79, 82–97, 98, 102, 107, 108, 110, 153
ANTONINUS PIUS 67, 82, 83, 84, 85, 94, 96, 102, 152
Apollinaris, Lucius Julius 132
Apollo 133, 134
Aquileia 123
Ardoch 37, 41
Areani 112, 121, 122
Ariovistus 7
Arles 123

Armenia 11, 54
Arras 115, 154
Arviragus 43, 149
Asia 4, 10, 82, 146
Atrebates 16, 20
Auchendavy 89
AUGUSTUS 5, 6, 8, 9, 10, 11, 12, 15, 16, 82, 148, 155
AURELIUS, MARCUS 12, 58, 82, 94, 96, 98, 99, 153, 159
Auxilia 9, 12, 13, 19, 25, 62, 92

Balmuildy 89
Barburgh Mill 86
Barcombe Hill 49
Bar Hill 90
Barochan 35, 37, 41
Barrock Fell 122
Batavians 27
Bearsden 92, 94, 95
Beckermet 77
Beckfoot 48, 72, 79, 80
Beneficiarius Consularis 63
Bertha 37, 41, 87
Bewcastle 60, 70, 107, 113, 133
Biglands House 73, 75, 78, 79
Binchester 28, 93
Birdoswald 50, 64, 66, 68, 109, 113, 115, 122, 123
Birrens 60, 70, 94, 107, 133
Birrus Britannicus 140
Bishopton 86
Bithynia 147
Blackstone Edge 30
Blencogo 48
Blennerhasset 31, 80
Blitterlees 115
Bochastle 37, 41
Boothby 49
Boresti 37
Boudicca 19, 20, 21, 23, 28
Boulogne 17, 111

Bowness-on-Solway 60, 61, 64, 66, 68, 72, 78, 80, 81, 121, 122
Brampton 48, 49, 52, 129
Brancaster 119
Braystones 77
Brigantes 18, 19, 20, 22, 23, 24, 25, 26, 27, 28, 30, 31, 32, 60, 69, 80, 83, 84, 94, 99, 110, 126, 127, 129, 137, 149
Brigantia (goddess) 60, 133, 135
Briglands 96
Britannia Prima 112
Britannia Secunda 112
Broomholm 44
Brougham 29, 30, 135
Brough-on-Humber 24, 28, 30, 129
Burgh-by-Sands 46, 47, 48, 62, 65, 68
Burnswalk 109
Burrow-in-Lonsdale 29, 132
Burrow Walls 72, 77, 115

Cadder 41
Caer Gybi 78, 116
Caerleon 39, 85
Caermote 51
Caernarfon 78, 116
CAESAR, GAIUS JULIUS 7, 8, 13, 15, 17, 146, 149
Caesarea 151
Caledonians 12, 27, 34, 35, 37, 38, 39, 53, 84, 99, 100, 101, 102, 108, 114, 120, 142, 151
Calgacus 38, 142
CALIGULA 16, 17, 149
Calpurnius Agricola, Sextus 96, 98
Camelon 35, 37, 41, 87
Campfield 76
Camulos 133
Capitolinus, Julius 83, 84, 147

Cappadocia 151
Cappuck 44
CARACALLA 13, 102, 105, 106, 108, 109, 153, 154
Caratacus 16, 18, 19, 23
CARAUSIUS 111, 112, 113, 118, 120, 154
Cardean 37
Cardiff 78, 116
Cardurnock 73, 74, 76, 78, 79, 108, 115
Cargill 37, 41
Carlisle 30, 31, 32, 42, 43, 44, 45, 48, 49, 50, 53, 55, 61, 80, 85, 99, 109, 110, 122, 124, 127, 128, 131, 133, 135, 143
Carpow 41, 105
Carrowburgh 64, 65, 133, 135
Carriden 86, 89, 110
Carron, river 88
Carthage 4
Cartimandua 18, 19, 20, 23, 24, 25, 26, 27, 28, 30
Carvetii 24, 28, 31, 80, 110, 126
Carvoran 46, 48, 49, 64, 70
Castle Nick 68
Castlecary 41, 89, 96
Castleshaw 52
Castlesteads 68, 109
Carzield 86
Ceionius Commodus, Lucius (S.V. Aelius Caesar, Lucius)
Chatti 12, 39
Chester 19, 25, 28, 29, 35, 39, 51, 52, 122, 129, 132
Chesters 61, 65, 92, 110
Chesterton 25
Christianity 135
Cicero, Marcus Tullius 6
Cimbri 1
Cirencester 19
Civilis, Gaius Julius 27
Classis Britannica 61
Claudian 123, 149
CLAUDIUS 1, 8, 15, 17, 21, 23, 25, 26, 83, 102, 146, 149, 151, 155
Cleddans 89
Cleaven Dyke 41
Client ruler 7, 10, 11, 16, 20, 23
Clodius, Publius 132
Clodius Albinus, Decimus 100
Clyde, river 32, 34, 35, 37, 40,

41, 42, 44, 60, 83, 85, 86, 87, 88, 102, 114
Clyro 19
Cocidius 133
Cogidubnus 20
Cohors VIIII Batavorum 45
Cohors I Tungrorum 44, 45
Colchester 17, 18, 20, 21, 69, 151
Colonia 4, 18, 20, 69
Comes Britanniarum 113, 122
Comes Litoris Saxonia 112, 118, 121
Comitia Centuriata 4
COMMODUS 96, 98, 99, 100, 147, 153
CONSTANTIUS I 112, 114, 115, 116, 120, 154
CONSTANTINE I 113, 115, 120, 135, 149
CONSTANS 115, 120
Corbridge 30, 42, 44, 45, 48, 50, 85, 86, 87, 99, 105, 110, 116, 122, 123, 128, 130, 133, 135
Corbridge (Red House) 28, 32, 43, 45, 53
Corio 99
Corionototae 31, 99
Coritani 84
Cornovii 84
Cote How 115
Coventina 133
Crackenthorpe 28
Cramond 105
Crewe 135
Croy Hill 88, 89, 90
Cumberland coast 62, 72–81, 92, 108, 115, 120, 143
Cunobelinus 16, 17, 18

Dacia 12, 50, 53, 70
Dalginross 37, 39, 86
Dalswinton 40, 44, 45
Danube, river 1, 11, 12, 35, 50, 54, 57, 97
Dee, river 25, 53, 112
Demetrius of Tarsus 125, 132
Denmark 118
Dexippus of Athens 149
Dere Street 70, 105, 131
Dicalydones 114
Didius Gallus, Aulus 18, 19
Dio Cassius 11, 20, 97, 98, 99, 101, 102, 105, 147

DIOCLETIAN 14, 111, 112, 113, 120
Dobunni 18
DOMITIAN 12, 33, 35, 39, 41, 44, 50, 146, 151
Doune 37, 41
Drumquhassle 37, 41
Duntocher 89, 90
Durotriges 17
Dux Britanniarum 112, 121, 122

Easton 48
Ebchester 28, 93
Eden, river 60, 61, 111, 140
Edinburgh 86
Egypt 135
Elbe, river 11, 12
Eller Beck 139
England 2, 15, 24, 27, 41, 55, 80, 93, 94, 108, 121
English Channel 16
Equestrian order 5, 8, 12, 13, 57, 146, 147
Eskmeals 77, 78
Eunapius of Sardis 149
Euphrates, river 1, 11, 57
Ewe Close 110
Exeter 17, 18
Exploratores 107, 112, 116

Falkirk 96
Farnhill 48
Faustine II 82
Fendock 37
Fenlands 60
Fife peninsula 87
Filey 121
Finglandrigg 47
Flavia Caesariensis 112
Flavius Martius 110
Flimby 78
Foederati 113, 117, 118
Forth, river 32, 34, 35, 37, 40, 41, 42, 44, 60, 83, 85, 86, 88, 102, 105, 114
Fosse Way 18
Franks 120
Frontinus, Sextus Julius 20, 30, 39
Fronto, Cornelius 58

Galatia 136
GALBA 26

GALERIUS 112
Gallicanus, Vulcacius 148
Gamelsby Ridge 48
Gask Ridge 2, 37, 40, 102
Gaul 7, 8, 15, 16, 25, 27, 28, 82, 119, 146
Genauni 83
Germans 1, 7, 20, 39
Germany 10, 11, 12, 20, 27, 28, 41, 58, 77, 94, 118, 132, 139, 142, 146
GETA 102, 105, 153
Glacis 88
Glasgow 86
Glasgow Bridge 89
Glenlochar 86
Gloucester 17, 19
GORDIAN III 147
Greatchesters 115
Greece 4
Greek city-states 4
Greeks 4, 133, 147, 148, 149

HADRIAN 12, 13, 44, 53, 54, 55, 57, 58, 59, 60, 61, 67, 70, 74, 75, 76, 77, 81, 82, 83, 85, 146, 151, 152, 158
Hadrian's Wall 2, 11, 18, 43, 47, 49, 50, 54, 55–71, 72, 77, 79, 80, 81, 83, 84, 85, 86, 87, 89, 91, 92, 94, 99, 100, 101, 106, 107, 108, 112, 115, 120, 127, 133, 143, 151
Haltonchesters 122
Haltwistle Burn 49, 140
Hardknott 50, 130
Harrington 77
Hellenistic kingdoms 4
Hercules 133, 153
Herd Hill North 73
Hermogenes 132
Herodian 101, 147, 148
Hcronbridge 52
Hiberni 114, 116, 123
High Crosby 49
High Rochester 44, 70, 107, 115
Hnaudifridus 113
Hod Hill 18
Holt 129
HONORIUS 124
Housesteads 63, 65, 109, 110, 113, 115, 122, 128, 135
Humber, river 112

Huntcliffe 121
Hygiaea 132

Iceni 19, 20, 21, 22, 23, 60
Imperium Britanniarum 115, 118
Imperium Galliarum 14, 111, 154
Inchtuthil 36, 37, 40, 41
Inveresk 105
Inverquharity 37
Ireland 35, 117, 123
irregulars 12, 70, 108, 112
Irthing, river 17
Isle of Wight 17
Italy 4, 6, 7, 9, 10, 15

Jalonus 133
Jarrow 55
Judaea 58
JULIAN 120, 148, 149
Juno Caelestis 135
Jupiter 133, 153
Jupiter Dolichenus 135
Juvenal 1, 43, 44, 149

Kaims Castle
Kelvin, river 88
Kent, river 53
King Street 29
Kinneil 89
Kirkbride 30, 42, 46, 48, 53, 64, 74
Kirkham 51
Kirksteads 99

Lake District 32, 50, 52, 80
Lampridius, Aelius 147
Lancaster 29, 51, 52, 78, 93, 113, 116, 117, 129
Latin language 16, 114, 132, 148
Latin rights 6
Learchild 44
Lectio 4
legions 4, 6, 9, 11, 12, 13, 17, 19, 26, 29, 35, 36, 39, 40, 44, 50, 101, 112, 155–60
   II Adiutrix 26, 39, 41
   II Augusta 17, 26, 61, 85, 92, 120
   VI Victrix 59, 61, 92, 153
   VI Ferrata 153
   VIII Augusta 17
   IX Hispana 17, 21, 25, 26, 28, 39, 58

   XIV Gemina Martia Victrix 17, 20, 26
   XVII 1, 11
   XVIII 1, 11
   XIX 1, 11
   XX Valeria Victrix 17, 26, 27, 28, 37, 61, 92, 154
Leighton 19
Leintwardine 19
lilia 89
limes 28, 40, 44, 45, 49, 86
Limes Germanicus 12, 37, 54, 76
Limes Raeticus 12
Lincoln 17, 28
Littlechester 29
Lollius Urbicus, Quintus 83, 85, 89
London 21, 154
Longthorpe 21
Lopocares 31
Low Borrow Bridge 115, 136
Low Carlingill 136
Low Mire 115
Lugdunensis 25
Lune, river 29, 53, 110, 111, 115, 133, 139
Lupicinus 121
Lurg Moor 87

Maeatae 84, 100, 101, 102, 108
Maenius Agrippa, Marcus 81
Magister 112, 121
MAGNUS MAXIMUS 122, 123
Maiden Castle (Dorset) 18
Maiden Castle-on-Stainmore 130, 136
Mains Rigg 49
Mainz 12
Malton 24, 28
Manchester 29, 132, 135
Maponus 134
Marius, Gaius 5, 9
Mars 133, 153
Marsyas 134
Maryport 31, 53, 72, 77, 78, 80, 81, 93, 121, 122, 129, 131, 133, 134, 135, 137, 143
Mastiles Lane 25
Maxima Caesariensis 112
MAXIMIAN III, 112
Mediterranean Sea 2, 11, 16, 133
Menteith (Malling) 37, 41
Mersey, river 29, 53

Middlewich 25, 29
Mithras 135
Mollins 35, 41
Mons Graupius 12, 35, 38, 39, 144, 151
Moray Firth 39, 105
Moresby 72, 77, 80
Moricambe 73, 74, 78
Mumrills 89, 92
Muncaster 79, 118, 129

Nene Valley 52, 129
NERO 8, 19, 22, 23, 26, 156
NERVA 148
Nether Denton 46, 48, 49, 50, 54
Netherby 60, 70, 107
Newbrough 46, 48
Newstead 40, 44, 45, 85, 87, 92, 107
Newcastle-upon-Tyne 55, 60, 68, 94, 129
Nicaea 147
Nithsdale 84, 85
North Sea 16
Notitia Dignitatum 108, 112, 118, 122
Numerus Barcariorum 117

Ocelus 133
Offa's Dyke 19
Old Carlisle (Red Dial) 31, 80, 128, 131
Old Kilpatrick 86, 89
Old Penrith 110, 128
Olympiodorus of Thebes 149
Ordovices 19, 25
Orontes, river 1
Osnabriick 11
Ostorius Scapula, Publius 18, 19, 20
OTHO 26
Outerwards 87

Pannonia 100
Papcastle 51, 98, 134
Parisi 23, 24, 28
Parthia 1, 11, 54
Pasture House 73
Paullinus, Gaius Suetonius 19, 22
Pausanias 83, 94
Pax Romana 2, 6, 8
Pennines 24, 25, 28, 29, 43, 136
PERTINAX, PUBLIUS HELVIUS 99, 100

PESCENNIUS NIGER, GAIUS 100
Petillius Cerialis, Quintus 21, 26, 28, 29, 30, 32, 39
Petronius Turpilianus 22
Pevensey 119, 120, 123
Picts 114, 115, 116, 120, 122, 123
Piercebridge 3, 110, 113, 131
Pike Hill 49
Platorius Nepos, Aulus 59
Po, river 4
Pollio, Trebellius 148
Pompeius Falco, Quintus 44, 54, 59, 66, 151
Pompeius Magnus, Gnaeus 7
Portchester Castle 119
Portus Setantiorum 129
Praetorian Guard 17
Prasutagus 20
Priscus 99
Procurator Augusti 13, 21, 22, 62
Ptolemy of Alexandria 37, 129
Pudens, Gaius Valerius 101

Quernmore 52, 129

Raedykes 105
Raetia 83
Ravenglass 51, 53, 72, 77, 78, 117, 118, 121, 122, 129
Ravenna Cosmography 131
Reculver 119
Red Dial (S.V. Old Carlisle)
Regensburg 12
Rey Cross 28
Rhine, river 1, 7, 8, 11, 12, 15, 16, 28, 35, 37, 50, 57, 59, 94, 96
Rhyn Park 19
Rianorix 135
Ribble, river 29, 53
Ribchester 29, 51, 94, 98, 131, 133, 134, 135
Richborough 17, 120
Risehow 73, 78
Risingham 70, 107, 115
Rochdale 30
Roman citizenship 6, 7, 9, 13
Roman empire 1, 14, 16, 17, 50, 57, 63, 70, 113, 124
Rome, city of 3, 4, 5, 6, 8, 13, 15, 16, 17, 34, 82, 124, 146, 148, 151
Roscius Aelianus, Lucius 39

Rough Castle 89, 91
Rudchester 122
Rudge Cup 69

Sacrovir, Gaius Julius 16
Sahara Desent 11, 57
Saint Alban 105
Saint Albans 21
Saint Bees Head 78
Sallustius Lucullus 44
Sarmatians 97, 98
Saturninus, Julius 132
Saxons 118, 119, 120, 123
Saxon Shore 78, 112, 116, 118, 120, 123
Scalesceugh 52
Scotland 15, 28, 32, 34, 35, 38, 40, 41, 42, 43, 44, 46, 53, 70, 71, 80, 83, 84, 85, 86, 93, 94, 95, 96, 97, 101, 102, 105, 106, 107, 115, 121, 122, 123, 126, 152
Scotti 116, 120, 122
Seabegs 89
Seneca, Lucius Annaeus 19
Senecio, Lucius Alfenus 101
SEPTIMIUS SEVERUS, LUCIUS 13, 41, 53, 84, 97, 98, 100, 101, 102, 105, 106, 107, 111, 112, 129, 135, 153, 159
Servian walls 3
Setantii 24, 28, 31
Severn, river 18
SEVERUS ALEXANDER 147
Sicily 6
Silloth 76
Silures 19
Skinburness 74, 78
Solway 23, 31, 40, 42, 44, 45, 48, 53, 61, 71, 80, 111, 121
Southampton 118
South Shields 46, 53, 71, 80, 105, 109, 111, 122, 129
Spain 7
Spartianus Aelius 44, 54, 66, 76, 147
Spurcio 135
Stainmore 28, 30
Stanegate 2, 30, 32, 40, 41–54, 57, 60, 62, 64, 65, 68, 69, 70, 74, 80, 127
Stanwick 25, 28
Statius 26, 27, 149

Stilicho 123
Stockton Heath 52
Stonea 60
Strabo 16
Stracathro 35, 37
Stageath 37, 41, 87
Strathallan 37, 41
Strathearn 37, 41
Suetonius Tranquillus, Gaius 17, 19, 44, 145, 146, 147, 148
Summerston 89
Swarthy Hill 75
Syria 1, 100, 147

Tacitus, Publius Cornelius 9, 12, 18, 19, 22, 23, 25, 26, 28, 31, 32, 34, 35, 36, 37, 38, 39, 40, 43, 44, 52, 63, 145, 146, 148
Taunus 76
Tay, river 32, 34, 40, 41, 87, 102, 105
Tectoverdi 31, 110
Tees, river 131
Templeborough 25
TETRICI 111
Teutoberg Forest 1
Teutones 1
Thames, river 16
THEODOSIUS I 79, 118, 149
Theodosius (comes) 121
Throp 49
Tiber, river 3
TIBERIUS 8, 11, 16, 82
Tigris, river 1, 57
TITUS 26, 33, 34, 35
Togodumnus 16
TRAJAN 12, 50, 54, 55, 57, 58, 59, 70, 82, 85, 146, 148, 158

Traprain Law 110, 126
Trebellius Maximus, Marcus 22, 26
Trent, river 18
Tributum 4
Trier 132
Trinovantes 19, 20, 21
Troutbeck 51
Tyne, river 23, 40, 42, 44, 45, 53, 54, 59, 60, 61, 71, 80, 105, 110, 121, 152

Ulpius Marcellus 98, 99, 107, 108, 153
Usk 19

Valentia 121
VALENTINIAN I 121
vallum 64, 65, 66, 92, 108, 127
Varus, Publius Quinctilius 11
Venutius 23, 25, 26, 28, 30
Veranius, Quintus 18, 19
Verica 16
Verres, Gaius 6
Verturiones 114
VERUS, LUCIUS 82, 98, 153
Verus, Gnaeus Julius 94, 95
VESPASIAN 12, 17, 18, 26, 27, 28, 33, 34, 50, 157
Vettius Bolanus 26, 27, 28
vexillation 18, 28, 30, 32, 39, 43, 45
vicarius 112
Victorinus 154
Vindex, Gaius Julius 25
Vindolanda (Chesterholm) 1, 2, 42, 43, 44, 45, 46, 48, 49, 50,

52, 99, 110, 111, 115, 122, 128, 130, 133, 140, 143
Virgil 30
Virius Lupus 100, 101
VITELLIUS 26, 27
Vopiscus, Flavius 147
Vortigern 124
Votadini 71, 84, 126
Vulcan 133

Wales 2, 15, 19, 20, 22, 23, 25, 27, 30, 112, 117, 121, 123
Wallsend 64, 68, 71, 80, 109, 115
Walton-le-Dale 29, 53, 129
Warrington 52
Wash 118
Watercrook 50, 93, 130, 133
Watling Lodge 86, 89
Waver, river 46
Whickham (Washing Well) 46
Whitchurch 19
Whitley Castle 111, 140
Wilderness Plantation 87, 89
Wilderspool 29, 52, 129
Willowford 61, 63, 68
Windermere 52, 53, 131
Woden Law 109
Wolsty Bank 73
Wreary Hall 122
Wroxeter 17, 19, 27, 28

York 25, 28, 39, 51, 105, 106, 112, 122, 125, 132, 135
York, Vale of 24

Zosimus 124, 148, 149